ON THE
CONTRARY

Books by
Sydney J. Harris

Strictly Personal
Majority of One
Last Things First
On the Contrary

Sydney J. Harris

ON THE
CONTRARY

HOUGHTON MIFFLIN COMPANY BOSTON

The Riverside Press Cambridge

1964

The Riverside Press
Cambridge, Massachusetts
Printed in the United States of America

*For David and Lindsay
With love*

As soon as we have thought of something,
try to see in what way the contrary is true.

SIMONE WEIL

CONTENTS

ON THE
CONTRARY

OF THE LIFE
OF THE SPIRIT

Man Is Blind to Those Unlike Him

If we can understand a saint, then we can understand a man. And if we can understand a man, then we can know how he ought to behave, and how he was meant to behave.

What is the one characteristic that all saints have in common? It is not piety or love of God, as commonly understood, for some saints did not believe in God (as we conceive Him), and many people are pious who are far from saintly.

The quality they all have in common is *Identification*. Through some mysterious process, only dimly perceived by the rest of us, they are able to identify with the full range of creation.

They identify with the leper and the criminal, with the disfigured and the stupid, with the thief and the alien, with the coward and the heretic, with the beast in the field, the bird in the air, the fish in the sea. They comprehend the *sharingness* of creation.

A saint is a man (and woman, too, of course) in his fullness, just as an oak tree is an acorn in its fullness. He is what a man is meant to be, a model, an archetype, a goal that is given us.

This is what all religion is about, despite the doctrinal differences. It is about the proper way to be a human being — the first and only lesson worth learning in life, and the ultimate end of all education.

The more creatures unlike oneself that one can identify with, the more fully one enters into humanhood. This is the whole message of the saints; this is why Jesus moved among the poor, the afflicted, the disreputable, the outcasts, the dregs of society.

At one end of the human spectrum, we have the pure egotist who cares for no one and nothing but himself; such persons are rare. Then we have the tribal types who are kind and loyal to their own family only. Then those who recognize the claim of the community, beyond the family. And then those who accept a nation composed of many similar communities.

This is as far as man has gone in his spiritual and moral and emotional development. He can identify only with the *similar*, and not with the *unlike*. He cannot see the similarities beneath the differences; the differences frighten and anger him. His identification is narrow, partial, and fatally provincial.

The parent who identifies only with his own children is better than the one who does not, but he is still limited — true parenthood means identifying with all children everywhere. Could we move a few steps farther in that direction, war would become as inconceivable as fathers slaying their own children.

A Blind Spot in the Crystal Ball

WHENEVER people say, "I wonder what life will be like thirty years from now," or whenever some journalistic visionary draws a portrait of life in 1990, it is always the material conditions of mankind that intrigue them.

We listen to speculations about our buildings, our highways, our merchandising, our scientific and technological changes. The portraits are attractive, if a little frightening — but none of them considers the most important thing.

Nobody asks, "What will people be like thirty years from now?" or "How will we behave with one another and toward one another in 1990?" We fail to ask this because most of us believe (mistakenly) that human conduct remains substantially the same, that "human nature doesn't change."

But while the basic nature doesn't change, different social orders bring out different traits and patterns of conduct in people. We do not behave like the ancient Romans or the medieval French or the Elizabethan English or even the nineteenth century New Englanders. For better and for worse, our attitudes and relations are vastly different today.

It seems plain to me that the essential question we must ask about the future is: "What sort of people is this society bound to produce?"

As our society becomes more urbanized, more mechanized, more militarized, more specialized, there can be no doubt that what is called the *ethos* of the American people will change along with our ways of physical living. Certain traits will be encouraged, and others will be repressed; certain kinds of knowledge will be highly rewarded, and others will be ignored or even frowned upon.

And this is why most speculation about the future strikes me as trivial and marginal. At the root of all our problems is always the *human personality;* and this is the last field of inquiry we seem interested in. Or, at most, we want to "adjust" the personality to fit the technical and social changes, rather than shape the culture to fit what we think a full human being ought to be.

We don't even think in terms of a full human being, as the old Greek philosophers understood it. We think of "economic man" and "psychological man" and "man the citizen" and "man the maker." Our pragmatic society is concerned with *functions*, not with *goals*, with "Will it work?", not with "Is it worth the human effort?"

What kind of children are we turning out? What attitudes and ideals and sentiments are we encouraging and discouraging? These are the proper questions for the future, and not space travel or electronic kitchens.

"Sympathy" Can't Solve Our Woes

"THERE's a lot of human sympathy in the world," said my friend, talking about some worthy project for which he was soliciting funds. "People are very willing to give to charity."

What he said was true — but I reflected that sympathy is not enough. It never has been. What is needed is more *empathy*, and that is rare indeed.

Sympathy is feeling *for* someone; it is a cheap and easy sentiment, especially when we ourselves are comfortable and unthreatened. Empathy is feeling *with* someone — it is projecting our consciousness into his suffering.

As an example, before I had children of my own, I could sympathize with those parents whose children were crippled or killed by autos. I felt sorry for them. But only after I had children of my own could I know, in the deepest part of my being, what agonies they were going through.

The consequences of empathy are much more than emotional; they are realistic and practical. As a father, I would rather crash into a brick wall than hit a little child with my car. But without this empathy, I might well seek for self-preservation first, and offer "sympathy" later.

One reason that I am less than rapturous in my acclaim of organized charities is that — despite their worthwhile work — they seldom if ever give us the opportunity to make the jump between sympathy and empathy.

Americans are perhaps the most generous people the world has ever known, and yet somehow we find that all our money and food and offers of friendship are not met with deep and abiding gratitude by the recipients of our favors.

This is not because, as cynics allow, those recipients are greedy or ungrateful people; it is, I suspect, largely because they are looking for empathy rather than sympathy, for a compassionate understanding of their needs and problems rather than for handouts that make us feel virtuous and benevolent while leaving us untouched by their plight.

The same attitude has been noted by welfare workers in families that are economically depressed, the ill, the homeless, the friendless. They take the groceries or the check, the clinic service or the clothes — but they feel that nobody is really interested in them as individuals, only as "unfortunate" statistics who are in some way inferior to the rest of us.

How the human race can jump this gap between mere sympathy and a binding empathy is a question that has vexed better minds than mine. But until we can project our feelings into the sufferings of others, we are merely buying off our consciences with the "sympathy" of material aid.

Religion Unites Only at the Top

THE IRONIC and saddening thing about doctrinal differences between people of different faiths is that the sharpest differences exist on the lowest level, where the people least understand what they "believe" in.

What I mean by that complicated sentence is that a Catholic philosopher such as Jacques Maritain, a Protestant philosopher such as Reinhold Niebuhr, and a Jewish philosopher such as Martin Buber have a great deal more in common with each other than any of them do with the rank-and-file members of their faith.

All doctrines become flattened and coarsened and vulgarized and emotionalized as they pass from minds that are acute and sensitive to minds that are merely receptive and unreflecting. In this passage, the emphasis shifts from the common core of belief to the differences; and the only way most persons know what they "believe" religiously is by knowing what they do *not* believe.

That is what John Erskine meant by his *mot* at Columbia University: "Most people have some sort of religion — at least they know which church they're staying away from."

Long ago, Jonathan Swift put it with his usual bitter precision when he observed that "We have just enough religion to hate one another, but not enough to love one another."

On the higher levels, as we read more deeply and widely in the field of theology, we find that a Maritain, a Niebuhr and a Buber have a profound respect and affection for one another's thought; they know that what binds them together in a common tradition is far more substantial than what divides them philosophically.

But, somehow, the churches themselves, as practical institutions for the transmission of beliefs and practices, have stressed the *separateness* at the expense of the unity. I don't mean that all churches should merge in a warm puddle of sentimentality, ignoring genuine differences. Yet the differences have become the "handle" by which most persons grasp their religion; for the *positive* concepts of a creed are too difficult and demanding for us to live with in our daily lives.

We live by the slogans, the symbols, the uniforms, the

school colors, as it were, of our own particular faith. These are tangible objects that mark us off from the others, and give us a feeling of solidarity within our own religious ranks. Stripped of them, we would scarcely know what we believe, in the most intimate and ultimate sense of believing.

Seeking Own Flaws Takes Courage

"WELL, I ALWAYS admired him," said a friend of mine about a locally prominent man who had just died. "Whatever else you might say, he had the courage of his convictions."

Any kind of courage, of course, is preferable to funk — but I often wonder why people so much admire a man with "the courage of his convictions" while they totally ignore a much higher and rarer kind of courage.

What I am referring to is the courage to *examine* one's convictions, and to revise them or abandon them in the light of such scrutiny. Convictions are dear to us; they are comfortable and familiar and reassuring; and it takes a genuinely courageous person to change his convictions when they should be changed.

Hitler had the courage of his convictions; Stalin had the courage of his convictions. What they lacked, of course, was the ability or willingness to alter those convictions, to give up their precious dogmas, to subject their passionate and fanatical beliefs to the cool and cleansing light of reason, and decency, and the living actuality of the human condition.

This is what takes real courage, of a high moral order: to say, "I was wrong, I was mistaken, I have changed my views." Not one in a thousand can bring himself to this act of heroic repudiation.

Courage is not a virtue, said Socrates, unless it is also wisdom. A brute is courageous on instinct, a criminal may be courageous out of fear, a soldier may be courageous in the vilest cause for the wrongest reasons. Courage becomes a moral virtue only when it is linked, through prudence, with the knowledge of what is right and proper for a man to be and to do.

To have the courage of one's convictions is better than to have the convictions without the courage, or simply to have no convictions; but best of all is the rare ability to submit one's convictions to the pitiless eye of reality, to examine them critically and regularly, to discover if they have become fossilized in our hearts and minds or are still living beliefs, with an authentic core of truth that corresponds to the outer world.

In this respect, the scientific spirit must be commended above all others; for it is the essence of scientific methodology to keep looking for evidence that will refute its own theories. Darwin entered into his notebooks every scrap of evidence that seemed to deny his theory of evolution; he had the courage to challenge his own beliefs, to search scrupulously for flaws in his own body of doctrine.

It is this capacity that makes the human being so admirable a creature. The courage of our convictions we share with the panther and the python; it is the courage to overthrow them when necessary that sets us above the brute world of the irrational and the appetitive.

The Perennial Skeptic Is Immature

"IN WHAT WAY have you most changed since your college days?" was a provocative question aimed at me from the audience recently, after I had finished addressing a university group.

It took me a few moments to absorb the question. Then I said, and I believe quite accurately: "In those days, I believed that almost everything was false; now I believe that almost everything is true."

When we are young, if we have inquiring, skeptical minds (as we then should), we are interested in puncturing the pretensions of most organized groups. We look for the foolishness, the inconsistency, the hypocrisy, the fraud in official religions, political parties, systems of philosophy and moral codes.

As we grow older, however, if we genuinely mature, we begin to be dissatisfied with this negative approach. What seems important is not the falseness surrounding a doctrine, but its residual truth. What can we extract from any body of thought that is usable in building up our own structure of reality; how can we fit together all these diverse blocks to make some sense out of conflicting and contradictory views of life?

The end of skepticism must be a kind of provisional certainty; for the person who goes through life a skeptic is as sealed off from reality as the person who goes through life adhering to one closed system of thought. After all, the skeptic who refuses to see anything as all black or all white is himself seeing things as all gray, which they are not.

The education we receive at school is only a preliminary to real education — which consists of finding and combining the various truths that subsist in different theories. This is hard, patient, and never-ending work. And it is why most people prefer to slump comfortably within a closed system, or to profess an easy skepticism about all beliefs.

There are truths in Marx, if you know where to look for them, and how to apply them; just as there are truths in Adam Smith. Catholicism and Christian Science, diametrically opposed in so many ways, both contain elements of basic truth which we ignore at our peril. There is scarcely any view held by man that does not in some way reflect a facet of reality.

All this does not mean that we should be lukewarmly "tolerant" toward all views, for we have an obligation to root out error wherever we find it. But it does mean that we can find truth in the most unexpected places, if our minds remain open to it. And that the man who concentrates on the folly of his opponents' beliefs will never acquire the power to understand them, to absorb them, or to overcome them.

Charity Goes Far Beyond "Giving"

THERE ARE three degrees of charity: giving, doing, and being. The lowest order is *giving* — anyone with a little surplus funds can give to make himself feel better or to assuage a guilty conscience.

Doing is a step upward on the rung of charity. It involves time and effort, and not merely the writing of a check. Here too, however, some people use their charitable work for neurotic motives that quite cancel out the good they try to do.

Being is the last and hardest stage of charity. Few of us ever achieve it — for it is a deeply rooted attitude of mind and spirit that permeates our whole approach to people, and goes far beyond attending board meetings, doing volunteer work, and making contributions to dinners and benefits.

Harsh though it sounds, I would suggest that without the last stage the first two stages are almost meaningless and futile in the long run. The giving and the doing are treatments of social *symptoms;* only the being can make us want to get to the *causes* of social evil and to wipe them out — not as a sentimental or humanitarian gesture, but because we feel genuinely involved in the life of mankind.

The word "charity" comes from "caritas," which means

simply "love" — and the Biblical "faith, hope and charity" is better rendered as "faith, hope and love." Greatest of these, we are told, is "love."

It is an interesting commentary that what we call "charity" today has become almost completely divorced from the idea of love; charity is an organized effort to help certain groups of people, through fund-raising, banquets, benefits, theater parties, bazaars and such social events.

Those who support and contribute to such charities may be, in most cases, superior to those who do not. But the danger here is that we sometimes think we can buy virtue for ourselves by these superficial means, without the necessity of loving those we give to and organize for.

Charity is always resented when it is devoid of personal respect or affection. When it becomes, as it sometimes does, a substitute for personal involvement — then the recipient can easily turn cynical and greedy. For what is given without love is accepted without grace or gratitude.

There is an old saying, "The good is the enemy of the best." Those of us in the first stages, of giving or doing, must not permit our sense of self-satisfaction to keep us from attaining the final rung of charity. Doing good is too often the enemy, or the counterfeit, of being good — and charity can easily become the counterfeit of love.

"Good" in the Universe Needs Evil

As I stood at the airport, waiting for the plane to bring my family back from Florida, I thought of the frightful risk involved in loving. If the plane had crashed, most of myself would have gone down with it.

And yet, there is no way to love without risk. When you commit yourself to another, when that other becomes an integral part of yourself, you have made yourself infinitely more vulnerable to the cold hand of fate.

The problem of evil in the world — which puzzles both believers and nonbelievers — can only be understood, I think, by the analogy with love. Without evil there is no good, just as without risk there is no love.

Those who cannot love are those who are afraid, or unable, to run the risks involved. They want to keep themselves safe and protected. They fear that their love may be rejected, or betrayed, or weakly returned. And some, indeed, fear being loved — they cannot stand the pressure of another personality bearing upon them.

Yet unless we are willing to take such chances, to accept the fact that in loving we leave ourselves wide open to disappointment or disaster, we cannot escape from the web of our own selfish egos. Love casts out fear, as St. Paul said — but fear also casts out love.

Likewise, it is the presence of evil in the world that gives good its only value. Try to imagine a universe without accident, without mortality, without sin; a universe in which nothing bad or unexpected could happen. It would also be a universe in which nothing was "good," for an attribute cannot exist without its opposite.

If I cannot take a risk for my child, what is the meaning of my "love"? If it cannot be jeopardized, either by my own actions, or by the child's growth, or by some unforeseen catastrophe, then the precious element of freedom has been lost — and without freedom all values are equally meaningless.

I don't mean to drag us all into deep metaphysical waters, but I simply think it is more honest and adult of us to accept the presence of evil in the world as a necessary part of its goodness. This does not mean that individual evils should be tolerated, but that it is our very *opposition* to evil that constitutes our particular goodness.

Without this opposition, without the constant struggle against fate, accident and our own flawed personalities, we would be beasts or angels, but not human beings. It is the bitterness of life that gives sweetness its savor, for each exists only in terms of the other — like love and risk.

"Soul" Gives Man Power to Refuse

A FRIEND OF MINE, who prides himself on being a hard-headed materialist, recently told me that he gets annoyed with my occasional references to the "soul."

"Since I don't believe in God or in any so-called 'spiritual' qualities," he said, "I'd like you to define for me what you mean by the 'soul' without mentioning God or going into religious matters that nobody can prove one way or the other."

I think it can be done so as to satisfy even my old-fashioned materialistic friend. The English word soul corresponds to the Greek word "psyche," which means the "inner self" of a person. That each of us has an inner self can be demonstrated without any reference to supernatural matters.

The brilliant French essayist Alain, in his book *Definitions*, gave what I believe is the best description of what people in all centuries and cultures — religious or pagan — have meant by the soul. I should like to quote two central paragraphs of his essay, to show how closely "lack of soul" corresponds to what we would call "neurosis" in modern parlance:

*

The soul is what refuses the body. What, for instance, refuses to flee when the body trembles, what refuses to strike when the body is provoked, what refuses to drink when the body thirsts, what refuses to take when the body desires, what refuses to give up when the body recoils in horror. These refusals are the prerogative of man. Total refusal is sainthood; looking before leaping is wisdom; and this power of refusal is the soul.

"The madman has no power of refusal; he no longer has a soul. They also say he has no awareness, and that is true. Whoever yields completely to his body, be it to strike, be it to flee, be it merely to speak, no longer knows what he does or what he is saying. One acquires awareness only through opposing self to self. . . . There is no such thing as a base soul; only a lack of soul. This beautiful word in no way defines a being, but always an act.

*

The neurotic lives only for self; he cannot oppose "self to self." He does not have the freedom of will to refuse the body; he is a driven creature, a slave to his own fears and appetites. He suffers from what moderns call "an impairment of psychic liberty," and what the ancients called a defect of soul. He is not what a human being should be — and what is proper to a human being can only be summed up in the word "soul," in the act that refuses the body for the greater good of the whole creature.

If Christ Returned on Christmas

IF THERE should be, on Christmas night, a second coming — would there not be soon a second crucifixion? And this time, not by the Romans or the Jews, but by those who proudly call themselves Christians?

I wonder. I wonder how we today would regard and

treat this man with his strange and frightening and "impractical" doctrines of human behavior and relationships. Would
we believe and follow, any more than the masses of people
in his day believed and followed?

Would not the militarists among us assail him as a cowardly
pacifist because he urges us not to resist evil?

Would not the nationalists among us attack him as a
dangerous internationalist because he tells us we are all of
one flesh?

Would not the wealthy among us castigate him as a
troublemaking radical because he bars the rich from entering
the kingdom of heaven?

Would not the liberals among us dismiss him as a dreamy
vagabond because he advises us to take no thought for the
morrow, to lay up no treasures upon earth?

Would not the ecclesiastics among us denounce him as a
ranting heretic because he cuts through the cords of ritual
and commands us only to love God and our neighbors?

Would not the sentimentalists among us deride him as a
cynic because he warns us that the way to salvation is narrow
and difficult?

Would not the Puritans among us despise and reject him
because he eats and drinks with publicans and sinners, prefer-
ring the company of winebibbers and harlots to that of
"respectable" church members?

Would not the sensual among us scorn him because he
fasts for forty days in the desert, neglecting the needs of
the body?

Would not the proud and important among us laugh at him
when he instructs the twelve disciples that he who would be
"first" should be the one to take the role of the least and
serve all?

Would not the worldly-wise and educated among us be

aghast to hear that we cannot be saved except we become as
children, and that a little child shall lead us?

Would not each of us in his own way find some part of
this man's saying and doing to be so threatening to our ways
of life, so much at odds with our rooted beliefs, that we could
not tolerate him for long?

I wonder.

Home Is Where the Spirit Lives

AT DINNER last night, we were discussing the American expatriates — the young people who, since the 1920's, have gone
abroad to study and write and live, and sometimes die.

One of the guests suggested that these expatriates were
simply running away from home. I ventured to disagree,
remembering a comment Kafka made in one of his books:
"There are some things that can only be achieved by a
deliberate leap in the opposite direction. One has to go
abroad in order to find the home one has lost."

Every man has two homes: a geographical home and a
spiritual home. And fortunate are those for whom the two
homes coincide. They seem to settle into themselves as soon
as they grow up, wanting no other environment and no
other stimulation than are provided by their family and
neighborhood and town.

Others are not so lucky. For them the geographical home
is not a spiritual home. They feel at odds with their community, with its attitudes and its limitations; and they must
wander through the world to find a place they can rest.

These people (except for the chronically restless) are not
running way from home; they are looking for it. And this is
particularly true of persons with acute sensitivity and imagination — of creative persons, that is.

Henry James, although coming from a distinguished American family, finally found his spiritual home in England; while his brother, William, was perfectly happy living on these shores. In our own time, T. S. Eliot forsook St. Louis at an early age to make his permanent home in London.

Contrariwise, many English writers, such as Aldous Huxley and W. H. Auden, have moved to America and become citizens in every sense of the word. Ibsen, the great Norwegian playwright, lived most of his mature life away from Norway. Chopin, a Pole, felt most at home in France; and Joseph Conrad, another Pole, was drawn irresistably to the English-speaking countries.

In one sense, nobody runs *from* home, but *to* home. Everyone is seeking for the warmth and acceptance and sense of peace he remembers from his early childhood, or feels he missed in childhood. The powerful appeal of Thomas Wolfe's novels to young people comes from his tortured expression of this drive to find a spiritual home.

Science Can Never Explain "Self"

WHAT WE CALL the "mind" or the "soul" or, more generally, the "self" seems to many scientists to be located in that central organ of experience, the brain. And it is certainly true that when the brain goes, then the spirit and the sense of identity seem to leave the body.

But the real mystery of the "self" has scarcely been touched by science. For science can deal only with the measurable — with what can be counted, felt, weighed, seen, or somehow recorded in a quantitative manner — and the inner world of the self is immeasurable.

The point is tellingly made by the distinguished zoologist at the University of Basel, Adolf Portmann. In his recently

translated book, *New Paths in Biology*, Professor Portmann
lays a cautionary hand on the investigators who would subordinate biology to the exact sciences, "to reduce life to a few
so-called elementary functions: irritability and motion, metab-
olism, growth, reproduction, heredity and mutation."

All such attempts are quite fruitless, Professor Portmann
warns, "because they ignore a crucial aspect of life: self-
activity and the independence of living forms."

For example, he asks us to consider the *Planaria*, a genus of
flatworm which is found in river gravel, and which has been
the subject of many experiments. If we cut a planarian in
half, we find that each part develops into a whole worm: the
front acquires a new body, and the back organizes *itself* a
new head, complete with brain, eyes and feelers!

Then he further asks us to reflect on the meaning of the
statement: "the back organizes itself a new head." What is
the "self" which creates a new brain? And, moreover, a brain,
he points out, whose function it is to guide the regenerated
organism as a whole.

"It does us good, from time to time," he adds, "to reflect
deeply on such matters, not only because the process of regeneration helps to explain all those healing processes on which
our own existence and well-being depend every day of our
lives, but above all because it brings us face to face with the
secret of the 'self' which lies hidden in every single individual,
in every separate creature."

The "seat of the soul" was thought by the ancients to be
in a pineal gland; others placed it in the liver, in the heart, in
various parts of the anatomy. Today we venerate the brain;
we equate it with "mind" and "soul" and "self." But the self
is not in an organ; it is, rather, in the *organization of life as a
unit*. To learn its secret, science is not, and can never be,
enough.

"*Authenticity*" *and Teaching*

DISCUSSING a common school problem, a parent recently asked me: "How is it that some teachers are able to control their classes with a very light rein, and have no disciplinary troubles, while others must shout and plead and threaten and still get nowhere with the troublemakers?"

I don't think the answer has much to do with teaching techniques or even experience, beyond a certain degree. I think it has almost everything to do with the "authenticity" of the teacher.

Notice I do not say "authority," but "authenticity." For genuine authority, which is more than a matter of official position and the ability to reward or punish, comes out of the depths of the personality. It has a realness, a presence, an aura, that can impress and influence even a six-year-old.

A person is either himself or not himself; is either rooted in his existence, or is a fabrication; has either found his humanhood or is still playing with masks and roles and status symbols. And nobody is more aware of this difference (although unconsciously) than a child. Only an authentic person can evoke a good response in the core of the other person; only person is resonant to person.

Knowledge is not enough. Technique is not enough. Mere experience is not enough. This is the mystery at the heart of the teaching process; and the same mystery is at the heart of the healing process. Both are an art, more than a science or a skill — and the art is at bottom the ability to "tune in to the other's wavelength."

And this ability is not possessed by those who have failed to come to terms with their own individuated person, no matter what other talents they possess. Until they have liberated themselves (not completely, but mostly) from what is artificial and unauthentic within themselves, they cannot communicate, counsel or control others.

The few teachers who meant the most to me in my school life were not necessarily those who knew the most, but those who gave out of the fullness of themselves; who confronted me face to face, as it were, with a humanhood that awoke and lured my own small and trembling soul and called me to take hold of my own existence with my two hands.

Such persons, of course, are extremely rare, and they are worth more than we can ever pay them. It should be the prime task of a good society to recruit and develop these personalities for safeguarding our children's futures; and our failure to do so is our most monstrous sin of omission.

Treating Symptoms, Not Causes

A RECENT public service advertisement by the President's Council on Physical Fitness was headlined with a large, bold-face quotation from Arnold Toynbee, the historian: "Of twenty-one notable civilizations, nineteen perished not from conquest from without, but from decay from within."

The ad went on to warn that the "soft living" of our times may bring a continuing decline in the physical and moral stamina of our children — and that parents should insist on a minimum of fifteen minutes of vigorous activity every school day for all boys and girls.

Of course, the "decay" Toynbee was describing was moral decay and not physical. While it is true that we need exercise, it is an absurd and misleading *non sequitur* to suggest that any of those civilizations collapsed because the young people couldn't do headstands or pushups.

Indeed, one of the worst of those ancient cultures was that of Sparta, which made a fetish of physical strength and fitness, and is the prototype of all Fascist states since then. The boys and the women alike were forcibly trained for deeds of strength and endurance, on behalf of the state — aggressiveness and duplicity were the cardinal virtues of the Spartans.

It is no accident that the Nazis, too, formulated a "Strength through Joy" movement, and aimed at developing the largest muscles in the service of its perverted nationalism. In fact, an overemphasis on the physical is almost always a sign of moral decay or corruption, in which the body is urged to take the place of the spirit.

The "soft living" to which we are addicted today has little to do with our physical aptitudes, and everything to do with our mental attitudes. It manifests itself in apathy about public affairs, indifference to the welfare of the less fortunate, heedless self-indulgence in material pleasures, and the cynical subordination of ethical values to economic considerations.

This moral infection is pandemic at all levels of our society, and in all age groups. Getting children to exercise fifteen minutes a day will be about as effective in combating it as brushing one's teeth every day to eradicate cancer of the jaw. It is another pathetically comical example of our tendency to treat symptoms rather than going to causes.

There is nothing wrong with a program of physical fitness, but to link it up with Toynbee and the fall of twenty-one notable civilizations is both an insult to history and a grotesque distortion of the kind of regeneration and rededication so desperately needed in these parlous times.

Machines Can't Teach Humanities

DURING A recent teachers' convention at which I spoke, one of the panel members asked my opinion of "mechanized" teaching by means of television, tape recordings and such impersonal devices.

I could only answer that mechanization is better than a bad human teacher, but infinitely inferior to a good one. Moreover, while certain subjects might lend themselves to impersonal teaching, the truly important ones depend upon direct human communication.

Geometry might be taught by an exceptionally clever machine; history could never be. At least the rudiments of botany or geology might be transmitted mechanically, but not even the rudiments of philosophy or ethics. Whatever teaches us to think, feel and behave more like men (which is why we call such subjects "the humanities") cannot be offered in a dehumanized fashion or it loses all meaning and impact.

All true communication is "personal," in the highest sense of the word. The most profound truths are manifested in persons, and not in propositions. What a man believes, in the abstract, cannot be divorced from *how* and *why* he believes it, *and what he does with it.* "A great teacher," as Professor M. V. C. Jeffries has said, "does not merely preach his gospel; he *is* his gospel."

Consider, for example, the question as to the "nature of justice." As Lord Lindsay put it: "The question as to the nature of justice was one which it was natural for Socrates to ask, and impossible for him to answer." Plato wrote the Socratic dialogues because he believed that "Socrates in his person and his life offered the real answer to the questions he propounded, and which his teaching never solved."

Such ultimate definitions as "justice" can never be adequately put into words, logically or philosophically. It is only through the character of another person that we can glimpse the existential meaning of such a term. First, we must learn to love Socrates; then, and only then, can we share with him his own love of justice and right-doing.

And, as person-to-person relationships tend to dwindle away in the complex and chaotic modern world, we find increasing skepticism about such "absolutes" as justice, truth, decency, and goodness. This skepticism is understandable because such terms can never be "proved" — they can only be communicated on an intensely personal level, and this level is rapidly being replaced by "mass communication," which can in no way be a substitute for the personal confrontation.

Good teaching, of important subjects, can never be mechanized. Even between persons, it cannot be transmitted only on the intellectual level. It is the whole living man who alone can bring us the truth.

When a Thou Becomes an It

EVERYONE is at the center of his own universe, like a spider sitting at the heart of his web. This is the condition of man, to be self-centered, in the most literal sense of the word.

And when we engage ourselves with another person, our own existence seems necessary and absolute, while the other's existence seems contingent and relative. We are essential to our world; he is not.

Yet, while this is our deep emotional conviction, on the intellectual level, we know it is not true. The other person is as real as we are. He, too, is the center of the universe; he is necessary and absolute to himself.

Treating ourselves as absolute, and others as relative is, of course, the primal sin. It converts persons into *things* to be manipulated, used and discarded; into *means* for our own ends, not for their ends. In Buber's terms, it turns a Thou into an It.

And when a Thou becomes an It — when the createdness of the other person is not viewed as necessary as our own — then there is no reason (beyond expediency) to treat the other as a person. All injustice and cruelty come, basically, from this distorted view of reality.

Seen in this light, the great commandment "Love thy neighbor as thyself" becomes something more than a sentimental injunction or a pious wish or even a purely religious precept. It becomes an imperative for mankind — a self-protective measure to keep us from wiping out one another, as we seem about to do on a global scale today.

The great commandment means that our neighbor, however he differs from us, is just as real, just as worthy and as worthless, just as much the center of creation. It means that the only way we can like some people is by loving them — by loving not the accidents of their personality, but the essential createdness of them, the residual humanity that makes us all much more alike than we are different.

The kind of love we are commanded to have is not a *feeling*, in the ordinary sense of the word. Nobody could be "commanded" to love his neighbor as he loves his mate or parents or children or friends. It is an *act of the will*, a turning of the whole person to the other, in open recognition that what unites us is much greater and deeper than what divides us.

Man will never lose his self-centeredness. He can only mitigate it, by accepting the realness of the other, and regarding him as an absolute. In the crisis of our times, the I can save itself only by reaching out to the Thou and saying "We."

When "Extraordinary" Is Ordinary

A STRANGE and rather wonderful paradox occurred to me the other day, while riding up eighteen flights in a crowded elevator. As I looked at the passengers around me, it seemed suddenly plain that what we call the "extraordinary man" is really the ordinary man.

By "extraordinary," I am not talking in terms of any special talent or prowess, but in terms of character, or rock-bottom decency, of the "niceness" that we immediately recognize as a sign of strength, not of weakness.

Such people are extremely rare, which is why we term them extraordinary. Yet I have the feeling that these few are the "ordinary" people, and we many are the "extraordinary" ones — even though in numbers we far outweigh them.

What do I mean by this odd statement? To understand it, consider the common cold. For the human organism, a cold is an unusual thing, an abnormal thing, an "extraordinary" thing, if you will. If a person were wholly himself all the time, if he were what he is meant to be, he would never have a cold. It is not a "normal" thing for men to have.

Now, this abnormal condition is something that almost everyone has at one time or another. Only a handful of people *never* have a cold. This, of course, makes them "extraordinary" — when, in point of fact, they are ordinary and we millions who get colds are abnormal. It is not a matter of numbers or statistics, but of departures from a norm.

It seems to me that the moral and psychic and emotional norm for man is also not to have a "cold" — that is, to be like those few individuals who immediately impress us with their decency and largeness of spirit. The only thing extraordinary about them is their ordinariness, which makes them so rare, valuable and respected.

They are what we ought to be, are meant to be, and could be. They represent the natural man, somehow uncontaminated by the infections that plague the rest of us, more or less frequently. They show us what it is like *not* to have a cold in the head, and we know instinctively that they, and not we, represent the basic form for mankind.

We struggle along with our self-created burdens, our vanities, our lusts, our pettiness, our piques and our resentments; and through all this, we think of ourselves as quite "ordinary" people. Perhaps it is worth considering for a moment whether we are the extraordinary ones, sniffing and blowing through life — and they are so ordinary, so much what man was designed for, as to seem freakishly remote from us.

Logic Can't Solve Everything

A COLLEGE STUDENT in Wisconsin writes to suggest that I should stress the great need for "logic" in all areas of thinking. He took a formal logic course last semester, and was dazzled into veneration by the precision and economy of this intellectual tool.

I recalled my own similar introduction to the elegant simplicities of formal logic more than a quarter century ago. After learning about the "undistributed middle term," the various fallacies, and the real difference between "contraries" and "contradictories," I wanted to make logic a compulsory course for all students everywhere.

My instructor, however, was wiser than I. He knew all too well the limitations of formal thought. "A logic course in itself is not of too much use," he said sadly. "It's in their basic assumptions that most people go wrong, not in their reasoning processes."

It took me a long time to appreciate the truth in his modest disclaimer of his subject. I was infatuated with the idea that if only people could be made to understand the syllogism and the principles of legitimate deduction, most fuzzy and emotional thinking would disappear.

He was perfectly right, of course. Logic can help us go from A to B to C; but it cannot by itself establish the rightness or the truth of A. And most of the basic controversies of mankind begin from different starting points that cannot be verified in logic.

The writers of the Declaration of Independence, for instance, held certain truths to be "self-evident" — that all men are created equal and endowed by their Creator with inalienable rights, such as life, liberty, and the pursuit of happiness.

Now, "self-evident" means incapable of proof. You either see it, or you don't. If you don't, no "proof" can ever make it evident to you. There is no logic in the world that can convince you, no argument on a strictly rational basis that can demonstrate the "truth" of this belief.

Such convictions are "suprarational." They either resonate in the inner core of us, or they strike no response whatever. If two disputants start from opposite views about the nature of man, both may proceed with utter logic and come out with completely different conclusions. Like a mathematical equation, there is no more in the end than you start with in the beginning.

Logic makes a fine servant, but a poor master. It can be used to "prove" almost any view, so long as its basic premise is accepted. What men feel about one another is, ultimately, more important than how they think.

Basic Knowledge Is Inexpressible

AFTER devoting a long and profound section of his book to the subject of "time," St. Augustine was forced to confess: "If nobody asks me what time is, I know what it is; but if somebody asks me what it is, then I do not know what it is."

What interests me about this frank and engaging statement

is not the subject of "time," but the subject of "knowing." How can we "know" something as long as no one asks us, but not know it when someone asks?

With his customary acuteness, St. Augustine takes us right to the heart of the problem of "knowing." He is saying that certain types of knowledge, by their every existence, are inexpressible.

I would go further and suggest that all *basic* knowledge is inexpressible. As a homely example, a famous chef once declared that the most important part of any food he prepared was not in the recipe, but in his mind.

In the same way, Schnabel "knew" a Beethoven sonata. His knowledge was not in the notes he played, or in the rests, or in the phrases. It was an incommunicable knowledge — he could play it, but he could not explain to his students how it should be played.

Human life progresses so slowly, if at all, because basic knowledge is incommunicable. Love — genuine love, not its many counterfeits — cannot be taught. Piety — the real sort, not its sanctimonious imitations — seems like a delusion to those who do not possess it. And honor is just a fancy word to those who live only for material goods.

We cannot understand what we do not possess, as the blind cannot know color. And how explain color to someone incapable of seeing it? We can explain wavelengths and intensities and radiant energies which stimulate the nervous mechanisms of the eye — but not scarlet and silver and sky-blue.

"Time" remains a great mystery — despite Augustine and Bergson and Whitehead and Einstein — because it is the existential fabric of our lives, and we cannot get outside of ourselves to explain it. We "know" what it is only as long as we do not have to express it.

For all the deepest elements in the human condition cannot be expressed, explained, defined or demonstrated. Not love, not piety, not honor, not the passion for knowing or the delight of making. Each generation must learn these for itself, slowly, painfully, after making the same old mistakes in the same old ways. Hegel may have been right when he sighed, "All we learn from history is that we learn nothing from history."

Why Evil Always Defeats Itself

IT IS A comforting thought on a grim day that what keeps the world from falling wholly into crime and corruption is the psychological fact that evil is a *separatist* thing, while goodness is a *unifying* thing.

We would be utterly under the rule of evil, were it otherwise; for evil is industrious, while virtue is too often apathetic; evil is cunning, while virtue is credulous; evil is attractive and exciting, while virtue makes no similar appeal to the senses.

But the one redeeming factor, the one element that tends to cancel out all the other advantages of evil, is that by its very nature it separates itself, not merely from the good, but from other evil as well. It is not only destructive; it is ultimately self-destructive.

Samuel Johnson put it pithily two centuries ago: "Combinations of wickedness would overwhelm the world did not those who have long practised perfidy grow faithless to each other."

Thieves fall out; thieves *must* fall out, for it is the essence of their character, the mainspring of their behavior. They can have no enduring loyalty to one another, no basic trust, no disinterested activity. What is anti-social in them in the beginning turns into anti-one-another in the end.

This is worth remembering in an age when evil seems ascendent, powerful, organized, and ruthless; when society assumes the dimensions of a magnified racket; when expediency becomes the mark of polity; when nations, like sophisticated gangsters, engage promiscuously in threats, bribes, blackmail, and all the lower forms of intimidation.

It is no mere sentimentalism to insist that — barring some cosmic cataclysm — evil cannot survive and flourish; for it contains the seed of its own destruction. Its center does not hold, it flies apart, it cannot cope with the one thing it wants above all — success.

For success, to have any meaning, requires order, coherence, unity, proportion, and equity. All these factors are alien to the spirit of evil. Most of all, success calls for cooperation at the deepest level — and cooperation is impossible for the separatist spirit.

Rival gangs kill one another off; within each gang, struggles for power disintegrate the group. Hitlers and Stalins cannot maintain "non-aggression pacts" for very long. Tyrants are assassinated by their own lieutenants. The same instinct that drives a man into wickedness drives him to dominate and destroy his associates in the enterprise. Evil in its very nature is self-defeating; in dark days, this truth is sometimes all that good men have to cling to.

The Deeper Meaning of Equality

THE FRIGHTFUL and ignorant arrogance of modern man is nowhere more clearly revealed than in his contemptuous attitude toward the words of his progenitors. He accepts what he finds comfortable, and rejects what he does not understand.

To take two of the most simple and obvious examples: Our

forefathers reminded us that "all men are created equal." Now, evidently, all men are *not* created equal — they are different in height, weight, background, mental capacity, moral character, and dozens of different ways. No two men anywhere on earth are exactly equal in such ways.

When modern man points this out, does he imagine that Jefferson and Franklin and the American Revolutionists were such idiots as to believe that men were created equal in such ways? Nobody above the mental level of eight would think that. So, obviously, the founding fathers meant something quite different, and much deeper, than these "equalities." But we do not bother to discover what they meant.

The second example comes from the Bible, where we are commanded to love our neighbors and love our enemies — apparently, as Chesterton said, because they are so often the same persons.

Along comes modern man and asserts that nobody can be "commanded" to love anybody. Love to us is an emotion, a feeling, and it cannot be turned off and on, it cannot be directed and channeled. Love, like the wind, bloweth where it listeth, and nobody can be told whom he should love.

How can anyone in his right mind imagine that this is what the wise men who wrote the Bible meant when they informed us that God commands us to love our neighbors? Didn't they know as well as we that people are bundles of likes and dislikes, attraction and repulsions, affections and aversions? Does anyone think that the priests and the prophets were so stupid that they thought this kind of love could be ordered, even by God?

So, obviously, something else is meant. The kind of "love" we are commanded to have in the Bible is not (at least, at first) a "feeling" or an "emotion." It is an act of will, it is a turning toward the object in a way quite different from the way in which we turn to our beloved sweethearts or sons or daughters.

Notice that we are not commanded to "like" people; we are requested to "love" them — which is both easier and harder. We cannot decide whom we will like; but in some peculiar way we can learn to "love" even those we may not like. Unless we understand this, the whole Biblical message eludes us — as, in a different way, the whole Declaration of Independence eludes us if we fail to grasp its meaning of "equality."

It is easy to prove that the past was wrong, stupid and misguided. All we have to do is to ignore the significance of what is said. Modern man has no trouble whatsoever in doing this.

Man: Creator of Destruction

WHILE DRIVING through a state park the other day, the children saw me carelessly tossing a dead match out of the car window, and reminded me of Smokey the Bear's warning: "One tree can make a million matches, but one match can burn a million trees."

This is more than a homely aphorism for children, and it says more than the dangers of being careless about fire. It strikes to the very heart of the human condition.

We can observe the same truth, on the children's scale, at the seaside. Six children may labor for hours to build a lovely and intricate sand castle — but in one second a baby can come along and wantonly destroy their achievement.

Man is a creature of creation and destruction. The creation requires labor, talent, skill, patience, cooperation, imagination, and often great courage. The destruction usually requires little except the urge to destroy; it calls for no distinctively human abilities.

Nature has loaded the dice against us. One fanatical assassin with a gun can change the course of history, no matter how many statesmen and savants are ranged on the other side. The work of decades can be undone in an instant, as a cathedral that took a century to build can be demolished with a well-placed charge of dynamite.

These are all the most obvious truisms — yet truisms seem to be the last things that human beings learn, accept, and act upon. Our capacity for violence and destruction has increased a millionfold in modern times, but our capacity for creation and for cooperation has lagged far behind.

Humanity has not yet begun to fight its real war — which is not the war of people against people, but the war of all of us against our own destructive tendencies, and against Nature's indifference to our fate. Better control of the physical universe, combined with better control over our own nature, is the only way to assure our survival as a species.

But we have not yet begun to regard man as a species. What L. L. White calls "the unitary nature of man" is dimly perceived by only a few in each country; the rest retain a primitive view of their own subculture as being the finest and the best.

The basic task of modern education is not to teach reading and writing and counting, but to teach young people (and older ones as well) what it means *to become a human being*. All other tasks are subordinate to this one, for if we turn out skilled technical animals who do not know what a human being ought to be, we are simply hastening our violent extinction.

Man's nature is not forever *given*, like the other animals, which cannot help being what they are. We make ourselves, as we make our history; and it is wholly up to us whether we use the trees for matches or set the matches to trees.

A Prejudice Isn't an "Opinion"

YOU HAVE TO earn the right to be wrong. This statement
would strike most modern ears as peculiar, if not perverse.
Yet I believe that unless we understand and respect what it
means, we cannot approach the works of the mind or the
spirit with the proper attitude.

Two qualified historians might disagree about the causes of
World War II; one might be right, and the other wrong.
But the wrong one has earned the right to his opinion, for he
has studied the subject earnestly and at length.

Two musicologists might argue about the respective merits
of Bach and Beethoven; one might be right, and the other
wrong. But here again, the wrong one has earned the right to
his opinion, for it is based on love, diligence, and seriousness.

And the right to be wrong can be won only in this way.
The works of the mind and the spirit — history, philosophy,
literature, the arts — are much more than a mere matter of
taste and preference. They demand our active collaboration,
our objective study, our willingness to lay aside our preconceptions and open ourselves to new possibilities and combinations.

The person who says "I know what I like" almost always
stigmatizes himself as an ignoramus. We like what we are
used to; what we expect; what reassures us and makes us feel
comfortable; what massages our egos and confirms our good
opinion of ourselves. That is all that "I know what I like"
really means.

Every man, we say, is entitled to his opinion. But "opinion"
is a tricky word; it should mean a "reasoned view" or a "judgment," and not just a prejudice. When a judge hands down
an opinion, it is based on something more than his personal
preference, it rests upon a tradition and an organized body of
knowledge in the field of jurisprudence.

Not everyone, of course, can be or should be, an expert. But all of us have an obligation to refrain from passing off our prejudices as "opinions." If we go to a football game, and do not understand what is happening on the field, we will not pretend to judge the teams or the players; but if we attend a play, a concert or an opera, we are quick to ventilate our prejudices, defending them as our "opinions."

They are not opinions, because in most cases they are not based on anything but subjective preference, like choosing vanilla over chocolate ice cream. And it is the most profoundly unconscious arrogance of the common man that he can evaluate uncommon works without even the minimum of expertise he would bring to a sporting event.

Was an Illusion Also Mourned?

Now THAT the initial shock has passed away, and the emotional numbness has worn off, perhaps we can begin to see a little more clearly the deeper feelings that were so stirred up by the murder of John Kennedy.

Beyond the sense of horror and outrage and pity, beyond the political and social and historical insult to our system, his assassination cut into the depth of our being also for another reason that may possibly tell us a good deal about ourselves and our unconscious view of human life in America in the twentieth century.

For here was the man who had everything — brains, ability, charm, youth, looks, money, family, power, fame, international respect even from his enemies. He seemed, in a way, immortal, the living embodiment of the American Dream.

And then, quite literally in the twinkling of an eye, he was no more. Gone, utterly gone, this bold and vital young man who only a moment before had been smiling and waving at the crowd. Done to death by an insignificant madman, in a tragedy that a dozen different "ifs" might have prevented.

Somehow, we had seemed to believe that we might be able to cheat Death. If we were rich enough and strong enough and smart enough — and, most of all, young enough — death might not dare to touch us, at least so frivolously, so wantonly, so insanely.

We may have grown up, a little, as a people in that moment; we may have begun to acquire what Europe and the rest of the world have long accepted as "the human condition" — a sense of the tragic that is not morbid or fatalistic, but mature and more accepting of man's limitations and the dark contingencies of nature.

If this could happen to President Kennedy, it could happen to each and any of us, tomorrow, tonight, the next minute. Of course, everyone has known this, in an abstract way; but not in an existential way. This is why we refused to believe it at first — could it happen here, now, to us, to such a man?

All these attributes — brains, ability, charm, youth, looks, money, family, power, fame — cannot avert one bullet, one blowout, one step in the dark. We cannot buy our way out. No matter how strong, how young, how rich, we are subject to the same caprices of fate as the Hindu beggar and the Zulu tribesman.

We mourned his death as a tragedy to him and to the nation; but were we also mourning the death of an illusion long and secretly held by us?

"Simple" Questions Are Important

SCIENCE deals with the commonplace, not with the extraordinary. It questions the obvious more than it investigates the strange and the exotic. This is a lesson the layman has not yet learned to apply to his own life, his own time, his own society.

The greatest advances in science have been made by watching a bean grow, an apple fall, a star shine. From Galileo and Newton through Mendel and Pasteur and Einstein, the revolutionary discoveries have all been made by examining the simple and the immediate.

How exactly did Einstein come to his theories of relativity, which have utterly transformed the world of the present and the future? By questioning a word that everybody "understands." While drudging away in a patent office in Switzerland, and working on his mathematical equations, he asked himself what was meant by "simultaneous."

Of course, everybody knows what "simultaneous" means — happening at the same time. But what exactly is "the same time"? No one human being among the millions who had existed until then ever doubted that he knew what "the same time" meant. A child of five could have told us. And yet, by questioning this simple, obvious idea, Einstein cracked open the whole universe like a nutshell.

Each scientific genius, at the crucial point of his career, went back to first principles. Each asked himself a question that any idiot could answer — and each found that the answer was not true, that the obvious was not so obvious after all, that the infinitely simple has locked within it the secret of the whole complex cosmos. A leaf, a stone, a star.

In our personal lives, we too rarely confront ourselves in the naked simplicity of our essential being. We almost never ask the questions which have "obvious" answers; only a child asks such questions — and we quickly shame him or shush him out of repeating them.

Science has made such enormous strides because it is not ashamed or afraid to ask such unsophisticated questions: Why doesn't an apple fall up, why doesn't a bean pod turn into a carrot, what time is it if you're traveling on a moonbeam?

Philosophy, on the other hand, has been a circular process because most philosophers have devised abstract systems and rules and theories, but have not observed themselves and their fellow men in their existential condition. The questions of our identity and our relationships, our proper roles as created beings, have been answered (if at all) by creed and custom, by rote and by rule. And not until we begin to ask the right questions will we begin to get a glimmer of a right answer.

Shrinking Globe Expands Hostility

A RECENT advertisement for an aviation company suggested that the new jet planes, by shrinking distances between nations, would also contribute to a greater warmth and understanding between peoples.

I see nothing in human history, or human psychology, to justify this naïve hope. In fact, quite the contrary seems to be the case.

It is not the *physical* closeness, but the spiritual closeness between peoples that create bonds of friendship and understanding. To live closely to someone we dislike or misunderstand only breeds wars and conflicts.

We delude ourselves in thinking that faster transportation or quicker communication can bring us together. It is the vast inner spaces of the mind and emotions that must be bridged, or else proximity is just an added source of irritation.

The worst wars have always been between the closest neighbors. The French and the Germans share a common border, but this is all they have shared for centuries. The English have abused their neighbors, the Irish; the Russians have always attacked their neighbors, the Poles; and America's only aggressive war was against her neighbor Mexico.

Closeness in time and space without closeness in spirit is more likely to result in murder than in mutuality. When a husband or wife has been mysteriously killed, the first person the police suspect is the surviving mate, not a strange burglar.

And most mortal crimes, indeed, are committed by relatives and friends, whose physical and social closeness is not matched by their emotional closeness. A dissident family locked tightly together in a house is the most explosive combination in the world.

The more the globe shrinks, in time and space, the more compelling becomes our necessity to find a spiritual bond linking the peoples of the world. Jet planes, in themselves, are only emissaries of discord and destruction, permitting us to extend to peoples far away the same hostility we express in our own small circles.

Modern technology has given us the facilities to live better; but it has also, at a frightening rate, given us the facilities to die faster. We can now kill people we have never seen, thousands of miles away, in a matter of minutes.

The real problem confronting the human race is not "how quickly can we get there?" but "why are we going there at all?" Our know-how may soon blow us all up, unless we can master the know-why of our deepest motivations.

Impulsiveness vs. Contemplation

WHEN Chesterton was once asked that tiresomely familiar question, "What book would you choose to have with you on a desert island?", he quite sensibly replied, "James' volume on 'Practical Shipbuilding.' "

He was doing more than giving a flip dismissal to this trite question. He was pointing out the absurdity of taking a situation out of context. Most of us would answer, with spiritual solemnity, the Bible or Shakespeare; but Chesterton, who was both a deeply religious and a widely cultivated man, saw through these pretensions.

On a desert island, of course, we would want a book that would help us survive and escape, if possible. For a man alone is no good to himself, even with the Bible and Shakespeare for company. Robinson Crusoe was going crazy until he came upon Friday.

Books of a spiritual or cultural quality must be a *supplement* to life; they cannot be a *substitute* for it. If the average man makes the disastrous mistake of substituting action for thought (which always ends in violence), the thoughtful man often makes the contrary mistake of substituting books for life (which always ends in sterility).

Indeed, perhaps the central task of any human life consists in achieving the proper balance, the correct tension, between the contemplative and the practical aspects. For both the man who thinks too much and the man who thinks too little tend to take the wrong action in a crisis.

The consideration of subtle moral, psychological and social values can immobilize a man from taking action with courage and dispatch; and, contrariwise, the ignoring of such considerations can plunge us into deeds whose consequences are quite the opposite of what we intended. Life is so hard to anticipate precisely because each event is an equation in which one term is hidden from us — the mysterious "x" that lies so deep within our own nature that we cannot see it.

What expert bridge players call "the feel of the table" — knowing intuitively when to pass and when to bid — is as important in living as in playing. The reflective man will nearly always pass, and the impulsive man will nearly always bid; but true expertise consists in cutting across the grain of one's nature when the situation seems to call for it.

It might almost be said that only if we learn how and when to violate the natural bent of our temperament can we cope with the unpredictability and perversity of human affairs.

2

OF THE
SOCIAL ANIMAL

What Makes a "Remarkable" Man?

IN THE recently translated book *Meetings with Remarkable Men*, by G. I. Gurdjieff, the author explains that by "remarkable men" he does not mean what the modern world calls "celebrities" or "personalities."

"From my point of view," he writes, "he can be called a remarkable man who stands out from those around him by the resourcefulness of his mind, and who knows how to be restrained in the manifestations which proceed from his nature, at the same time conducting himself justly and tolerantly toward the weakness of others."

I found this three-part definition of a remarkable person to be one of the best I have come across, an excellent yardstick for judging the stature of men, living and dead, who have influenced society.

Of course, such a man must have resourcefulness of mind. This is, in a way, the easiest, for it is freely given to some as a gift, like musical talent, or coordination of body, or the flair for making money. Some of the world's worst men have had exceeding resourcefulness of mind.

The second and third, however, are the real keys to remarkableness. Consider the author's subtle and tactful phrase, "who knows how to be restrained in the manifestations which proceed from his nature."

This means, as I understand it, that the man of exceptional mental abilities and drive must learn to discipline himself so that his egotistic drives do not overwhelm his capacity for doing good. All that is self-centered, idiosyncratic, vainglorious, must be subdued to the special gifts he has been endowed with. This is the hardest task for artists and writers and all persons with creative talent.

The third consists in "conducting himself justly and tolerantly toward the weaknesses of others." Here, again, most men with resourceful minds tend to be impatient with and contemptuous toward those who are slower, weaker, less able to cope with inner and outer problems. Just as lack of restraint is the typical sin of the creative man, lack of tolerance is the besetting vice of the productive man, the maker, the builder, the leader, the manipulator of institutions and movements.

A truly remarkable man, Gurdjieff seems to be saying, requires three balanced components to his nature: intellectual prowess, spiritual diffidence, and emotional stability. When any one of these is lacking, what we have is only a part of a man, no matter how impressive his achievements, or how commanding his personality.

And such men, of course, can be counted on the fingers of one hand in any generation. But this is the standard we should keep fixed in our minds, for judging not only others but ourselves as well.

Is the Negro a Man — or Not?

Is THE NEGRO a man, or is he not a man? This is the root question that the times have put to us, and we must answer it unequivocally. For this is, at bottom, what the current race conflict is all about.

Either the Negro is a full-fledged human being, and a complete American citizen, or he is less than a human being and incapable of citizenship.

If we believe the first, the Negro must be assured of all his civil and legal and human rights. If we believe the second, the Negro should be stripped of citizenship and made a ward of the state. No middle course is possible.

Most Americans, on both sides of the issue, refuse to face this central point. The Negro should be treated just like everyone else — no better, no worse — or else he should be confined to a reservation, returned to Africa, or sent back to slavery.

Any other "solution" is just hypocrisy and foolishness, and only postpones the ultimate day of reckoning. Is the Negro a man, or is he not a man? Once we answer this question honestly, all the other answers will fall into place, painfully but surely.

I happen to believe he is a man (though grievously flawed by centuries of abuse), created by the same God who created the rest of us. To treat him any differently is, to my mind, an act of profound impiety.

Those who think otherwise should not make concessions they do not believe in. They should not hide behind the deception of "separate but equal" schools or any such other mumbo-jumbo. They should frankly ask that the Negro be assigned to a subhuman status in our society.

If we do not think the Negro is a man, we should both

ignore his "rights" and absolve his "responsibilities." If he cannot live anywhere, work anywhere, eat anywhere, go to school anywhere — then he should not be asked to pay taxes, to fight for his country, to give his time, his labor or his loyalty to enterprises in which he cannot fully share.

The white man has made the Negro what he is, and has kept him where he is. Nobody knows how far the Negro can go up, because he has never had the chance; we only know how far he can go down — and it frightens us terribly — because we have pushed him down. We have refused to let him live decently, and then we accuse him of the sin of indecency.

Do we think the Negro is a man or not a man? We can no longer squirm and back away from this crucial question. For already having postponed it so long, either answer we decide upon will bring anguish to millions.

Oh, for the World of the Artist

WATCHING the great Pablo Casals conduct a chamber orchestra in a Bach suite (in the closed television-circuit program for the National Cultural Center last month), I was forcibly reminded again that the world of performers and artists is in many ways a model of what the outer world ought to be.

Despite the backbiting and envy and childishness of so many performers, there is an immense respect for talent and ability, skill and discipline, imagination and interpretation.

The world of the artist is supremely the world of the *individual;* compared to it, business and trade (which use the word "individualism" too often as a synonym for making more money without restraint) are impersonal and anti-individualistic. The modern corporation, indeed, is a prime example of high-level collectivism.

In the arts, a man or woman is judged *solely and wholly* by what he can do and how well he can do it. There is a true democracy of merit, which means that there is also a true aristocracy — made up of those who have proved themselves as individuals, regardless of their background, their national origin, their private failings.

The veneration given to Casals by his fellow musicians is a moving example of what the entire human family was meant to be. This dumpy, bald, hobbling, ailing old man, without money, without power, without even a country of his own, commands the utmost respect of artists throughout the world — because of his vast ability and his fierce dedication to the highest goals of his craft.

What an artist (if he is really an artist) wants to be is the *best* — not the biggest or the richest or the most famous. His end is a *value*, not a commodity; and true civilization can survive only when we place values above commodities. The least practical, and most destructive, thing a society can do is to enshrine the practical above the "idealistic."

What is immensely appealing, in a deep human sense, about the arts is that they remain one of the few areas in which true individualism can flourish; in which the creator and performer is a person directly communicating with other persons; in which his ancestors, language, connections, and superficial traits are totally subordinated to his professional skill.

A state which cannot produce and sustain such art is doomed, however tall its buildings or powerful its armaments; and both "democracy" and "individualism" can be measured by the ways in which those who are gifted in other areas shape their lives to give fuller expression to the higher parts of their nature, and not merely to the appetitive part we share with all animals.

The Nature of a "Serious" Man

ONE OF THE chief reasons that people don't get the right answers is that they don't ask the right questions. They think they are being serious when they are merely being solemn.

The other evening, at a little gathering, a man turned to me and asked what I thought about the Congressional election trends. I murmured some polite evasion. He then asked me about the Cuban situation. I shrugged noncommittally.

He became exasperated and charged me with a refusal to be "serious." I said I would rather play bridge than engage in the kind of futile discussion he was proposing. And I told him why.

Like most people, he thinks the Big Questions of the day are the important ones. But he never stops to ask the Little Questions that are forever at the bottom of all fruitful discussions.

How can we have an effective dialogue about the election or the Cuban situation, or any other large subject, until we agree on some common aim? Unless we both understand what is meant by "the good life," we will be arguing at cross-purposes all night — which is why most political debates end exactly where they begin.

The serious man is not the one who keeps trying to interpret news events, or analyze trends, or influence voting patterns. The serious man is the one who examines the underlying foundations of his beliefs and convictions. And, in this respect, not one person out of a thousand is truly serious.

What is the nature of the human animal, his limitations and his potentialities? Is it possible to have peace without justice, or justice without virtue? And what do these words actually mean, if anything?

Until we can begin to answer some of these fundamental

questions, we can't decide what the purpose of society ought to be. And until we can decide what the purpose of society ought to be, we can't know what we are voting for, or fighting for, or arguing about.

The man who thought I was frivolous because I preferred bridge to an election analysis couldn't realize that I preferred bridge because I was serious and he was frivolous, and I refused to pretend that he was asking important questions when he was only massaging his ego.

It is better to play a game and know you are playing than to play and think you are in earnest — because in the latter case you are never really earnest, but only using phrases in their pompous and shallow news-commentator sense. When I double two spades, everyone at the table knows exactly what I mean.

We're All Alike — and Different

THE DISTINGUISHING mark of a good mind, it seems to me, is the ability to hold two conflicting ideas at the same time, and to be dominated by neither.

This is extremely hard to do. Consider the two propositions: "Everybody is different" and "Everybody is pretty much the same." I believe that both these statements are true, and that a realistic view of life consists in holding them in balance at all times.

If we are dominated only by the first proposition, "Everybody is different," we become the most arrant kind of individualist. If we overstress the uniqueness of the individual, we ignore the fact that man's nature is basically social. The consequences of such a view are usually despotism, oligarchy, or fascism.

If we are dominated by the second proposition, "Everybody is pretty much the same," we become the most insensitive kind of collectivist. If we overstress the common denominator of mankind, we ignore the fact that it is the spirit of individuality that gives meaning and flavor and delight to human existence. The consequences of such a view are often mass mediocrity, sheepish subservience, and Communism.

Proust, in his great novel, remarks that "The universe is the same for all of us, and different for each of us." The same for all of us — we have the same needs, the same loves, the same fears, the same rights, the same responsibilities. And the man who denies this in the name of "individualism" becomes a dehumanized creature.

Different for each of us — for each is a distinct unique personality, with his own way of looking at life, his own independence and autonomy, his own freedom to make decisions, his own end in himself. And the man who denies this in the name of "society" cruelly sacrifices personal values for abstract social ones that can never be realized by collective action.

Humanity is perpetually in the position of a charioteer with two horses wanting to go in opposite directions at the same time. If we give in to one or to the other, we cannot avoid crashing over the precipice. Like every good horseman, we must give each steed just the right amount of freedom and the right amount of control. To determine these degrees, and the proportions between them, is the continuing human task.

It cannot be done if we allow either conflicting idea to run away with us, out of fear, or greed, or simple ignorance. The skillful combination of opposites is almost the whole art of living.

Culture Mustn't Claim Too Much

THE CANT that is spoken in the political sphere is equaled, if not excelled, only by the cant that is spoken in the artistic and cultural sphere. The most absurd and inflated claims are made by proponents in both worlds.

I was, therefore, pleased to read recently the transcript of some talks given by Artur Schnabel, the pianistic genius, a few years before he died. Among other blunt and honest comments, Schnabel had this to say:

"All my life I have heard this talk about the power of art to bring people nearer to each other, that world peace will come only if more music is circulated and exchanged. Yet I have seen people deeply moved — as deeply moved and affected by music as is possible — and the next morning they would go into activities which you might call criminal and inhuman."

The fact that the Russians love Van Cliburn's artistry, and we love Gilels or some other Russian performer, has absolutely nothing whatever to do with our extramusical activities, either individually or nationally. The Germans were the greatest music-lovers in the world — they would sob over Schubert and moan over Mozart — but the cause of international understanding was not forwarded one inch by such appreciation.

And, much as I applaud their good intentions, I feel the same way about the people who devoutly believe that speaking a common language would make mankind act more like brothers. There may be some good practical reasons for an international language, but it is sentimental nonsense to think that it would promote amity among mankind.

One of the most distressing lessons on history, in fact, is that the fiercest wars and persecutions often obtained among peoples who spoke the same language. The early Greek city-states fought among themselves with unparalleled ferocity; so did the later Italian cities and duchies. The English behaved most atrociously toward the Irish, and our own Civil War indicates that a common tongue did not prevent horrible fratricide.

Music is not an "international language," nor are any of the arts. There are only two things that will bring people closer together — one of them is positive, and the other is negative. The positive thing is love, and the negative thing is fear.

And since we are not good enough to love one another, we will be brought together (if ever) only by fear — by the very real fear, which exists today as never before, that destruction is indivisible, that we are all sitting in the same little boat in the middle of the sea, and to drill a hole under anyone's seat is to sink us all. This is the one international language time will force us to learn to speak.

The Glories of Maladjustment

THE CULT of adjustment in our time urges us to adjust to our environment and our society, as though adjustment were a good thing in itself. But if we are asked to "adjust' to something bad, then the better we adjust, the worse we become.

A persuasive argument might be made, indeed, that man should be called the Maladjusted Animal. It is because man is basically maladjusted that he is unique in nature, and dominates the natural world.

The anteater, the beaver, the bird, the insect — all are perfectly adjusted to their environment and their society. This is why animals have no history, but only a repetitive biological process. The ant is a thousand times more efficient, and better adjusted, than we are — but no ant knows anything more, nor can do anything differently, than his grandfather.

In the introduction to his interesting new Pelican book, *Personal Values in the Modern World*, Professor M. V. C. Jeffries tersely and effectively brings out this point: "If we take efficiency, pertinacity, fortitude, dexterity, as the measures of excellence, we cannot claim any natural pre-eminence for man. It is, in fact, not success but failure that marks man off from the rest of the animal creation."

The author then goes on to say: "It is because man is maladjusted — which is evident in the chasm between aspiration and capacity, vision and performance — have there arisen all the distinctively human activities: scientific inquiry, artistic creation, philosophical speculation, and (the supporting condition of them all), historical experience."

Historical change, Professor Jeffries reminds us, is peculiar to man, and lifts human life on to a plane of its own. "When Caesar landed in Britain, when the Pharaohs built their tombs, when men first learnt to make fire — ants' nests were no worse and no better organized communities than they are now."

We are concerned with education precisely because we are a maladjusted animal, because we are not determined by our structure and environment but are able to change and adapt external circumstances. Rather than "adjusting" to the earth, we have adjusted it to us. This is both our glory and our despair. We have the power to learn, which other animals do not, but also the power to fail, which other animals do not.

Each new plateau reached by the human race has been the result of some maladjustment — and it is no accident that personally maladjusted individuals have usually been responsible for our ascent to a higher level of comprehension and ability. Society has a right to ask that we cooperate for the common good, but not that we acquiesce in the common beliefs.

Portrait of a Twentieth-Century Man

HE IS A short, chunky, near-bald man, with a shrewd eye, an aggressive jaw, and a ready joke for nearly all occasions. His beliefs are firm and explicit, in every realm, from the economic to the psychological to the aesthetic. He is a man who knows his own mind, and expresses himself freely and pungently.

In economics, he believes that the economic factor is the most important in human life. Ideals and spiritual qualities are all very well in their place, but it is money that makes the mare go. What most deeply influence men's decisions are their economic needs and drives.

In psychology, he is suspicious and disdainful of any Freudian interpretations. Psychoanalysis should be banned, he believes, because it holds that unconscious psychic factors determine our conduct — and he will have no truck with such mystical interpretations of life.

In aesthetics, he is against all "modern" manifestations. He despises abstract art as a corrupt, degenerate and infantile activity; he will have nothing to do with music that is not traditional and familiarly melodic. In literature, he prefers facts to fancy; he wants a "message" to be got across, in plain, everyday language.

Indeed, "practical" is the keyword of his nature. He will use ideology when it suits his purposes, but what he wants to see is a huge industrial machinery operating at top productive power, a high standard of living, and an administration that is cool and efficient, with emphasis on technical and scientific developments.

He is ardently nationalistic, although he may pay lip-service to such concepts as "humanity" and "brotherhood." He wants his nation to be first in everything, from missiles to marathons; and his entire foreign policy is based on national self-interest. What is good for his country, he firmly believes, is good for the world.

He is, in short, a completely modern man: pragmatic, materialistic, bourgeois in his attitudes toward the arts, uneasy in the presence of psychological subleties, utterly convinced that with the right political party in the saddle and the economy booming, most of the people's problems would be solved.

What he most dislikes are intellectuals, fanatics, artists who will not sensibly serve the needs of the community in clear and simple terms, people who will not work hard at their jobs, beatniks of all sorts, religious cranks, promiscuous and immoral citizens, and those who flirt with alien creeds.

His name: Nikita Khrushchev. Do you recognize him in yourself?

Who Oversees the Overseers?

THE COMMONWEALTH enforces morality on its citizens — but who enforces morality on the commonwealth?

We are punished, as individuals, if we lie, steal, use violence or kill — but what effective restraints prevent the commonwealth from doing the same?

What is murder for a citizen in peacetime is bravery and glory in wartime. What is theft for an individual is conquest for a nation. What is lying for a person is diplomacy in foreign relations.

There is a common morality among citizens of a community; but there is no common morality among nations. Nations are above the law; they make their own laws, and break them at will — if it serves the "national purpose," if it is for "self-defense." And every war is, of course, for self-defense.

When our children look at the behavior of nations, throughout history and up to the present day, what can we tell them about their own morality? How can something be "wrong" if an individual does it, and "right' if an institution does it? Especially since institutions are supposed to exist for the benefit of individuals, and not the other way around.

Who has custody of the custodians? This ancient Roman question has not even yet begun to be answered. The commonwealth is the custodian of our conduct, but its own conduct is often at shocking variance with what it prescribes for us.

This is perhaps less true in a democracy than in a totalitarian society — but who would say that the American people decide where we are going, what we are doing, and how we are doing it? If we plunge into war, will the American citizenry have any more to say about it than the Russian citizenry? Do we have the information, the time, the resources at our disposal, to make such an irreversible decision?

The world has grown too big and too small at the same time: too big in its complexity, and too small in its dimensions. What affects one affects all — and yet the problems are so intricate, the variables so many, the controls so sensitive, that everyone feels paralyzed and ineffective and overwhelmed, like an ant in an avalanche.

All people everywhere want basically the same things for themselves and for their children. It should be the task of governments to reconcile these common ends with the functions and needs and different systems of each society. Instead, the differences are exaggerated, and the common ends obscured. Can anything short of a global catastrophe bring us to the light? That is the only question worth asking today.

Radical Righters Are Fascists

IT's AN interesting peculiarity of our social order that while the term "Communist" is flung around frequently and often carelessly, its opposite number, "Fascist", is hardly used at all.

In Europe, this is not the case. People have no hesitancy in speaking of the right-wing radicals as "Fascists," for this is what they are. To speak of them as "extreme conservatives" is a foolish contradiction in terms.

And it seems quite plain to me that there are many more Fascists and Fascist sympathizers in the United States than there are Communists and their sympathizers — unless, of course, you care to adopt the Fascist line and suggest that everyone who favors staying in the U.N. and retaining Social Security is a Red fellow traveler.

We seem to be so exercised about Communist influence in this country, which is negligible, both in numbers and in appeal to the American temper. Yet, year by year, one sees a Fascist spirit rising among the people, although it is called by many other and softer names, and has even achieved a certain dubious respectability in some circles.

There is no reason why there shouldn't be a Fascist movement in this country; nearly every nation has one. But it should be called by its right name, and it should be willing to accept the consequences of its position, as the Fascist parties do elsewhere.

It has no business masquerading as "Americanism" or "conservatism" or "patriotism," when its whole philosophy of man is based on a hate-filled exclusiveness that would shock and affront the conservative American patriots who founded this country.

What is distressing about this movement is the tacit or open support given to it by men who genuinely think of themselves as "conservatives," and who do not understand the implications of right-wing radicalism any more than the German industrialists understood what would happen to them when Hitler swept into power with their support.

Just as Communism always begins with an appeal to "humanity" and "equality" and ends with inhuman despotism, so does Fascism always begin with an appeal to "nationalism" and "individualism," and ends with a military collectivism far worse than the disease it purports to cure.

These twin evils are the mirror image of one another. It would be the supreme irony if, in rejecting the blandishments of Communism, we fell hysterically into the arms of Fascism disguised (as always) as Defender of the Faith.

Whose Face Is That in the Mirror?

THE SENSELESS murder of the President was a mirror we were forced to hold up to ourselves — and we did not like, or believe, the image that we saw.

"How could it happen here? In this day and age? In our country? I thought such things happened only in history. In Europe. Somewhere else and long ago."

These were the reactions of Americans. They bespoke a tremendous ignorance and delusiveness about ourselves. For, as I have written many times in the past (and have been assailed for so writing), we are a violent people who do not know the range and force of our primitive feelings.

Why should it not happen here? The last three Presidents out of four have had assassination attempts on their lives. Nowhere in Europe is this true; in most such countries, the chiefs of state walk about virtually unguarded.

In this day and age? This is the age of the most ferocious war the world has ever known, the most bloody dictatorships, the gas ovens, the concentration camps, the bombings of Hiroshima and Nagasaki by a "peace-loving" nation.

In our country? Why not, with our staggering homicide rate, our casual and callous auto fatalities, our shocking prevalence of firearms, our frontier relish for combat and conflict, our contempt for courts, our cynicism about the effectiveness of orderly processes.

If anyone still doubts this, consider the cry of applause that went up from the crowd gathered outside the Dallas jail when it learned that the presumed assassin of the President had himself been shot down.

This reaction is, to me, more appalling and more revealing than anything else in the whole nightmare of the weekend. Here was a man not known for sure to be the killer. He had not confessed, not been brought to trial, not defended, not sentenced. And he was killed while in the very hands of the police.

And the crowd outside shouted its approval of this bestial, stupid and irrational act. This is frightening, this is disgusting, this discloses the profound failure of our society to instill in its citizens any real sense of civilization, any idea of the meaning of law and justice. This is what turns our country into little better than a jungle.

If this dreadful murder of a President makes us see ourselves more clearly, makes us re-examine our feelings, makes us determined to purge the violence within each of us and all of us, it will not have been in vain.

Why We Can't "Sell" U.S. Abroad

A HIGHLY PLACED advertising executive has recently bemoaned the fact that America has been unable to "sell itself" to the rest of the world. Why is it, he asks, that America has raised advertising to its ultimate potency in terms of products, and yet we apparently cannot use these same powerful techniques to sell "the American way" abroad?

There are two answers to this, I think. First of all, we do not agree on what we are "selling" as a nation. We are confused and divided as to what "the American way" actually consists of.

A country is not a product, with a constant level of quality and a standard brand. It is a vast plurality of ideas and emotions, institutions and attitudes. It is, moreover, a unique blending of democracy and anarchy, capitalism and socialism, egalitarianism and class-consciousness.

Secondly, it is impossible to sell something you are too close to. We do not have a cool perspective on our nation because we live in it and we love it, with all its faults and imperfections. And a man is a bad salesman when he is too emotionally involved in the object he is trying to sell.

For example, it is an amusing irony that advertising agencies can sell anything — except themselves. The one product they cannot seem to hold is their own services. Every week, according to that interesting journal, *Advertising Age*, dozens of accounts shift from one agency to another. The advertising business is in a perpetual state of flux, and no agency can be sure that a large account may not suddenly decide to turn elsewhere.

This is because the agencies are too close to themselves to examine their own flaws with a candid eye; and also because they are curiously ineffectual in *selling themselves* to their accounts. They may be able to persuade the public to remain loyal to a brand, but they are much less successful in persuading the account to remain loyal to an agency.

Salesmanship requires enthusiasm, to be sure; but it also requires objectivity — and we cannot be objective when our deepest desires and drives are intimately involved.

America cannot be sold abroad, as we sell a soap or a soft drink, because we have too little perspective and too much passion. When we understand ourselves better, and love ourselves a little less, we may find that the rest of the world might not have to be "sold" on us.

What Good Is a Phony "Image"?

I was pleased to read that at a recent meeting of advertising people in New York, the director of creative projects at NBC news told the group that the worst word ever coined by advertising people is "image."

As reported in *Advertising Age*, he said that "substance and truth are the important things, rather than image, even if the picture is at times unpleasant."

The "image" is what the public sees and hears; the reality behind the image may be quite another thing. If we labor heavily and expensively at the image, and make the public believe what we are not, then there is little incentive to change the reality itself.

There is the same difference between the old-fashioned words "character" and "reputation." A man's reputation is what others have been trained to think about him; his character is what he really is. If he devotes most of his efforts to improving his reputation, for its own sake, then his character will inevitably suffer.

"We must change our image," says a company — but an image must be a true reflection of reality, or it is a fake. And the only permanent, meaningful way to change an image is to change the substance behind it.

The substance cannot be changed by publicity, by promotion, by advertising — but only by a radical re-examination of one's goals, standards, and values. This is hard work, and often unpleasant to face, but it is the only ultimately rewarding way to merge the reality with the image.

What others think of us is, of course, important; and we do not want them to have a wrong conception. Yet, merely dressing up our image to please and flatter and beguile the public is a form of prostitution, unless the inner self conforms to the outer appearance.

When a professional group, such as doctors or lawyers, feels that its image has become somewhat tarnished in recent years, it usually opens a barrage of publicity about the "dedication," the "service," the "high ideals" that animate these professions. Rarely is any attempt made to remedy practices and reform procedures that have tarnished the image.

It is generally considered sufficient if the public is persuaded to adopt a newer and brighter image; but this, too, will fail the test of time if the substance is not altered — and successive campaigns will have to be more intense and hysterical to offset the renewed cynicism.

"Image" is a word we should all forget as quickly as possible. It is a debased currency, whose purchasing power decreases the more we inflate it with publicity.

Television's False Defense

THE CONSTANT theme of the hucksters in the field of entertainment — which today means mostly television — is that they are "giving the people what they want."

Those of us who deplore the moronic offerings in mass entertainment are sneered at as eggheads who are out of touch with reality. The hucksters insist that not only are they giving the public what it wants, but the public loves it.

Both these propositions are demonstrably false. As a glaring example of their falsity, I cite a recent syndicated television column out of Hollywood with the headline: "40 Nighttime Shows Destined for TV Ax."

The story said: "At least 40 of network TV's current crop of weekly nighttime shows will be dropped by summer. About half of this number were series which made their debuts last fall."

If the hucksters know what the people want, and are giving it to them, how does it happen that the majority of TV programs lead so brief a life and undergo so suddenly tragic a death? Why is programming in such a constant state of chaos and confusion? Why is the search so desperate for "new" material — which usually turns out to be as ghastly and unimaginative as the old material?

I submit — on the overwhelming evidence itself — that not only do the producers and networks not know what the public wants, but the public itself does not know until it gets it.

It is a false assumption to hold that the demand creates the supply; in the arts and entertainment, it is the supply that creates a demand. There was, for instance, no "effective demand" for off-Broadway theater; but the supply continued until the habits of theatergoers were changed, and today off-Broadway theater is the most vital and fruitful aspect in American drama.

There is never a demand for anything that is good until it comes along and takes hold of people. This it cannot do unless it is given a chance, unless time and care and money and energy and patience are expended upon it. Advertisers well know this — there is no demand for a new product, generally speaking, until repetition and exposure over a wide area and for a considerable time generate such a demand.

It is nothing less than a downright lie to suggest that the TV producers are giving the people what they want — and the frantic activity in changing program formats every few months exposes this lie. And it is equally mendacious to suggest — as one recent book does — that the viewers on the whole are "satisfied" with their TV fare. If they were, television would not be the programmatic lunatic asylum it has become.

Don't Judge a Book by Its Uses

THE OTHER evening I heard a man arguing that a certain book should be suppressed because it contained material that could be "dangerous" and "harmful" if it fell into the wrong hands.

His attitude — so common and so wrongheaded — reminded me of what Jacques Maritain, the great Catholic scholar, had to say on the same subject: "If books were judged by the bad uses man can put them to, what book has been more misused than the Bible?"

In the fifteen hundred years since it was codified and made canonical, the Bible has been used by innumerable sects and rulers to justify (and indeed to exalt) the burning of witches, the torture of heretics, the practice of slavery, the extermination of peoples, the subordination of women, the custom of polygamy, and scores of cruelties, barbarities and bigotries of the most odious nature.

Almost anybody can use almost any book for almost any purpose. I have been recently going through a collection of Nietzsche's works. All most people know about him was that he apostrophized the "superman" and that the Nazi movement seemed to take much of its philosophical impulse from Nietzsche's writings.

But a careful reading of his work shows quite the contrary. He was violently anti-German, and considered himself a "good European." Some of his finest passages indict nationalism and war; he opposed anti-Semites as vulgar and brutish. His "superman" was the diametrical opposite of Hitler's "Blond Beast." And he anticipated many of Freud's deepest insights into the irrational character of prejudice and hate.

Our own founding fathers provide a similar example. We can find in the speeches of Washington and Jefferson and Madison and Franklin enough to provide us with ammunition for nearly any cause. I could easily compile a selection of Jefferson that would make him sound like a revolutionary Marxist; and a selection of Franklin that would make him sound like a pacifist and a toady to King George.

To repress a book because it contains "dangerous" or "harmful" material would be to extirpate 90 percent of the world's great literature — for the greater a work of art is, the more universal, the more embracing, the more it can be misused for every perverted cause.

The only book that cannot be dangerous or harmful is the bland book, the meaningless book, the insipid and characterless book that discourages thought, feeling and reaction. And it is such books that proliferate when controversial works are suppressed; censorship, whether in Russia or America, always leads to the tyranny of the commonplace.

"Realists" and the Death Penalty

ONE MAN is opposed to capital punishment. Another man is in favor of it. Question: which man is the "sentimentalist"?

Most people would answer, I think, that the man who opposes capital punishment is the sentimentalist. He is the "bleeding heart," the idealist, the one who is "soft on criminals."

This is how words continually betray us. For all the facts we have available indicate that the man who opposes capital punishment is the realist, while the man who favors it *does so for emotional reasons and no other*.

In a new pamphlet, *The Unexamined Death*, an analysis of capital punishment by Hans W. Mattick, formerly assistant warden of the Cook County Jail, the author states in his conclusion, "The evidence indicates that those who favor capital punishment are sentimentalists, pure and simple."

The hardheaded and practical people are those who have actually examined the evidence and found that "capital punishment is irrelevant to the homicide rate." It is indefensible on any rational grounds, and is simply a form of legalized vengeance or "corporate murder."

There are, I believe, good moral and psychological reasons for abolishing the death penalty. But I am not concerned with them here; what interests me in Mattick's brief and pungent study of the subject is the overwhelming evidence that *capital punishment prevents no murders*. It does not do the one thing its proponents insist it can do.

What capital punishment does do is to provide society with an unjust and irrational outlet for its anger and fear. Furthermore, it permits us to close our eyes to the multiple causes of crime by getting rid of the symptoms only. Meanwhile, the crime rate continues to increase everywhere, despite more stringent penalties.

I have argued the case against capital punishment in previous columns, and I have never seen a factual refutation of it. But what is most ironic in this whole controversy is that the label of "sentimentalist" should be attached to the opponent of capital punishment, while the proponent smugly believes himself to be the "realist" in the matter.

If realism means understanding cause and effect, if it means proportioning the methods to the ends, if it means being for something because it really works in fact, if it means refusing to be swayed by emotional considerations — then it is the opponents of the death penalty who are realists, in any meaningful sense of that abused word.

(For a free copy of *The Unexamined Death*, write to the John Howard Association, 608 S. Dearborn St., Chicago, 5, Ill.)

Why Should Killer Show Remorse?

"THE KILLER showed no remorse."

In how many newspaper stories have we seen this sentence, or its equivalent? We are expected to be surprised that the perpetrator of a brutal crime is not immediately overcome with shame and repentence.

But in the modern age, in our society, the shame lies in being caught, in going to jail, in failing. Most criminals regret they were caught, and resolve — not to get caught again.

The emotion of remorse belongs to the conscience; and conscience is not an automatic mechanism within the human mind. It must be built in, carefully and patiently, during the early years.

We live in a success-oriented society. Our criterion is "getting away with it," and we respect the man who gets away with it, if his loot is large enough. We despise petty criminals not so much because they are criminals but because they are petty.

Children grow up not listening to what we say, but watching what we do. Their conscience is shaped by our conduct. If they see that the law can be twisted out of shape by those with the right connections and the power to do so, then they want connections and power.

Why does the automobile mean so much to boys as young as fourteen and fifteen? Because it means so much to their fathers. Because it has become a deep emotional symbol of status and influence and independence. This is why, by far, most car thefts are committed by boys too young to vote.

Why are the most abominable sex crimes perpetrated by youngsters who in our fathers' time would do no more than wreck a fence on Halloween? Because sex, along with success, has become a mainspring of our social order; because most of the material goods advertised in American life are keyed to the seductive lips, the soaring bosom, and the shapely leg.

It is not enough to blame "the parents" for the delinquencies of their children. The parents, too, are victims of our seductive drive for profit and pleasure as final goals in themselves. In a real sense, all of us are "the parents" of all young children — because we help shape the culture and determine its values.

Young people learn from everyone around them; family influence has declined as technology brings more things into the home and takes the children more easily out of the home. They are exposed to a hundred influences unknown or unobtainable a few generations ago. They are exposed to everything except that old-fashioned notion of "conscience."

So why should the killer show remorse?

Three Factors Really Deter Crime

THE PEOPLE who would increase punishment for crimes are not stupid; they are just innocent of any historical sense. For the whole history of mankind has shown that severity of punishment does not reduce or deter crime.

Punishment has become less severe over the centuries not because we are more humane or sentimental than past generations, but because hard experience has shown that punishment in itself is futile.

Men used to be subjected to the most horrible tortures and deprivations for even the pettiest of crimes; but the crime rate did not decrease with this treatment. When pickpockets were publicly hanged on Tyburn Hill in England, other pickpockets used to circulate among the crowd during the executions.

There are only three things that really deter crime — the *swiftness* of punishment, the *sureness* of punishment, and the *justice* of punishment. It has nothing to do with the length

of confinement (which merely brutalizes men), or with the
privileges that are given or denied in prison.

If we are not able to work out any rational and effective
preventive program for crime, it is our obligation to see that
our penological system is sensible and workable.

The crime rate is embarrassingly high in the United States
because punishment is slow, it is anything but sure, and it has
only the vaguest relationship to justice.

The length of sentences depends upon the criminal's wealth
and type of legal help more than upon the seriousness of his
transgression. Court procedures are slow and cumbersome.
It is the poor and stupid criminal who gets the heaviest sentence — so the aim of criminals is to become rich and cunning,
and thus avoid the harshest penalties.

It may surprise people who point to England's low crime
rate to know that the average prison sentence there is shorter
than in the United States. But the English system of justice is
swift and sure — money and politics do not intervene between
the prisoner at the bar and the judge on the bench.

Meting out heavier sentences is fanatically idiotic (and
cripples the reformative powers of prison), as long as the
lawbreaker knows that skillful legal talent and the right connections can long postpone or easily ameliorate his punishment. There is not a penologist or a prison warden in the
country who is not painfully aware of this contradiction.

When we demand greater punishment for lawbreakers, we
are really confessing our inability to cope realistically with the
corruption of justice in our amoral society.

Wanted: A Heavenly Housekeeper

THERE is a lot of talk about honesty in advertising, and most
of it is directed at the massive million-dollar sales pitches. But
I would venture that most of the dishonesty in advertising

comes from people like me, when we insert a "Help Wanted" ad in the classified sections.

We advertised for a new maid last week, and our invitation sounded as though we were offering nectar and ambrosia in the Garden of Allah. You know — Own rm., TV., pvt. bath, pd. vacation, Blue Cross, etc.

Actually if we had been honest, we would have advertised something like this:

Wanted: General housekeeper, cook, maid, child care, laundry. Must be sober, industrious, faithful, cheerful, thrifty, brave, clean and reverent. Willing to slave from dawn to dusk, and even later. Must love our children like a mother, treat our house like a church, serve our guests like royalty, put up with our careless habits, sacrifice days off for our convenience, have no or little personal life, and be perfectly content to stay in a small cell (pvt. room) when not actively working.

"No pension plan. No fringe benefits. No inducements that are offered by commerce or industry. Small pay, long hours, boring duties. If fascinated, call at once for interview."

It must be recognized, of course, that this sort of fraud cuts both ways. In the "Situations Wanted" columns, the job-seekers perpetrate the same grandiloquent deception, by representing themselves as "Exp., Cap., Rel., Eager, Intel., and Attctv."

If they too, had been wholly honest, they would have advertised something like this:

"Wanted: position with family of two employed adults and no children; am indifferent housekeeper and poor cook; Saturdays and Sundays off; no dinner guests served; am moderate alcoholic with arthritis; expect advances on salary; hate country, and will not accompany family on summer vacation; no heavy work; regard children with detached hostility; can operate washing machine but am world's worst ironer. Smoke in bed. Require 21-inch color TV set."

I've never known a family who frankly said, "We're stinkers to work for, and you can't blame the last four maids for quitting without notice," nor a domestic who ever admitted, "I'm only doing this because I can't do anything else, but don't expect me to do it well."

At any rate, if you know someone who's looking for nectar and ambrosia in the Garden of Allah, there's this marvelous family named Harris, whose children make Albert Schweitzer look like a delinquent, and who do practically everything around the house themselves, except clean the ashtrays . . .

Judgment Isn't Tied to Intelligence

ONE OF THE most serious mistakes we can make is to confuse the thing we call "intelligence" with another thing called "judgment." The two do not always, or necessarily, go together: many persons of high general intelligence have notoriously poor judgment.

One reason I cling tenaciously to the democratic doctrine is that I respect the overall judgment of the people, even though the average intelligence may be relatively low. Let me explain what I mean.

Every psychologist knows that, generally speaking, the larger the group the lower the intelligence level. When you expand a group of one hundred into a thousand, your intelligence curve flattens for the group as a whole. This can be demonstrated without any dispute.

Now, because of this phenomenon, there are those who maintain that democracy in a large society, such as ours, is unworkable and self-defeating. With 180,000,000 people, the average intelligence must be low indeed — and how can we then expect the electorate to rule themselves rationally and wisely?

But such people reckon without that quality known as

"judgment," which is not directly related to intelligence as such — a fact that is painfully known to the wives of many intellectual men.

For instance, it has also been proved by extensive psychological tests that *the larger the group, the better the judgment.* If you ask a dozen persons to estimate the weight of a desk telephone, the answers will vary widely, and the median answer is likely to be quite inaccurate.

But, if you ask twenty-four persons, and then forty-eight, and then double that again, by the time you have asked a thousand persons, the excesses on both sides have canceled each other out — and the median answer will be uncannily accurate.

So, while the collective intelligence of a large group is low, the collective judgment of a large group is quite high — and often much better than the individual judgments of the most intelligent persons within the group.

This is the rationale of democracy as a system of governing, apart from any moral or historical or political reasons. The more people who are enabled to judge a matter — provided, of course, that the society gives these people enough information on which to make a judgment — the more valid is this judgment likely to be.

When democracy does not work, or works badly, it is not because the intelligence of the "mass" is low, but because native judgment is impeded by lack of information, or emotional blocks, or the cumbersome machinery of administering a democratic society. It is not a lack in the people themselves.

Blue-Collar Men in White-Collar Jobs

I WAS CHATTING with a British auto mechanic who is now working in the United States. "Living conditions are wonderful here," he said, "but the standards of work wouldn't be tolerated anywhere in Europe for a moment."

The man is a craftsman of a high order, and he is appalled at the sloppiness and negligence going into many American products. "Most of the men here don't care how poorly they do their jobs," he shrugged.

I am convinced that the main reason for this lies in our insensate drive toward a college education for everybody, ending in a white-collar job, which alone confers "status" in our society.

American parents, on the whole, do not want their sons to be artisans or craftsmen, but business or professional people. As a result, millions of youngsters are being prepared for careers they have little aptitude for — and little interest in, except for the dubious prestige.

I know a newly-married couple near Pittsburgh who have just moved into their first house. The husband has drifted unsuccessfully from job to job in the business world since they were married.

Yet, almost single-handed he has transformed their ramshackle house into a thing of taste and splendor. He is magnificent with his hands, but he will not use them for occupational purposes because somehow it is thought to be "demeaning" in our society.

But he — and many thousands like him — would be both more prosperous and happier performing tasks of manual and mechanical skill. His family would be horrified at the thought, however, and he would be ashamed and embarrassed. Good family, good school, nothing to do but work in an office and drink too much.

Our culture has elevated the businessman to a status unprecedented anywhere in the past. The price we pay for this is an alarming, and growing, scarcity of willing apprentices in the field of craftsmanship.

There is little incentive here for an artisan to be proud of his work, if he cannot be proud of his position. Shoddy goods and poor servicing are not so much an economic matter as a psychological one. The pay is high, but the prestige is low.

The young man near Pittsburgh would be leading a much happier and more productive life in overalls than in a button-down shirt. He would also pay off his mortgage faster, but we have made clean fingernails a symbol of superiority that keeps many from doing at all what they can do best.

Nations Can Be Betrayed by Slogans

IF A NATIONAL slogan is repeated often enough and loudly enough, everybody begins to believe it, even if it has no truth. A people can easily hypnotize itself into taking The Word for The Fact.

I was talking to a German visitor from Hamburg the other night. He was born just before the First World War, and grew up during the German depression and Hitlerism.

"All during my early years," he said, "I had heard about our pressing need for *Lebensraum* — for more living room for the Germans. We were cramped, everyone said, and could not prosper until Germany expanded.

"I never questioned this slogan, nor did most of the German people. We bitterly resented the Treaty of Versailles, and felt that it kept Germany from any future economic growth. This was a large part of Hitler's great appeal, among other things."

It was not until Germany began to rebuild after the Second World War, he said, that the whole theory of *Lebensraum* collapsed into nothingness. Today, West German production is phenomenally high, employment is almost total, and the people are thriving.

"What is interesting about this situation," he pointed out,

"is that today we have less *Lebensraum* than ever. Our nation has been bisected and we are cramped for space — but this has nothing to do with our economic progress."

There are many factors responsible for Germany's industrial revitalization, but the problem of "space" has been shown to be irrelevant. Yet millions of Germans fought and died for this frightful illusion, not once but twice.

The slogans of other nations have been nearly as pernicious. For a long time, the ruling thought in Britain was "colonialism." It was believed that without her "profitable" colonies Britain would become destitute. Actually, colonialism soon began to cost Britain more than it gave her. Wisely, she cut her losses before they were fatal.

The Soviet people have lived under slogans for forty years, most of them bearing little relation to reality. Marx and Engels, were they alive today, would scarcely recognize what has happened to their concepts under the brutalized and cynical sloganeering of Lenin and then Stalin.

And we ourselves — are the American people exempt from the vice of living by slogans rather than by realities? Do our practices square with our preachment? Would our definition of "the American way" satisfy the founding fathers? Let us at least ask ourselves these questions.

Can a Nation Really See Itself?

NOBODY really knows what he looks like to others, no matter how often he may stare at himself in the looking glass. I wonder if this is as true of nations as it is of individuals — that we remain ignorant of the way we look to others?

Not long ago, in a motoring magazine, I was reading an interview with Stirling Moss, one of the world's greatest rac-

ing drivers, whose skill and courage are undisputed throughout the world.

He was speaking about the difference between American
and European motor races, and underlined the point that "in
Europe you don't get one driver pushing another . . . Drivers
don't chop each other off."

Over here, in America, he added, "I rather felt in the sports
car races that if you weren't prepared to push, then you
wouldn't get by . . . Racing has enough hazards; racing should
allow the best man to win rather than the one who is prepared
to literally push other people off the road."

We like to think of ourselves as a gentle peaceable, sports-
manlike people; and it shocks and saddens us when we hear
Europeans speaking about the "pushy" Americans. Are we
like the man with bad breath, who is the only person in the
room oblivious of his offense?

Anyone who has seen the English patiently queueing up
for buses, or for theater tickets, or at any booking office, must
surely have contrasted their behavior with the way Americans pile rudely into a crowded bus. And although motoring
habits are pretty bad all over the world — something in the
nature of a car seems to bring out the worst in men — yet
nowhere else in the world is there so much carnage on the
highways as in America.

We are often accused of being uncivilized, underbred, and
crude, and a lot of this criticism may spring from envy or
ignorance or malice; but are we sure that such accusations are
wholly without foundation? Do we really want "the best
man" to win, or do we reserve our admiration for "the one
who is prepared to push other people off the road"?

Where does courage shade off into recklessness? At what
point does aggressiveness become savagery? When does "the
will to win" become the overriding lust to win at all costs?

Where does "individualism" drop into anarchy and indiffer-ence and the bloody law of the jungle?

These are questions that, as a people, we rarely ask our-selves; for we are so busy priding ourselves on our gentleness, our generosity, our peaceful instincts. But when one of the world's great motoring champions begins to question our unnecessary roughness on the racing course, perhaps it is time for us to take a more searching glance at ourselves in the looking glass.

No "Freedom of Choice" in Clubs

AT DINNER the other night, a member of an exclusive club was defending the club's policy of limiting its membership to white Anglo-Saxon Protestants with the proper prep school credentials.

"We want to be free to choose our associates in the club," he said, "and we think that this freedom of choice belongs with life, liberty and the pursuit of happiness."

Now I have no objection if any private club or organization wants to limit its members to red-haired men with one leg and a maternal grandmother named Fortescue-Fortescue.

It is our privilege to be as silly or as exclusive or as narrow as we like. What I object to is calling this "freedom of choice" or "freedom of association." It is the exact opposite of these.

When a club arbitrarily limits its membership to one kind of person, it is denying itself freedom, rather than granting it. It is cutting off from possible membership all those who — despite their high personal qualifications — do not have red hair, one leg and a grandmother named Fortescue-Fortescue.

The members of an exclusive club actually have voted away their own freedom of choice. No matter how much they may like and respect a man named Steinberg or Shaughnessy, they cannot associate with him in the intimacy of a club setting. They might invite an Einstein to talk to the group, but never to join it. This is one reason exclusive clubs are so infernally dull — sameness inevitably leads to boredom.

It is also said by the proponents of this archaic system that, after all, it is a "social" club only, and therefore no one is really hurt by not being allowed to join for reasons of ethnic or religious differences.

But this, too, is a delusion and a hypocrisy. The city club and the country club are much more than "social." They are where business associations form and where deals are made. A firm would be mighty reluctant to hire an executive who would not be welcome in the city club or the country club, for this would be an unfair handicap to business success.

As I say, we have a right to be as foolishly "selective" as we like. But we will not be grown up until our selectivity is on a personal basis. Clubs should be as "aristocratic" as possible, in terms of seeking the "best," but as democratic as possible in seeking the best out of the widest possible base of candidates. To do less than this is to make a mockery of the phrase "freedom of choice."

Let's Get Rid of the People!

THE RECENT ban on folk singing in New York's Washington Square park is only a logical step in the whole philosophy of park commissioners in America.

Most parks already ban ball-throwing, bicycle-riding, roller-skating, and walking on the grass. Indeed, any activity that has the slightest tinge of human enjoyment is frowned upon as an infringement upon "clean" and "attractive" parks. The ultimate is "No People Allowed"!

Actually, this attitude is a symptom of the administrative

mind generally. To the administrative mind, man *was* made
for the Sabbath, and not the Sabbath for man. People interfere
with their neat little plans.

Just imagine what wonderful hospitals we could run if the
patients didn't get in the way. Think of the gleaming labora-
tories, the antiseptic rooms, the faultless corridors, the impeccable charts, if only doctors and nurses were allowed to popu-
late the nation's hospitals.

And the libraries. Perhaps things have changed since I was
a boy, but then the book borrower was considered a necessary
nuisance by most public librarians, who felt that we simply
interfered with the Dewey decimal system and the perfect
uniformity of each book in its proper place on the shelf.

Public housing, too, would approach the ideal if only we
could find a way to get rid of the tenants. They tend to eat,
which creates a nasty garbage problem. They also tend to
breed, and you know what children can do to walls and win-
dows, lawns and driveways. If people would only go live
somewhere else, we could have the most admirable public
housing system in the world.

Even in commercial establishments — where the public is
an absolute *sine qua non* of survival — one still finds evidence
of the administrative mind at work.

For instance, I have been in many restaurants where the customer is regarded as an unwarranted intruder on operating
procedures. The cashier is too busy going through yesterday's
checks to make change for your bill; the hostess is too involved
with rearranging tables for dinner to give you a table for
lunch; the manager, of course, is upstairs, working on reports.

Institutions tend to become ends in themselves. Parks were
originally designed for public pleasure, but after a time they
become transformed into a System of Procedures — and the
procedures take precedence over the public. Once we allow

singing in the parks, we might next get dancing, and the kind of fun people used to enjoy in the public squares. And then what would happen to Ordinance 639–B, subsection 2? It appalls the administrative mind.

Beware of the "Perfect" Argument

A few weeks ago on that splendid television program, "At Random," I listened to a man who seemed to be more or less of a spokesman for one of the new African governments.

He was plausible — quick, ready with facts, eloquent, smoothly reasonable, and unfailingly courteous. Yet I was suspicious of him the moment he opened his mouth, and the more he talked, the more I distrusted what he said.

Curiously enough, in the delicate art of persuasion, there is such a thing as being *too persuasive*. And this is precisely where "official spokesmen" usually fail: they have what mother used to call "a plaster for every sore."

An honest person, with a mind that is not entirely closed, will never seem so fully rounded in defense of his position. There are gaps in his thought; there are facts he does not have available; there are flaws that he is willing to admit; there are points he will permit the other side to score.

But the propagandist is smooth as a pebble, without a crack in his armor — and this, which seems to be his strength, is really his weakness.

We are not, ultimately, persuaded by someone who seems to have all the right on his side. We know that life is not that simple. We know that justice does not reside exclusively on one side of the fence, that no group (like no individual) is merely an innocent bystander in conflict and dissension.

Some months before, I heard another official spokesman, this time for the United Arab Republic. It is my own view that both the Arabs and Israelis have made some serious mistakes, have committed offenses against basic morality. But the more plausibly he defended his own position, the more I swung over to the other side. Nobody, I thought, could be that right.

We instinctively recognize fairness and the groping for painful honesty on the part of a speaker. We are much more likely to believe a man who stumbles a little, who is at times frankly embarrassed by an inconsistency in his reasoning, who is unafraid to display the chinks in his argument, and freely lets the cool air of differences ventilate his mind.

Rabid partisans, of course, cannot do this; the Communists have all the answers taped, immovably and eternally; so have their opposite numbers, the John Birchers and company. And none of these extremists can ever win an argument (or a country) on reason or logic; the Communists win on hunger, and the Fascists win on fear and frustration.

It is when the propagandist seems most plausible, most unassailable in his facts and inferences, that we know we are not listening to a Man but to a Line — and a Line is always a Lie.

Experts Are the Safest Drivers

SHORTLY after I bought my first sports car, I picked up a flock of motoring magazines, to learn a little about the strange new world I was timidly entering.

What impressed me first of all, and most of all, was the repeated emphasis on "safety" in all these racing journals. On the track, or on the road, the driver who neglects safety is considered a moron and a menace.

And I wished that more of the young men who tootle around town so carelessly in their hopped-up cars would read what all the great racing drivers and teachers have to say about safety as a primary consideration in driving.

These young men are being killed at the rate of 8400 a year. Auto accidents slaughter more Americans between the ages of sixteen and twenty-five than any other type of accident or disease. Ignorance, arrogance and carelessness are the three horsemen that accompany the fourth horseman of Death in motoring fatalities.

Contrary to popular opinion, if such young men knew more about cars and about racing, they would drive more prudently. It is the pro who knows how vulnerable he is, how thin the line between courage and folly.

Racing experts are unanimous in declaring that they feel safer taking a specially equipped car across the Bonneville flats at 400 miles an hour than in driving an over-powered, under-steered, nose-diving, tail-wobbling stock car down a highway at seventy miles an hour. "I'm scared to death in highway traffic," admits one racing champion, who knows how much there is to be frightened about.

As an interesting sidelight on racing philosophy, another American expert pointed out that "the aim of racing is to win at the slowest possible speed." Ponder this curious sentence for a while, and you will see that it makes great sense.

The racing driver wants to win — but not by much. A nose is as good as a mile, so long as you pass the flag before the others. The experienced driver holds his car down to the *slowest possible speed* that will enable him to win. Anything more would be foolish and perhaps fatal.

Contrast this mature attitude with the driving habits of the young men you see on the highways every day. Their aim is to go as fast, and as recklessly, as possible; to prove that they can beat you at the getaway and pass you on the straight. When you see an idiot of this kind, you may be sure of at least one fact about him — he is not an expert, and he would be ruled off every racing track in the world.

Menu for Today: "Human Interest"

A LADY writes in to complain that my column lacks "human interest" appeal. "You spend too much time on philosophy, psychology, the arts and all that stuff," she charges resentfully.

Well, what one person calls "human interest," another calls piffle, and I personally feel that the phrase has been twisted and distorted wholly out of shape. Most "human interest" items are inhumanly preoccupied with the trivia of personality, like this:

Did you know that Franz Schubert was eighty-seven years old when he wrote his most famous operetta, *Blossom Time*, which is the life of his father, J. J. Schubert, the famous theatrical producer?

Did you know that "Fatty" Arbuckle, the old-time movie comedian, was really a midget who drank forty bottles of soda pop each morning before going on the set, in order to bloat himself to the proper dimensions?

Did you know that Bolero wrote his most popular song, "Ravel," while acting as a courier for General La Fayette in the French-Indian Wars?

Did you know that Leonardo da Vinci invented the zipper in 1382, but buried the secret of his discovery in a vault because Queen Isabella refused to permit the use of anything but laces on women's corsets?

Did you know that Pascal refused to marry Cleopatra because her nose was too long, and that this international incident was the real cause of the break-up of the Holy Roman Empire?

Did you know that Shakespeare tried to write a play about

King Henry seven times and failed, before he finally wrote his successful *King Henry VIII?*

Did you know that Audubon's bird-hunting expeditions were financed by a committee of patrons including Florence Nightingale, Sir Percival Wren, Stephen Crane and Jerome Robbins?

Did you know that we call someone a "hero" today because of an ancient Greek athlete named Hero, who swam across Lake Marathon for his beloved, a beautiful princess named Leander?

Did you know that London policemen are called "Bobbies" after Robert de Lyon, an Italian detective, who cracked the Jack the Ripper case and revealed the criminal to be Oscar Wilde? Even today, there is a statue of him in every Lyon's corner-house in London!

Did you know that an obscure stenographer named Elsie Smith invented the first typewriter that was also a cigar humidor, which is named in her honor the "Smith-Corona"?

Did you know that nothing paralyzes the intellect so swiftly or surely as a morbid addiction to this sort of human interest?

The Big Question — "How Much?"

OUR NATIONAL temper is most revealed not by the answers we give, but by the kinds of questions we ask. This is demonstrably true of individuals; and it is true of countries as well.

I know a man who is successful, intelligent and tasteful. Yet despite his taste he cannot refrain from asking "how much money" does any person or organization make.

If he hears about a famous pianist, it is not long before he wants to know "what he grosses" per week. If someone has bought a country estate, he cannot resist asking others how much they think it cost. He does all this quite unconsciously, and would be embarrassed to learn about his *gaucherie*.

As a people, we tend to do much the same thing. Our first questions about people or things or institutions are always the same: How much? How large? How tall? How long? We seem obsessed with size, quantity, wealth, the physical and material statistics of everything from a concert pianist to a cathedral.

We do not realize this, but the rest of the world does. Just as the English have a reputation for reticence, and the French for frugality, we have an international reputation for vulgarizing the unusual.

This passion for quantifying the world so that "qualities" become lost among numbers might almost be said to be our national neurosis; and it explains, in large part, the so-called "numbers game" that is making a jungle out of television and popular magazines and other media of communication.

Television shows, for instance, come and go with stunning rapidity; if a program doesn't catch on within a few weeks, it is scheduled for the axe. This means it has to attract tens of millions of viewers. The quality or depth of interest of these viewers are not taken into consideration — merely their raw numbers. But there is no loyalty, no stability, no persistence, in mere numbers.

The height of a building tells us nothing about its architectural virtues or flaws; the size of a man's income tells us nothing about his personal value; the length of a freight train is irrelevant to the commodities it carries — half the cars might be empty. And a magazine with eight million tepid readers, who were practically given a subscription at one-third price, may be less durable and less effective as an advertising medium than a magazine with one million enthusiastic readers.

All this preoccupation with size and quantity bespeaks a basic insecurity in our national life; it is no accident that our folk-hero, the Westerner, is always impossibly tall — how else would we know he is fated to be successful in the end?

Are the Beatniks Meaningless Rebels?

DURING a panel discussion at a college recently, several of the audience asked me what I thought of the Beatniks. When I asked them, "Which Beatniks?" they were stumped for a reply.

Like any other group that is too easily identifiable by a word, the Beatniks are composed of many different types, ranging from a few true individualists with taste and talent to a great mass of imitators with neither.

On the whole, I find the emergence of a Beatnik movement more healthful than otherwise for our culture. I think it is good to have protest, however futile or foolish it may seem; and good to have a reminder that our substantial, materialistic, middle-class values are not the only values in life, and maybe not the most important ones.

Of course, many of the Beatniks are fakers and deadbeats. But, then, so are many persons in other strata of life. I know a considerable number of young men in business who wear clean shirts daily, have impeccable family connections, and titles on their office doors — and they, too, are simply paid loafers who happen to have jobs because of affluence or influence.

In the 1920's America had a bohemian movement in the arts that proved most fruitful: out of it came many of the best novels, plays, paintings and music we have had in the twentieth century. Greenwich Village was dirty and casual and disrespectful and flippant — but it was also creative and imaginative and aware that man is more than a feeding and sleeping animal.

The Beatnik movement may exhaust itself in meaningless

rebellion, and may become a refuge for the merely bitter, the lazy, the prematurely disenchanted, the undisciplined who confuse their restlessness with independence. On the other hand, if out of it there emerges a handful of men and women with something new and striking to say, with a fresh vision of society, with a challenging approach to the problems of personal existence — then it will be worth all the beards and sandals and the other nonsensical insignia of the tribe.

A civilization must tolerate, must give room and air and liberty, to its cultural dissidents as well as to its political dissidents. One of the marks of social health is its permissiveness to be different, for the best as well as the worst grows out of eccentricity. The Beatniks may be dirty, but the ultimate influence can be a cleansing one.

Fine Police: One Answer to Crime

MOST PEOPLE innocently think that the way to "do something" about crime is by concentrating on the criminals.

This is looking into the spyglass at the wrong end. The only way to cut crime is by concentrating on the police. Police work must be turned from a trade into a profession — with professional standards, professional prestige, and professional pay. Any measures short of this will leave American cities wallowing in lawlessness.

As long as political influence can be brought to bear on the police department, the honest and independent policeman will become increasingly cynical about promotions.

As long as patrolmen are paid less than many skilled laborers, the force will not attract the caliber of men who are so desperately needed.

As long as the payoff — by restaurants, hotels and parking lots, among others — continues to operate as flagrantly as it does today, our young people cannot help but feel contempt for the forces of law.

These are facts the public refuses to face. The public wants criminals put in jail — but crime *prevention* is the only way to achieve crime *reduction*.

Anyone who has visited England, for instance, knows what a police force ought to be like. The men are well-trained, courteous, and proud of their jobs. They respect themselves, and the public respects them.

Crime in England is low not because punishment is severe — the average jail sentence is shorter there than in America — but because it is swift and certain. No delays, no fix, no payoff. The British public would not try to bribe a policeman. And the police, on the other hand, do not bully and badger the public. They recognize that a civil servant is supposed to be civil, as well as to give service.

We are sentimentalists about crime, although we call ourselves realists. We think that tougher judges or longer sentences or stiffer laws will reduce the crime rate — but this is futile daydreaming.

What reduces crime is the knowledge that the police are above influence and avarice; that they are well trained and well paid; that they are recruited from clean-cut young applicants eager for the life, and not sadists or misfits who talk and think and act pretty much like the men they are pursuing.

Some American cities have been highly successful in creating and sustaining such a police force. We will not be a civilized nation until every city has done the same.

How Can You Beat Mozart?

ONE OF THE reasons for abstract art, and atonal music, and experiments in writing has rarely been mentioned, much less discussed, either by the practitioners of the arts or by the critics. And that is the "unbeatability" of great traditional art. How can a modern composer hope to compete on the same terms with a Mozart, or a modern painter with a Rembrandt? The possibilities in those directions were long ago exhausted creatively.

Mozart I consider to be the greatest composer who ever lived; yet he was not a radical or an innovator. He simply carried to the most sublime height the musical fashion of his day. To compose in the style of Mozart today would be ridiculous.

Beethoven well knew this. His own music, when first performed, was assailed by the critics and public as "dissonant" and "harsh" and "revolutionary." He was forced to break with the Mozartian tradition simply in order to assert himself and to express his peculiar genius.

In painting, likewise, we can go no further in representational beauty than the masters of the seventeenth and eighteenth and early nineteenth centuries. What they did they did so superlatively well that no room was left in that direction for further effort.

When James Joyce wrote *Ulysses,* that landmark of modern fiction, he was trying to break out of the formalized structure of the traditional novel, to use words and feelings and ideas in new combinations and on deeper levels of apprehension. Whether or not he succeeded or failed, the significant fact is that he felt that the conventional novel was blocked off from creative progress.

Modern art, of course, has proved a boon to inferior talents. Since it is largely incomprehensible to the layman, it permits mediocrities to masquerade as "original" creators, and allows any foolish novelty to adopt the pose of boldness and profundity.

But surely geniuses like Picasso and Stravinsky do not need to hide behind the obscurities of modern art; Picasso can paint superbly in the classical style, when he wants to, and Stravinsky could easily write a traditional symphony of high quality, if he cared to.

Such men reach out for new forms just as architects try to design new types of buildings adapted to the age and the changing concepts of mankind. Why should anyone today build another Gothic cathedral? What would be the point of it?

Ninety percent of modern art is mediocre or false; but ninety percent of art in all times was the same. What has remained has been the ten percent that was fine. We must learn to discern the false and encourage the fine.

A "Sick" Comic's Views on Life

"I CAN'T UNDERSTAND the rise of those 'sick' comics," said a man the other day. "They attack everything, and they're against everything. They seem to take a perverse pleasure in turning all our traditional values upside down."

As a matter of fact, I happened to be reading the comment of a famous "sick comic" not long ago. His bitterness, his cynicism, his rancor, his iconoclasm, were evident in everything he said.

He was irreligious: "All religions issue Bibles against Satan, and say the most injurious things against him, but we never hear his side."

He was misanthropic: "All that I care to know is that a man is a human being — that is enough for me; he can't be any worse."

He was contemptuous of the American success story: "All

you need in this life is ignorance and confidence, and then success is sure."

He mocked our social conventions: "Good breeding consists in concealing how much we think of ourselves, and how little we think of others."

He despised our political system: "Ain't we got all the fools in town on our side, and ain't that a big enough majority in any town?"

He deprecated our American institutions: "In our country we have those three unspeakably precious things: freedom of speech, freedom of conscience, and the prudence never to practice either."

He attacked our civic life: "In the first place God made idiots; this was for practice; then he made school boards."

He maligned the U.S. Congress: "It could probably be shown by facts and figures that there is no distinctively native American criminal class except Congress."

He derided ecclesiastical authority: "A man is accepted into church for what he believes, and he is turned out for what he knows."

He perverted our moral axioms: "The moral sense enables one to perceive morality — and avoid it; the immoral sense enables one to perceive immorality — and enjoy it."

He expressed contempt for old age: "Well enough for old folks to rise early, because they have done so many mean things all their lives they can't sleep anyhow."

He scorned the pretensions of friendship: "It takes your enemy and your friend, working together to hurt you to the heart, the one to slander you and the other to get the news to you."

The name of this sick comic? America's favorite for a century. The fun-loving, irrepressible national figure, Mark Twain.

Those Chinese Are So Backward!

THE CHINESE COMMUNITY in Chicago — and in New York and San Francisco, and other cities that have one — celebrated its New Year on January 27. And what a bust it was. The Chinese New Year festivities included three days of introducing the Year of the Rabbit, 4660. But it wasn't anything like the way in which we celebrate the Christian era in 1963. I guess the Chinese just don't know any better.

There were no wild parties, no drunkenness, no automobile collisions at high and erratic speed. Instead, the heathens had a parade, followed by special movies and a Chinese opera.

The men didn't put on silly hats and slobber all over a nightclub table. Instead, following an old pagan tradition, they paid off their outstanding debts to meet the new year with a clean slate. And the women didn't even have sense enough to get loaded on champagne and ruin their new party gowns. Instead, they made their homes spotless, preparing to greet the new year by turning a new domestic leaf.

There were also absolutely no reports of Chinese juvenile delinquents hitting the beer bottles, filching their parents' cars, or similarly celebrating the Christian era's welcome to the year 1963.

For a long time now, the Chinese community has been a blot on the civic records of American communities. They just don't seem to want to participate in our national folkways.

They refuse to accept their rightful share of our alcoholics, our reliefers, our prostitutes, our delinquents, our deadbeats, our criminals, our reckless drivers, our fraudulent insurance claimants, our whole resplendent tapestry of urban living.

They won't even celebrate the new year in the American Way and in what has come to be the accepted Christian spirit.

The police blotter on any holiday — Chinese or Western — is almost totally devoid of their names. And the family courts and welfare agencies are shamefully snubbed by them.

I think we have a sacred obligation to send more missionaries to these benighted people. True, they seem to be backward in picking up our civilized practices, but with a little guidance and good will, I am sure we can get them to take part in our communal activities.

And, when they have forsaken their old-fashioned heathenish ways, maybe next year, or the year after, they will join the rest of us in proclaiming the Christian new year as decent, forward-looking people should — hats, horns, hooch, homicide and all. We can but hope.

The Steinbecks Are Disappearing

WHEN JOHN STEINBECK was awarded the Nobel Prize for Literature this year, his award probably marked the end of an era in American writing. Steinbeck is about the last of the "self-made" writers.

After being graduated from high school in Salinas, California, Steinbeck spent a year or so at Stanford and then left to go into newspaper work. With the exception of Sinclair Lewis, who received a degree from Yale (and then also joined a newspaper staff), most of the older generations of writers did not have the dubious benefits of a college education.

Ernest Hemingway left school to become a cub reporter; he had no college training at all. William Faulkner spent less than two years at the University of Mississippi, and then quit. Eugene O'Neill took a year at Princeton, and left hastily. All these men were Nobel Prize winners.

In the generation of the 1920's and 30's, such pre-eminent

writers as Sherwood Anderson, H. L. Mencken, Carl Sandburg and Ring Lardner were utterly divorced from the academic community — indeed, much of their literary satire and scorn were heaped upon the American colleges and universities in those decades.

Today, all this has changed. Not only do the bulk of writers take their degrees (and often go on to graduate work), but most of them continue to be associated with colleges as lecturers, instructors, or "poets-in-residence." From year to year, they travel the academic circuit, generously subsidized for the prestige of the university.

It is still too early to tell how this new relationship will affect the output and the quality of their creative work. The old class of professional writers was independent, irreverent, and sometimes militantly anti-intellectual. Heresy was their stock-in-trade.

The new breed has been quietly domesticated: they lecture, they preside at seminars, they patiently participate in writers' "workshops." They lunch with the Dean, dine with the President, and parade before the trustees on ceremonial occasions.

Creative writers should, of course, be the critics of their society; when they become a part of the Establishment, it is moot whether they have gained more than they have lost. Certainly, a university should harbor talents; but does a talent do best in a harbor or on the open seas?

Steinbeck and his immediate predecessors lived their professional lives on the open seas; like the buffalo and the whooping crane, they are a vanishing species on the American scene. The organization man is now gazing peacefully even in the groves of Academe.

The Negative Character of Power

ALTHOUGH Lord Acton said many wise and witty things about the nature of power, all that we remember is his famous aphorism that "Power tends to corrupt, and absolute power corrupts absolutely."

One of the most neglected aspects of the problem of power, however, has rarely been touched upon, even by so discerning a critic as Acton. And that is the predominantly *negative* character of power.

The power to create negative feelings is much greater than the power to create positive ones; this is true in every realm. As a drama critic, for instance, I have learned over the years that it is possible to keep the public away from a play I dislike; but it is impossible to make the public attend a play I happen to like.

Or, if a newspaper opposes a bond issue, it is much easier to defeat the issue than it would be to pass it with the paper's support. Most power turns out to be veto power: it can prevent, but it cannot promote nearly as well.

And what makes power precisely so dangerous is this negative character. If power does tend to corrupt those who hold it, is it not largely because the holders become cynical about their *positive* power?

A President, in his larger sphere, faces the same problem as a drama critic. He can prevent the legislature from enacting measures he disapproves of — but his positive power to get his own legislative program enacted is much weaker.

Dictatorships, of course, are almost always successful on a negative basis. Both the Russian and the German revolutions of our time were based on negative programs — on "liquidating" certain elements in the population. Hate, envy, despair, rage, fear — all these negative emotions are played on by revolutionary leaders to achieve their power.

A positive program, on the other hand, is rarely able to summon enough political or social power. A campaign based on decency, generosity, rationality, farsightedness, and constructive proposals does not rouse us to action. Every politician has known this since the Romans began feeding Christians to the lions.

The corruption of power, I am convinced, comes not so much from the untrustworthiness of those who hold power as from the elemental fact that they can effectively exercise their power only in negative terms. When a drama critic knows that people will not attend Shakespearean productions, no matter how enthusiastically he praises them, he becomes twice as vicious in denouncing second-rate plays — for power curbed in one direction always extrudes violently in the opposite.

Laments Passing of Old Tycoons

"GIVE ME the old-time tycoons," remarked my friend at lunch. "The ruthless operators who hired and fired without any sentimentality or hypocrisy."

"Why do you say that?" I asked — and then remembered that he had just been "let go" from a job he had held for fifteen years, after a merger between his company and a larger one.

"Because there's nobody I can blame, nobody I can be angry at," he said. "And that frustrates me, that starts my ulcer popping again."

"Have a glass of milk and explain yourself," I said soothingly.

"Well," he went on, "as you know, I worked for a big company. Everybody there was pretty decent. The pay was good, the working conditions were more than tolerable. We had all kinds of fringe benefits. All the executives were warm and sympathetic toward your problems.

"The thing is, though," he continued, "that they were just as warm and sympathetic when they let me go. Quite a few of us in the smaller company were squeezed out in the merger, you know. It wasn't our fault, and it wasn't theirs — and that's just the trouble, I guess."

"Why does that make it worse?" I inquired.

"Somehow, it's so impersonal," he said. "Individually, the men are all decent there. Yet the important decisions are made in an impersonal way by that legal fiction known as 'the corporation.' Everybody in authority was 'sorry.' Everybody tried to be 'helpful.' Each one said 'If it was my decision, you would have been kept.'

"And that's the whole point — it was no one's decision, except that fictional character. And you can't attack a fictional character; you can't argue with it; you can't appeal to its better nature — because it has only one nature.

"If I'd been fired by an old-fashioned tycoon, who didn't like my work or my personality or the way I wore my ties, I could at least understand it. There would be something tangible to hate or to accept. But this way, I feel as if I've been smothered by shadows — and you can't strike back at shadows."

"Why do you want to strike back?" I asked.

"Because I feel I've been done an injustice," he replied, "and all the executives I've talked to agree it was unjust. You know, the creed they live by is 'individualism,' — but I can't find an individual in the company willing to take the responsibility for knocking me off."

3

OF WAR
AND PEACE

The Prophet Deserves an Ear

In 1933, the great Christian mystic and philosopher Nikolai Berdyaev wrote a little book called *The Fate of Man in the Modern World*. It has just been reissued, more than a quarter of a century later, in a paperbound edition. (Ann Arbor Paperbacks. $1.75)

It is fascinating and frightening to read this book today. All his predictions have come uncannily to pass: the rise and decline of Nazism, the Second World War, the course of Russian events, the awakening of China, India and Africa, the threat of aggressive nationalism everywhere.

This quiet thinker, secluded in what practical men would contemptuously call his ivory tower, has turned out to be the most accurate prognosticator of our time. For in his ivory tower — which he describes as "Christian personalism" — he has been able to look down and chart the sins and errors of both Russian Marxism and Western materialism with devastating impartiality.

Berdyaev sees the life of the free spirit violated everywhere

— crushed by the despotic collectivization of the Communist state, and distorted by the shortsighted individualism of the bourgeois capitalist state. Nor is he an apologist for institutionalized religion, which he insists has surrendered to Caesarism and nationalism.

Whatever we might think of Berdyaev's ultimate solutions to these problems (which space does not permit me to set forth in detail), it should be chastening for us to reflect that it is always the prophet in our midst who deserves to be listened to — although it is usually too late when we are ready to pay respectful attention.

It is only in the ivory tower that we can achieve perspective, that we can rise above the day-by-day battle of contending forces, that we can take the long view, and assay the consequences of our actions and beliefs to our children and grandchildren. Down below, there is only sound and fury, and ultimate purposes are neglected for immediate "gains" that turn out to be fatal illusions.

What our age requires most of all is stepping back from the scene of combat, a withdrawal from involvement in daily events, so that we can shape our means to our final goals. Otherwise, we are the agents and victims of world affairs, not their creators or collaborators.

Nearly thirty years ago, Berdyaev foresaw the fix we are in today; even then he called for "a lessening of the sovereignty of national states" and a "movement toward a world-federation of peoples" as the only means of saving us from the global holocaust we are now facing. "One fears that the world will attain such an order," he wrote, "only after a considerable portion of humanity has been wiped out." Let us pray that he was wrong.

We Live in Two Worlds at Once

WE WERE walking down to the beach, on the last day of vacation. It was a morning fresh from the hand of God — sun and sky and wind and water, and birds coasting above the cliffs, and children tumbling about the sand.

It was impossible to believe, at that clear and suspended moment in time, that the other world actually existed — the world of bombs and warplanes, of revolts and repressions, of organized bitterness and official cunning and mechanized ferocity.

On a morning such as that, there comes a sudden, piercing knowledge that mankind is living through its own nightmare, that everything we call "real" in the big world is a feverish fantasy, that the only truth of existence resides somewhere here, between shore and sea, sand and sky.

Not that Nature is kind or benevolent; I do not subscribe to that sentimental fiction. But Nature is at least indifferent to our ends; it provides a setting which we can enjoy or mutilate or obliterate entirely. It gives us a choice of action, for good or ill.

The other world — the world of headlines — gives us no choice of action. We are mute walk-ons in a global drama we have neither written nor directed. As in a nightmare, we are controlled by forces we cannot comprehend.

Mankind has always known anguish and loss. But with a sense of purpose, with a feeling for the future, with a faith that goodness was recoverable, that wholeness and saneness were the ultimate and attainable ends of the pathetic and noble human struggle to find a meaning and a place in the universe.

We have become dehumanized. We now think only of "survival," like some blind, groping animals clawing their way underground. And not even survival as a people or a nation, but as a tribe, a clan, a family, defending its dwindling supply of water and food and air by machine guns aimed at their own neighbors.

Is the Greek dream, the Hebrew dream, the Christian dream, come to this — that we abdicate our humanity, call ourselves powerless before the forces of history, and retreat to our underground caverns, for the sake of a bestial "survival"?

Man was made to stand on the shore, to celebrate the sun and the sky, to use the wind and master the water, to care passionately for the children tumbling about the sand. He was made to grow in the image of his Father, to embrace his fellows everywhere, to open the doors, to feed the hungry, to return good for evil. Nothing is harder, but anything else is sure damnation.

No More Time for "We" and "They"

IT IS NEVER We who want the war. It is always They who want it.

They may be the Persians or the Spartans or the Carthaginians or the Yorkists or the Confederates or the Communists. There has always been a They.

But, from their side, We have always been the They. And, to them, We have always wanted the war. So, out of mutual fear and misunderstanding and dislike, We and They have always gone to war.

Obviously, there is only one way to end war before we end the human race. And that is for all of us to become a We. I know this is a foolish, impractical, impossible, idealistic solution. It has always been that.

But nothing else has ever worked. For thousands of years, the world has been guided by the practical, the possible, the realistic. And it has always failed. The next war has always been born within the peace treaty of the old one.

We have tried everything else — pacts and alliances and defense and extermination of the enemy and a League of Nations and a United Nations. We have patched and sewed, prayed and threatened, and ended by making new weapons for the new war against the new enemy.

Only now we have reached the end of that road. War has now become something bigger than We and They. We can no longer march off to war to protect our women and children — war is now coming to us, and the women and children will die along with the men, who have no place to march.

The human race is signing a suicide pact in its sleep. Events are slipping out of our control. No nation is "free," no nation is "sovereign" any more. Every nation owns the seas and the skies. The wind bloweth where it listeth, and radioactivity has no citizenship.

War has suddenly become obsolete as a means of deciding national differences. People everywhere in the world are beginning to know it, but governments do not yet know it. Governments are still a century behind the times, planning to fight with weapons they cannot control.

But there is no creative dialog between the people and their governments: none in Russia, and very little more here. The people feel carried along by forces they can neither guide, restrain nor comprehend. In the great Democracy, we have little more to say about war and peace than in the great Dictatorship. "What can one person do to stop it?"

We can think. We can speak. We can call for new ideas, for a personal, a moral, a humanitarian approach to world problems. If we are going to die, we can at least die as a consequence of our beliefs, not like animals, stunned and hopeless, in a war that nobody really wanted.

We Live in Two Kinds of "Time"

THE STRANGE, nightmarish quality of living in the world today comes from the odd juxtaposition of two kinds of time. For we are living both in "real" time and in "psychological" time.

In terms of "real" time, we are living on a globe no bigger than a walnut, and just as easy to crack. Or, to change the metaphor, modern science has packed us all into a tiny rowboat in the middle of a large sea, and a hole drilled under anybody's seat will drown us all.

But in terms of "psychological" time, most of us are still living in centuries past, stirred by ancient grudges, controlled by obsolete prejudices, driven by buried fears.

What brought this shocking contrast most vividly to mind was a recent item in the newspapers about riots between the Flemings and the Walloons in Belgium. When I read the item, I felt rather like Mark Twain's Yankee pulled back abruptly into King Arthur's Court.

This bitter dispute between the Belgians of Dutch ancestry and those of French descent seems as unreal and irrelevant as the fight between the Guelphs and the Ghibellines, or the Yorkists and the Lancastrians.

In "real" time, it is not only far too late to be a Fleming or a Walloon (except on commemmorative occasions), but it is too late to be a Belgian. It is almost too late to be merely a European — and Europe is just getting around to that idea in "psychological" time.

In an article not long ago, a scientist remarked that he had been accidentally locked up all night in a museum room with exhibits of dead crabs and lobsters. The experience so unnerved him that when the guard opened the door in the morning, the scientist embraced him, saying, "Thank God — you don't know how good it is to see a vertebrate again!"

It is too late to be anything but vertebrates, but members of a species called homo sapiens — the only species that seems bent upon its own destruction. We now have the tools to do what no other living creatures have ever been able to do before: to arrange our own extinction.

This is the prime fact of "real" time today; in the light of which, the rioting Flemings and Walloons seem as anachronistic as the Battle of the Frogs and Mice. Mankind is haunted by its past — like a neurotic patient, it cannot throw off its bondage to infantile memories, and remains fixed in an attitude of childish antagonism — living compulsively in psychological time, and unaware that real time is fast running out on all of us.

Can Freedom 'Win' the Next War?

I HAD a strange and disturbing dream last night. I dreamed that the atomic war had finally burst upon us. And I dreamed, also, that the United States had "won" it.

Of course, sixty million of our citizens were dead, and millions of others were dying. But we had knocked out Russia and China; the Communist threat was no longer with us.

Our side was now the undisputed victor in the war for world supremacy. Now it was our task to rebuild our economy and our society from the wreckage — almost half of our people dead or dying, our industry reduced to a fraction of its productive power, our biggest cities destroyed.

What could we do? Of course, it immediately became evident that the central government would have to assume extraordinary powers — perhaps for ten, twenty or thirty years. Prices would have to be regulated, and strict priorities given to everyone.

A "free society," as we now understand it, was no longer

possible. In order to survive its dreadful wounds, the nation would have to forgo the luxuries of competition, would have to concentrate on collective welfare rather than on individual benefit.

The men who had pulled us into war, crying, "Life wouldn't be worth living under Communism!" found that, having won the war, we were now living under something very much like Communism. We had defeated the enemy abroad, only to find it among us at home.

For the tragic paradox of the next war is that, in order to fight it, in order to survive it, in order to "win" it (if such a word has meaning), we will grow more and more to resemble our enemies. We no longer have Patrick Henry's noble choice between "liberty and death." There will be no such thing as "liberty" for those who survive the next war.

There is now a qualitative difference in war that has never existed before. The next war will not be merely bigger and noisier and more expensive than any of the others; it will be "lost" before it is begun, for its devastation will be so great that only a rigidly controlled and collectivized nation will be able to recover from it within a century.

This is why war as an instrument of national policy is no longer possible. If we lost it, we would perish or become slaves; if we won it, we would be forced to enslave ourselves to the rules of an ant society, and would have no choice but state socialism for the indefinite future. The military effort required to "crush communism" would so deplete us that the state here would have to be more powerful and centralized than ever.

As I say, this was only a dream; perhaps a nightmare; perhaps a vision.

Our Society Has a Split Personality

THERE ARE days, many days, when the world seems a cold and terrible place. So much cruelty, so much bestiality so much greed and indifference and blind anger.

Yet what we call "the world" is something different from the people who make it up. This is the enormous and stunning paradox of human society — that the institutions we have created, the mechanisms we have devised, are so much worse than we are.

For the people themselves, everywhere, are fundamentally decent. They are honest and well-meaning and wanting the same things for themselves and their families: a modest sufficiency, a little peace, a little pleasure.

I have been reading a new book written by a dope addict shortly before she committed suicide. It is a compelling and frightening book, for she and the other addicts seem nicer people than those around them. The police, the courts, the neighbors, the relatives, the whole machinery of our vast social order rolls its wheels mercilessly over these sick and helpless people.

Her story — authentic to its last gasp — is a bitter indictment of our behavior in the mass. There is no compassion, no understanding of the tragic plight of the addict. Our prisons are subhuman, our courts are Kafka-like nightmares, our police are coarse and venal, our whole apparatus of society is an expression of our fear, hostility and ignorance.

If, however, we examined each of these oppressive persons as an individual, we would find them kind and decent in their personal relationships — loving their children, supporting their parents, feeding stray cats, contributing to charities.

There exists a tremendous schizophrenia between our private and our public morality. Our attitude toward addicts is only one dramatic facet of this split. Individually, we would not treat dogs the way we permit migrant workers to be treated in this country. Our frightful housing situation shocks us only when a baby is bitten to death by rats; we think nothing of the others who die more slowly, suffocated by the slums.

And this schizophrenia, of course, is projected outward to the world. Nations behave toward each other as they never would to their own people; diplomacy and war confer a spurious legality upon the most immoral acts. We will not see an end to any of this until we fit together the two parts of our being, and learn to act institutionally in the kind manner we act personally.

Why a Man on the Moon?

WE KNOW what we need the money for — schools, hospitals, mental health programs, housing, transportation, help for the destitute. And we don't know where the money is coming from.

But we know where an immoral amount of it is going: $20 billion for our "Man on Moon" project. One-fifth of our total national budget to put a man on the surface of our desolate satellite. An American man.

And for what reason? Despite all the fancy-sounding and pseudo-scientific phrases by the administration, Governor Rockfeller was substantially right in calling it a "publicity stunt."

The chief reason is "national prestige." We want a "good image" on the moon. We want to beat the Russians there, but the place to beat them is here, by demonstrating to the peoples of the world that we are dedicated to peace, abundance, and justice.

An unmanned flight to the moon would cost a fraction of what we are contemplating, and would provide us with 95 percent of the scientific information to be got from a manned flight. Scientists know this, but scientists are not running the space program; the government uses their specialized knowledge, but is not deeply influenced by their opinions.

Besides, as Rockefeller sensibly pointed out, there is an excellent chance that the Russians will beat us there, anyway. Since they cannot compete with us in terms of providing for their citizens, it is psychologically most necessary for them to focus on their technological achievements. (Just as it is essential for them to win Olympics medals by sending "amateurs" who are coached and treated like professionals.)

The "prestige" of the United States depends not upon races — either to the moon or the end of a taboggan slide — but upon an unyielding devotion to the principles that made our birth as a nation the most inspiring event in Western history.

It depends upon our taking seriously — as we have not in the past — the Declaration of Independence and the preamble to the Constitution. It depends upon living up to ourselves in peace, and not merely dying up to ourselves in war; for, as Alfred Adler astutely remarked several decades ago, "It is easier to die for one's principles than to live up to them."

Twenty billion dollars to plant an American flag on the wastes of the moon — when a fifth of our citizens are still living in dire poverty, and two-thirds of our budget goes for military expenditures — is a shocking example of national irresponsibility and immaturity. The sophistication of science must not be used for such simple-minded goals.

Man's Ingenuity Is Misdirected

A FRIEND in from Washington was telling me about our complex and elaborate defense program — our warning sys-

tem, our lines of communication and our enormously in-
genious means of anticipating a sudden attack.

He told me nothing secret, of course, and nothing in detail;
just the general outlines of the program, and its vast technical
ramifications. As I listened, I became more and more glum.
His story did not make me feel safe, but sorry. The contrast
was so appallingly great — between our technical ingenuity
and our lack of machinery for keeping and holding the peace.

If one-fiftieth of the brains and money and time and energy
the nations put into arms went into devising a world system
for peace, we would be well on our way toward a solution
of present international difficulties.

Why should so much of our intelligence and cunning and
resources go toward creating a war apparatus, and so little
toward the common problems that face the human race: food
and shelter and disease and population explosions and economic justice?

It is not enough to blame the Russians for this impasse; long
before Communism was even a word, nations behaved in
exactly the same manner.

The difference today — the dismal and depressing difference — is that now we have the scientific and technical ability
to provide a decent habitation, and subsistence, for most of
the world. Imagine what the tens of billions spent for armaments could mean in terms of productivity in every corner of
the globe.

The problem extends far beyond politics; it is the central
moral problem of humanity, of survival itself. Are we to
perish wholly, because we mobilized our vast resources for
annihilation, and not for creation? Is it the final irony of the
human race that we deliberately use our wealth and skill and
intelligence for mutual destruction?

And this problem cannot be solved at the political level, the
diplomatic level, the ideological level; it can be solved only

at the moral and spiritual level, only when enough people stand up as individuals to protest against this lunatic betrayal of the human race.

How can we invent such magnificent machines, devise such brilliant technical systems, cooperate in such scientific ventures — and yet fail to use any of our God-given reason to construct a world order that is sane, just, and truly civilized? Our means are miracles of ingenuity, and our ends are barbarous remnants of prehistoric times. We are living in the most crashing paradox of history; and it may be the last one.

The Nightmare Race for Energy

THERE ARE two main reasons for war: one is external, and the other is internal. One is in the world; the other is in the mind.

The external reason is "gain," of one sort or another — land, minerals, property, slaves, gold, and all the familiar fruits of conquest.

The internal reason is "fear" of one sort or another — fear of being attacked, of being outstripped or outshone, of being dishonored, or simply the animal fear of the strange, the different, the unfamiliar.

When these external and internal reasons converge — as they do with periodic regularity in human history — a war is inevitably set off. They represent an irresistible combination of explosive factors.

All this has changed today, but we still do not know it. The external reason is fast disappearing in modern society: science has begun to conquer the secret of *energy*.

In the past, the national drive for slaves, for coal, for oil, for arable land, has been the desire for increased energy which can then be translated into wealth. It required an immense amount of hard work to attain and harness this energy effectively.

We are now on the threshold of liberating thermonuclear energy. By discovering the principle of magnetic heat insulation, scientists have demonstrated that within our lifetime the thermonuclear generation of electricity could be in global use.

What this means, of course, is that the material well-being of everybody everywhere could be raised to a reasonable level. There would no longer be "underdeveloped" countries; the vast inequities of wealth and poverty in most parts of the world would be equalized — not in the Communist way of taking away from the rich, but by giving to the poor from this unprecedented surplus of thermonuclear energy.

This is not a dream. It is not a utopian mirage. The very same technological advances that make the next war so frightening and so incredible contain the potential for *removing the material causes of war*. And this is the supreme irony of our time: we are so close to man's perennial hope of well-being, and yet never before so close to extinction.

It is a nightmare race we are engaged in. Can we restrain our internal reason — our fear, our hate, our lust — long enough to create an adequate organization of society that will utilize these new sources of energy for peace and security? Can we tame the beast within us until we have created abundance for all? This is the first, and perhaps the last question facing mankind today.

A Handful of Fool's Gold?

As WE ENTER the fateful year of 1964, I am somehow reminded of an entry in the log of Peary when he was trying to reach the North Pole more than fifty years ago.

On this trip, he traveled a whole day toward the North, his sled dogs unflagging in their speed. At night, when he checked his bearings to determine his latitude, he found to his surprise that he was much further south than he had been in the morning.

All day, it seems, he had been driving toward the North on an immense iceberg drawn southward by an ocean current.

And sometimes it occurs to me that we are all standing on this iceberg, racing forward in one direction, while the very ground beneath us moves implacably in the other direction.

With tremendous speed and power, we are moving toward discoveries and inventions that utterly dwarf Peary's conquest of the North Pole. In medicine, in technology, in food supply, in materials and techniques and processes, we have made more progress in the last fifty years than was made in the previous five hundred.

Yet, at the same time, the ground we are standing on steadily seems to move backward, drawn not by ocean currents, but by social currents too vast and deep for us to comprehend, much less to control.

As we check our bearings to determine the latitude of the human condition at this point in history, we are more surprised and appalled than Peary to learn that we are "farther south" than our fathers or grandfathers were.

The first two thirds of the twentieth century have witnessed a monumental regression from the hopes and aspirations of the nineteenth century. For now, with all the new techniques at our disposal for mastering nature and controlling our own destinies, we appear farther than ever from our goals.

The gigantic iceberg we stand on is the whole world; and no man, no nation, can alone change the current in its course. But, hopefully, unlike the ocean currents, the social currents are not immutable. They are made by us (however slowly, however unconsciously), and can be redirected by us. But not while we continue to race against each other.

Perhaps we shall never know unity (which is not unanimity), or harmony (which is not uniformity), but then our children and their children will have inherited from us only a handful of fool's gold. Nearly two thousand years after the birth of Jesus, it may possibly be time for us to take His message seriously, or to stop pretending that we do.

We Need Preventive Statesmanship

LIKE A dilatory patient who goes to see the doctor six years after the onset of a hacking and chronic cough, the human race is concerned only with symptoms and not with diseases, only with cures and not with prevention. We are now looking for a pill to cure our cosmic cancer.

"What can we do about Cuba?" asks the worried citizen — and there simply is no satisfactory answer any more. Six years ago, or more, when the corrupt and repressive Batista government was ruining the country, we asked no questions about Cuba.

When it was perfectly evident that Hitler was about to overrun all of Europe, we asked "What can we do about the Nazis?" The only answers were war or surrender; the disease had progressed too far and too fast.

Nobody was much concerned about Germany in the years between the Armistice of the First World War and the Depression — years when the Nazis were making the most out of Germany's impoverished condition. Likewise, by the time the Bolsheviks took over Russia in 1918, it was already too late for the world to do anything but fight or accede to it.

Preventive medicine has grown enormously in the last few decades; but there still is no preventive statesmanship, no inoculation against the virus of war and tyranny and revolution.

We supported, both actively and passively, Batista's rotten administration in Cuba. Anyone with a grain of political sense could have foreseen that the pendulum would some day swing to the other extreme — that a Castro is the logical outgrowth of a Batista, as the terrible excesses of the French Revolution followed the excesses of the French monarchy.

In physics, every schoolboy knows that "action and reaction are equal." The same is true in the political life of mankind. The repressive Czarism was followed by the even more repressive Bolshevism; indeed, no nation with a history of democracy has ever voluntarily become totalitarian. Both Communism and Fascism have succeeded *only* where liberty had never been known before.

Cuba is a symptom, not a disease; Berlin is a symptom, not a disease; Korea and Vietnam and a half-dozen others are all symptoms and not diseases. And there is little that one can do about a symptom while the disease persists.

They are all symptoms of the world's neglect, its indifference, its narrow self-interest, its unwillingness to face the obvious fact that preventive statesmanship is the only way to keep the peace. Whatever we "do" about Cuba today will be wrong.

Now We Face an Anonymous War

MANKIND has known all sorts of wars in the past — land wars, sea wars, air wars, wars of aggression, of independence, of defense, of retaliation, of attrition.

Now we are faced with the possibility of an utterly new kind — the anonymous war. It will soon be no longer possible to know who is attacking us. How are we going to cope with *that* kind of warfare?

This is no soft-headed fantasy of my own. The concept was expressed not long ago by the tough-minded defense analyst Herman Kahn, in his keynote address at the annual honors dinner of the Institute of Aerospace Sciences in New York. Kahn told the technically sophisticated group:

"Anonymous warfare would certainly complicate the problem of deterrence. For example, with different nations deploying submarines with Polaris-type missiles, it might be impossible to determine who fired any particular-missile. The same uncertainty can exist even for missiles fired from land or outer space."

With three, four, or a half-dozen nations owning atomic submarines, capable of firing at either coast from the ocean, how would we retaliate? Who would we hit back? Where would our bombers fly to? What war would we declare?

These are real and imminent questions, not hazy speculations. And this is why, in past columns, I have stressed the importance of our realizing that the next war will be *qualitatively* different than all others — and not just bigger and louder.

The possibility of anonymous attack is another reason that war is no longer feasible as an instrument of national policy. There are no longer two enemies drawn up on either side of a clearly marked line. It is no longer a chess game, but more like a bomb tossed into a crowded theater. Such old-fashioned concepts as "tactics" and "strategy" mean little when we do not know who hit us, and where to hit back.

Today we are worried about the Russians. Tomorrow it may be the Chinese or three other countries that have mastered atomic fission and built the fatal weapons. In the light of such developments, all our traditional notions of defense and counterattack and security have suddenly become obsolescent.

What we desperately need, as I have said before, is a revolution in our thinking to match the revolution in our scientific and technical lives. Future wars are unfeasible because they cannot be won, only lost. If we can persuade ourselves of that truth, perhaps we can begin to persuade the rest of the world of it, too.

Close Neighbors, Like It or Not

WE SPEAK glibly of the "shrinking" world of today — but do we actually realize how much the world has shrunk since our nation was founded?

When the original thirteen colonies decided to federate, they were much "larger" than the whole world is today. In 1776, the fastest courier required twenty days to take a copy of the Declaration of Independence from Philadelphia to South Carolina.

This was about 575 hours to travel a distance of 350 miles as the crow flies: an average rate of about .61 miles an hour. A commercial jet today can easily go 610 miles an hour, or 1000 times as fast.

Since the world is about 24,000 miles around, if we divide it by 1000 (the number of times greater than our speed of travel is now), this represents a world only twenty-four miles in circumference compared to the world of 1776.

Consider a world that is only twenty-four miles around — about the distance from the north end of Chicago to the south end. And, of course, if we computed the same way for wire or telephone communication, the whole world would shrink to the size of a pea.

But this is the world we live in. Vietnam is no further than a drive out to the picnic grounds. Paris is a brief spin to a drive-in movie. Moscow is less than half a length of the city away. With a globe only twenty-four miles in circumference, compared to 1776, what validity is there in Washington's words warning us to beware of "entangling alliances"?

We are entangled right up to our eyeballs, like it or not. The world has become one city, in time and space. We cannot avoid being entangled with our neighbors, because the whole concept of distance has been so radically changed that a global war can now be declared, waged and lost in fifteen minutes.

Psychologically — much less politically and socially — we have not been able to catch up to these facts. We are not prepared for such proximity; we can barely endure our neighbors across the street, and now we are asked to cope with those across the world.

It is almost too much to bear in too short a time. Technology has plunged us into a tiny goldfish bowl together, and we are all swimming around furiously, wondering what happened to the spacious pond we used to live in. It is the most severe test of humanity that one can imagine. If the world goes to war, it may be more out of frustration than out of hostility.

"Insanity" in World Leadership

ABOUT A quarter century ago, W. H. Auden, the British poet, termed the twentieth century "The Age of Anxiety." The phrase took hold; in fact, Leonard Bernstein titled his symphony No. 2 "The Age of Anxiety" when he composed it in 1949.

I think the term is outdated. In the last half-dozen years, we have gone beyond the Age of Anxiety, and we have entered the Age of Schizophrenia. Our personalities are no longer merely disturbed — they are split, from top to bottom, among the leaders and among the people.

To me, the most obvious and appalling evidence of this schizophrenia can be seen in the hydrogen bomb testing by both sides. The split between what we *know* and what we *do* was baldly and accurately summed up by Ambassador Lall of India at Geneva this spring, when he said: "It will be of no help to the future to say that the purpose of further testing was a 'search for security.' No security can be found in this way — and the leaders of both sides have said so. The leaders of both sides have said that there can be no security through the perfection of weapons of mass destruction."

Ambassador Lall continued: "This is such a basic contradiction that it tremendously increases the apprehension of the world. Obviously we are standing near a very dangerous precipice if the very countries which announce that they cannot find security in the development of weapons still go ahead and develop weapons of mass destruction further and further."

What George Orwell called "Double Think" in his satire *Nineteen Eighty-Four* has come to reality twenty years earlier than he thought. In their speeches, both President Kennedy and Premier Khrushchev agreed that atomic war would be suicide, that no nation could be the "victor," that war as an instrument of national policy is no longer feasible.

Nevertheless — and "nevertheless" is always the sign of schizophrenia — both countries are going ahead with the spiraling arms race, both are testing, both are preparing furiously for "defense" in a war which cannot be defended. It is the ultimate irony that all we can agree upon is that everybody will lose.

If an individual behaved that way, he would promptly be

placed in a mental institution. But when nations behave as irrationally, their sanity is hardly questioned — and those few who dare to question it are branded as lacking in "patriotism." The world, as Balzac grimly predicted, is becoming an insane asylum run by the inmates.

Nuclear Killing Is Cheapest Yet

THOSE CITIZENS who are disturbed and alarmed about the "high cost" of our arms program have not really studied the economics of modern warfare. The total picture is bright indeed.

The billions we are spending for armaments may seem high, but in reality the cost of killing men (not to mention women and children) has become cheaper than ever before. It is almost, one might say, a bargain.

It has been estimated that in the American Revolution, it cost about $500 to kill a single man. During the Civil War, the cost rose to about $5000. In World War I, it was $25,000; in World War II, it was $65,000.

Thanks to the brilliant technological innovations of the last dozen years, in a nuclear war we will be able to kill a man for only $50. As Norman Cousins has pointed out, "a hydrogen bomb with the power of twenty million tons of TNT costs no more than $250,000. If TNT had been used, the cost would be more than $10 billion."

Nuclear bombs have extremely high explosive power per dollars of investment. When you double the destructive power, you don't add much to the cost; even when you increase the power a thousandfold, the cost is low.

Attractive as this is to us, from a sound bookkeeping point of view, it is also democratic — the nuclear bomb is a boon to the smaller, poorer, more backward nations. After the

initial investment, the smaller countries can afford to stock-
pile enough bombs to blow up half the world. This gives
them a parity with the larger nations, and allows the less
privileged peoples of the world to share the blessings of the
more advanced nations.

At last, war is becoming thoroughly democratized. In the
darker ages behind us, only large countries were able to wage
effective war — usually against their smaller and fatter neighbors. In the atomic age, however, even a third-rate power can
amass enough bombs to blow our planet into the next galaxy.
The nuclear bomb offers real equality of opportunity to all.

On a cost-accounting basis, not many men were killed in
World Wars I and II. The ratio between fatalities and total
war expenses was embarrassingly low. Men were hardly
worth murdering at those exorbitant prices.

Modern efficiency, however, has finally caught up with
the facts of extinction. The cost of living may be rising
steadily, but the cost of dying become a source of fiscal
gratification. When you can kill tens of millions at only $50
a head, you are pretty near the break-even point.

I hope that these warm and encouraging words give heart
to the disturbed among us. No dollar the government is
spending brings such a high return on investment as the
nuclear bomb program. You can be dead certain of that.

Try to Imagine a Million Fires

THE DAY I arrived in New York last month, I heard nothing
but the scream of fire engines from morning until well past
midnight. As you may have seen in the papers, the five
boroughs of New York together turned in 1000 alarms on
that Saturday in April.

The fire departments were taxed to their limits, and in some cases beyond. A grave water shortage developed late in the day. A wave of fires on southern Staten Island involved more than half of New York City's Fire Department alone.

In our muted discussions of atomic attack, we think mostly of the cataclysmic impact of the bomb. But, according to physicists I have read and listened to, the consequences of fire from such an attack are equally appalling. And the 1000 alarms on this Saturday would be infinitesimal compared with the conflagration begun by a single H-bomb.

How can we begin to imagine the unimaginable? This question, I think, is the clue to most of the passivity and fatalism of the public toward atomic warfare. Just as no finite and mortal person can *really* comprehend infinity or eternity, so none of us can actually grasp the apocalyptic quality of the next war.

Some things are too small to grasp — nobody, for instance, can really visualize the world of subatomic matter — and some things are too large. Man is a creature of the middle distance, and his vision is limited to objects in the middle ground.

It is no accident that the few philosophers of science in our time have pointed out the quite remarkable fact that the human species is, with almost mathematical exactitude, midway between the largest order and the smallest order of magnitude in the universe.

We stand in relation to the proton as the universe stands in relation to us. Such a concept is nearly inconceivable, except in a scientific formula, which robs it of all concreteness and existential meaning. But what a wonder, and a bafflement, that a creature'so equidistance from both magnitudes should be able to understand and (partly) control both of them.

There is no doubt in my mind that the human race is approaching its ultimate moral crisis. We have gone too far to turn back, we have opened too many doors that will not close again, and perhaps released too many demons that will refuse to be put back into their bottles.

The 1000 fires in a day were extinguished by heroic efforts; but we now have the capacity to start 1,000,000 fires simultaneously, with no capacity to extinguish them. Perhaps the most crushing paradox of our time is that never before has mankind been so powerful — and men so powerless. This is what we do not want to think of.

Lesson in the Metropolitan Mess

EACH TIME I visit New York, I think that the traffic cannot possibly be any worse — but it always is. On my latest visit, a few weeks ago, I walked the two dozen blocks from my hotel to the theater every night, in order to be on time.

If we want to understand international relations, the simplest analogy lies in a city itself. A city generally does nothing about its problems until the situation gets so bad that only radical remedies will work.

Most cities began one-way streets too late. They restricted parking too late. They built superhighways only when the traffic was so congested that the superhighways were obsolescent by the time they were finished.

Every American metropolis today faces the immense task of turning itself around, of demolition and rebuilding, of cutting out the cancer at its core, of coping with staggering problems of slums and race relations and poor schools and high taxes and the utter lack of planning that has characterized the growth of all large communities.

If we have not had the foresight to come to terms with relatively small problems within a given city, how can we expect that our relations with the world outside our borders can be any more rational?

"Too little too late" may be the epitaph of Western civilization. The modern twin menaces of Communism and Fascism — which are stronger than ever today, in various guises — could have been effectively aborted without great wars and widespread suffering. But we lacked the foresight, the concerted will, the energy to make the effort.

The most important part of medicine is preventive medicine. Everybody knows this. But we have not applied this knowledge to the social areas, whether it is traffic, or slums, or juvenile delinquency, or war and dictatorship. We spend, for instance, billions on prisons and reformatories, but hardly a dribble to erase the social and psychological conditions that create crime and delinquency.

Which American, private or public, was really interested in Cuba during the long dark years of Batista's regime? It was an exotic isle, a pleasure spot, a gambling haven. That it was rottenly overripe for revolution did not concern us — until a Castro looms up ninety miles from our shores, to our shocked surprise, fear and indignation.

No business could exist for more than a year without planning ahead, without spending considerable sums on research and development. But cities go on for years, countries for decades, building useless highways and unnecessary jails, stockpiling arms and making ineffectual treaties, in the name of "realism," while reality slowly crushes them to death.

Sometimes There Is No Solution

"ALMOST everything happens to you if you live long enough."
This is what a wise old man of my acquaintance told me

many years ago when I came to him with some problem that was bothering me at the time.

It is a simple sentence I have never forgotten. And it is remarkable how comforting that thought can be in times of stress or crisis. The only way to avoid trouble is to avoid living.

Americans, particularly (because we have been so favored by geography and history), tend to think of life as a series of problems and solutions. But less fortunate peoples, in other parts of the world, know better. Life is *not* a series of problems and solutions — it is a predicament.

There are some problems that have no solutions. There are some questions that have no answers. There are some situations that must simply be lived through, and cannot be worked out.

It is this kind of acceptance, of stoicism, that seems to be lacking in our ebullient American nature. We cannot bring ourselves to believe that life is a predicament, and not a group of neat equations that we can solve satisfactorily. This is as true in our national outlook as it is in our personal viewpoints.

Part of our resistance, and resentment, and frustration about the present world situation springs from this attitude. We simply cannot believe that the continuing crisis in international affairs cannot be solved or resolved by turning the right key, or taking the right posture, or being more aggressive or being more conciliatory.

Yet, all the realistic evidence points to the fact that we are going through a long period in which there are no satisfactory solutions. The Russians cannot be wished away, or frightened away, or talked away, or even fought away. They are here, and we are here, and the alternative to living together — in some uneasy symbiosis — is surely dying together.

This is what we find so unpalatable: that we are no longer

the sole masters of our own destiny, that we are caught up in a web of history, and we cannot act with the freedom and boldness we have long been accustomed to. Control of atomic fission gave us unprecedented power — but it also made us the slaves of its consequences.

The world is now balanced precariously on the edge of a precipice. Survival calls for delicacy, for the ability to sustain the tension without fight or flight. We have no answers, because new questions have been propounded by our scientific breakthroughs. The ultimate test of our maturity may consist in our willingness to accept the predicament, and to treat it with tact, not with cowardice or bravado.

They Were Wrong About Steam

IN A periodical called *Hogg's Weekly Instructor*, published in Edinburgh, Scotland, one of the issues in March 1845 contained an article on "Steam — Its Influence on Society."

Reflecting the widespread view held at the time of the introduction of steam power, the article proclaimed:

"It is not difficult to see how railroads and steam navigation will promote the peace of the world. Sovereigns will avail themselves of it, as well as the people. The rulers and ruled of different nations will meet face to face; and instead of believing, as hitherto, that they are natural enemies, they will soon discover that they are sworn friends. But for steam, it is not likely these visits would be made!

"But there is another way," the article continued, "in which steam power will promote peace. We know that the more destructive the weapons of warfare, the less likely will the nations be to proclaim war, and the more speedily will their disputes be settled when they do. Consider the changes necessarily produced in the art of war by the use of steam-ships! Think of their facility of access to any shore! Think of their fearful accuracy of aim and their destructive power, and we shall have fewer national quarrels . . ."

This is the illusion that has, falsely, nourished mankind since the invention of the catapult and the longbow. Each new military device, each new instrument of destruction, has been hailed as an end to future wars. The devastation would be "too terrible to contemplate," and nations would be forced to make peace in the future.

Such voices are still strong among us today. Yet everything in history proves them wrong. In the century following the hymn to steam in 1845, the world experienced its most horrible conflicts, generation after generation. The weapons became more wicked, and the casualties more widespread. Air power only added a new dimension to mass murder.

There is no record of a nation piling up arms and not using them; indeed, the very existence of arms acts as an incentive to hostile action. The physical fear of retaliation by enemies with equally formidable arms has never been a deterrent for very long. To say that armaments "prevent" conflict is to say that germs prevent disease.

Toward the end of his life, Napoleon himself admitted that "The more I study the world, the more I am convinced of the inability of brute force to create anything durable." Moral power is the only force that can prevent war, not physical power. The profound appeal of a man like Pope John XXIII is worth more than a hundred divisions of fighting men — if we but permit his wisdom and compassion to awaken our stunned consciences.

The Last Dozen People on Earth

WHEN THE last dozen inhabitants of the earth crawl out of the rubble and find themselves miraculously still alive, they

will start the tedious and heartbreaking task of rebuilding a
civilization — that is, if the world is still inhabitable, which
is unlikely.

They will then, and only then, begin to educate themselves
and their children — mutations permitting — in the lessons
nobody paid attention to before the Big Bang.

They will point out that nationalism is impossible, that the
remnant of mankind must forever unite or perish. They will
see clearly (and how painfully!) that war against our own
kind is the supreme act of treason toward God and man.

They will comprehend the piercing truth — as ancient and
ignored as Isaiah and Jesus and Buddha — that our species is
indissolubly one; that not color, nor national origin, nor religious belief, nor political conviction, can divide man from
man in any essential way.

These distinctions will, after the Big Bang, seem as trivial
and irrelevant as the differences in height or weight or color
of eye or pattern of fingerprint.

And they will teach their children — if there are still children who are teachable — that it was not the Communists
who "started" the last war, nor the Fascists who "started" the
one before that, nor the Kaiser, nor Napoleon, nor Caesar,
nor Hannibal.

It was, rather, the absence of law for all men, the wild
anarchy of nations, each pursuing its own selfish ends, each
blaming the others for greedy motives and evil ways.

There will be no "good guys" and "bad guys" in the history books of the future — if there is a book, if there is a
future. For "bad guys" are created by the "good guys" who
are too self-concerned with their own prosperity, their own
success, their own dominance, to recognize that prosperity,
like peace, is indivisible on this shrunken globe.

The last dozen inhabitants will not preach a new philosophy, but a very old one. And they will, finally, be forced to practice what they preach — for the words of Isaiah and Jesus and Buddha will be justified in every demolished city, every stricken land, every polluted sea, every cubic inch of poisoned air.

After the Big Bang it will happen, as was promised to us, that the meek shall inherit the earth. But what an earth, what a price to pay for learning the first lesson handed down to us!

Bombs Kill People, Not Ideologies

GLANCING through a magazine the other day, I stopped at an advertisement for Japan Air Lines, inviting Americans to fly to the Orient with "perfect hospitality in the tradition of Japan."

The ad went on to speak of "the enchantment of Japan," "the classic Japanese manner," "the calm beauty of Japan," the delicacy, the courtesy, the charm of the Japanese culture.

All too true, as any visitor can testify. And then I thought back to less than twenty years, and wondered if those could be the same people we were fighting — those "apes," those "inhuman monsters," those "grinning little devils," those "yellow fiends."

Now they are our allies and our friends, as they should be; and so are the Germans, and so are the Italians. And I wondered about another ad, twenty years hence, if the world should survive and rebuild after an atomic catastrophe.

I could see the four-color splash for Samovar Air Lines. The charming Russian stewardess serving tea to the American passengers. The (completely truthful) statements about Russian warmth, Russian hospitality, Russian service in the classic Muscovite tradition.

For there is no doubt that those of us who are left — if any are — after the next holocaust will do the same as we have always done: will make friends and allies out of our former enemies, will suddenly perceive their virtues and their talents, will admit them as full-fledged members of the human race, will even help rebuild their economy and restore their civilization.

The truly terrible thing about the war spirit, about the fear and hate and hysteria it generates, is that it forces us to think and talk and feel in terms of abstractions — those "Communists" this time, those "Fascists" last time.

But those we are fighting and killing are people — men, women and children — not political, geographic or economic abstractions. They are, in the main, as decent and fearful and confused as we are. And they regard us as abstractions as much as we do them.

It is only after the conflict that enemies emerge as people much like us, hoping the same things for their children, full of the same anxieties and prayers and puzzlements. It is not abstractions we kill, but people.

Communism is an idea, and it cannot be killed — any more than Fascism was killed the last time. An idea can kill itself off, but it cannot be murdered; this is the fatal mistake in all ideological warfare. All that can be murdered are their children, and ours.

A Case of Treason Against Man

IF YOU threw a stone at random down Main Street, America, and another stone at random in the center of Moscow, you would most likely hit two average persons — one an American and the other a Russian.

And if these two persons were brought together in a room

for a couple of hours, or a couple of days, I have not the slightest doubt that they could reach an amicable agreement about living together in peace.

Yet, multiply them by several hundred million, add government officials, put them under different flags, give them different anthems, and dress them in different uniforms — and you have Cold War creeping into Hot.

Nations almost always behave more badly than the people who compose them. The average German would have been appalled if he knew what the Nazi government had done. The average Englishmen could never have perpetrated the stupid cruelties of his government in the nineteenth century.

This, as I see it, is the central problem of mankind: to meet each other on a one-to-one basis, on the common denominator of humanity. We have never been able to do it yet, but I am unwilling to relinquish the hope that some day we will.

All human life is *personal*; everything else is an abstraction. The Government, the Empire, the People's Republic — all these are simply emotional barriers to understanding and cooperation.

The idea called "nationalism" can be a creative and loving force, if it inspires citizens with loyalty to the highest ideals and the best traditions of a people.

But too often it is used as a mask for greed, as a justification for "legalized" murder, as an excuse for violating God's commandments to treat one another as parts of the same body — the body of mankind.

The highest loyalty we can have is not to a neighborhood (even if that neighborhood is as large as America or Russia), but to the imperishable vision of brotherhood, which is written large in every Bible of every creed.

This is a personal duty that each of us bears; but governments try to persuade us that our overriding duty is to the

Flag, the Empire, the People's Republic. This is blasphemy against God and treason to man's best interest.

We in America have perhaps sinned less than many others, for we have not coveted what they possess. We have not needed to, being large and rich and relatively far from ancient feuds. But when we lose sight of *people*, and think only of *powers*, we are losing the dream that made us great.

Of Seat Belts and the World's Safety

"WHAT'S WRONG with the world?" said the young man to me yesterday.

I'll tell him what's wrong with the world. It's simple — depressingly simple. I don't use the seat belts on my car.

That's what's wrong with the world. One could write a hundred books on the subject, and the core of the trouble would still remain — I don't use the seat belts on my car.

I had them installed when I bought the car. Everyone should have them. The cost is small and the protection great. I even suggested that seat belts should be made mandatory on all automobiles, as an essential safety measure.

But I have never used them. Not once. On short trips, I feel it doesn't pay to bother. On long trips, I want to feel unconfined. On medium trips — well, I just don't.

Is this a trivial matter? What does it have to do with "what's wrong with the world?" Everything, I think. For what is wrong is that we don't use the *intelligence* we have. Our knowledge is not related to our actions.

I had enough sense to put seat belts in the car. Every little neuron in my brain tells me that nobody should drive anywhere without using them. But my brain does not guide me when I climb into the car.

I am guided (or misguided, instead) by a vague complex of

feelings I do not fully understand or at all control. By apathy, by insolence, by a curious kind of fear — the fear that if I acknowledge the danger of driving a car by using the belts, I may provoke the fates into causing an accident.

These are all irrational sentiments — foolish, frivolous, and perhaps fatal. Yet they are the masters of my intellect. Sitting at my typewriter, I am ardently for the belts; sitting in my car, I ignore them.

And is this not a true representation of the world itself? Doesn't the human race have the intelligence and the might to create a world of peace and prosperity? Doesn't everybody, everywhere on earth, want fundamentally the same goals?

But we do not use the intelligence we have. In 3300 years of civilization, there have been 8000 "peace treaties," each designed to prevent war — and each lasted an average of two years. All except maniacs want peace; but we will not wear the safety belts that can prevent war.

What's wrong with the world is lying right in my car, immaculate, unused, and waiting for the inevitable smashup.

4

OF MEN

AND WOMEN

How Our Attitudes Become Frozen

A MAN I have known, on and off, for years arrived from New
York recently, and we had a long lunch together between
planes. I ventured to ask him about the state of his pre-
viously turbulent domestic life.

"It's a curious thing," he said ruefully. "About six months
ago, I decided to reconcile myself to the situation and live
out my life with Susan as peacefully as possible. I make every
effort to be nice — but I've been nasty to her for so long that
I find it impossible to change."

His plight — which is real enough — reminded me of the
old story about the vaudeville knife-thrower who had used
his wife as a target for years, outlining her body on the board
with only a hair's-breadth between her skin and the knives.

One day he learned that she was unfaithful to him, and
decided to kill her during the evening performance, when it
would look like an accidental slip of the knife.

He tried for a week's performances, and couldn't hit her
— he had practiced just missing her for so many years that his
reflexes wouldn't allow him to come any closer.

Most of us are in the emotional position of the knife-thrower. Our attitudes toward those around us tend to congeal with time, and even when we want to change them, we often find that fixed habit makes us revert to the old and easy attitudes — even when we have, in a way, outgrown them.

"Habits, if not resisted," warned St. Augustine, "soon become necessity." The habits of the mind are even stronger than those of the body. It is easier for a man to quit smoking than to stop bullying his employees; the first merely satisfies a physical craving, while the second soon becomes a consuming spiritual necessity.

There is a great danger in our reactions becoming rigid toward anyone with whom we work or live in close association. It is commonly observable that young people are nicer to strangers than they are to their own parents: this is because they resent the parents' fixed attitudes toward them as they grow older and demand to be treated as emergent adults, not as infants.

We periodically re-evaluate our possessions, our position, our standing in terms of material achievements and goals; it is a pity that most of us are not able, also periodically, to re-evaluate our attitudes that have grown encrusted with habit. After all, the core of neurotic behavior consists in reliving the past without knowing it.

You Needn't Be Big to Be a Bully

WHEN we think of the word "bully," we commonly conjure up the picture of a red-faced, blustering man with hands like hams and a voice like a foghorn.

This is the bully of fiction and melodrama; it is not the bully of real life — who is more likely to be pale and soft-spoken, sickly and long-suffering. Of course, the fictional bully exists, but he is comparatively easy to cope with. For one thing, you know exactly where he stands, and his loud-mouthed ranting can be ignored or firmly opposed. A simple show of moral strength is often enough to deflate him.

But not so with the soft-spoken bully, the "sensitive" tyrant. He (or, more usually, she) is devilishly practiced in the black art of making those around him (or her) feel guilty and unworthy.

We have all seen the small, quiet wife with the martyred expression, who seems to be dominated by a vigorous and de-manding husband. Yet, in many cases, she is skilled in do-mestic tyranny, and while seeming to make untold sacrifices for her unappreciative family, actually manages to get her own way in every important matter.

The obvious bully just needs a puff of opposition to blow him over. The subtle and "sensitive" bully cannot be blown over, for it would seem a cruel injustice to oppose someone so frail, so prone to headache and heartache, so meek and un-demanding.

But the demands of weakness can be more powerful than the demands of strength. We are proud to resist a monster; we are ashamed to resist a mouse. And, with true psychologi-cal cunning, the mouse plays upon our sense of shame and guilt and ingratitude.

More husbands are driven to drink and infidelity by this kind of subtle bullying than by any open marital conflict; more daughters make hasty and ill-advised marriages because of it; more sons remain tied to the silver cord, resentful but ineffectual, because of it.

The soft-spoken and long-suffering tyrant exacts a high price for the role of seeming to be imposed upon. If you can make those around you feel guilty and ungrateful, you have forged bonds of servitude that are stronger than any physical chains. You have enslaved the psychic apparatus of freedom.

Using the three-dimensional technique of Freudian analysis, we are only now beginning to understand this devious despotism, beginning to learn that the big man with the big voice is only a cardboard caricature of the true tyrant in family life.

Sex and the Nature of Things

SPEAKING of the way in which the pendulum of popular opinion swings from one extreme to the other — as I was the other day — reminded me of a recent comment I heard made by an outspoken college girl.

"Sex is a natural activity," she said, "just like eating or sleeping. Why should we treat it any other way, and surround it with mystery and taboos?"

Her Victorian grandmother thought exactly the opposite about sex — and the grandmother was wrong. But what the college girl cannot see is that, in her own fashion, she is just as wrong as her grandmother was.

Sex may be a "natural" activity, but it is natural in a quite different way from all other personal functions. Eating and drinking and the rest are *individual* actions; sex, by its very nature, is an *interpersonal* action.

Now, no action in which another person is involved can be wholly a matter of individual choice or taste. Sex is not a private function, but a social one; and everything social must be governed by conventions, or society would fall apart.

The modern cult of "freedom" in sex is as unrealistic as the Victorian cult of "repression." The Victorians thought that sex was never to be discussed; the moderns think that hardly anything else is worth discussing. Both are perverted views.

Sex is not "natural" in a personal way, because it involves a great deal more than the body: It involves the mind and the emotions, the social patterning and the future of two persons.

It is a joining of two worlds — the biological and the emotional. Unlike the lower animals, who reproduce more or less at random among their own kind, man is a subtle blend of body and mind, which must work together for his greatest good.

It is healthful that we have cast off many of the veils that shrouded sex in the Victorian age; the subject needed daylight let in. But there is a difference between letting in daylight and throwing a spotlight upon it. To cast out the darkness, it is not necessary or desirable to cast out decency and decorum.

There is an old English saying about "throwing out the baby with the bath water." In our zeal to get rid of prudery, we must not dump overboard the standards of behavior that make sex a distinctively human activity. When it becomes less, we are betraying our real natures.

How Can a Lady Start Her Car?

"MEN ARE PECULIAR about cars," said the woman sitting across the breakfast table. "Especially when they see a woman trying to start one on a cold day."

"What do you mean?" I asked, sipping my coffee innocently.

"Well," she said, "my battery was low the other morning, and I had a little trouble starting up. About five men stopped, one after the other, to give me tips on starting a car in cold weather—and no two of them said the same thing.

"The milkman was the first. 'Pump the gas pedal before you turn on the ignition,' he advised, 'and then pull out your choke a little.' The next man said, 'Don't touch your gas pedal — pull out your choke all the way, and then turn on the ignition.'

"A third man passing — watching my unsuccessful efforts with both these procedures — said, 'Put your foot down on the gas pedal all the way, and then turn on your ignition, but leave the choke in.'

"This didn't work either, and another man came by. 'Pull out your choke halfway,' he advised, 'and put the car in low gear as soon as you turn on the ignition.'

"Finally, I had to call the garage — and the garage man who came over to give my battery a booster advised a totally different way of starting it in cold weather. Now I'm completely confused about it."

"All that proves," I said, the male on the defensive, "is that different cars start with different techniques. Some of those ways might work for one car and not for another. They were just trying to help."

"It's the same with getting out of snow or mud," she went on. "A man can't resist telling a woman driver how to do it. And all they ever say is 'Turn your wheels, lady!' They don't even tell you which way to turn them — they just love to shout 'Turn your wheels, lady!' "

"Well," I countercharged, "it's a fact that women seem to have more trouble getting cars moving than men drivers do."

"Of course," she said icily, "because we're self-conscious about it. Women are a minority group as drivers, and we feel that men are critical of us. So this makes us nervous, and we look even worse than we are. And men don't try to help — they just want to show their superiority."

"I'll tell you how to get your car started on a cold morning," I said helpfully. "Keep it in a heated garage overnight, my dear."

Somehow, for reasons that elude me, I never did get a

second cup of coffee that morning. Women are peculiar creatures, aren't they?

"*Feminese*" *Is Greek to Most Men*

A HANDY little guidebook that nobody seems to have written yet would be a pocket dictionary of phrases, translating Feminese into English for new husbands.

Ordinarily, it takes a husband several years to decipher what his wife is saying, and what he is expected to reply. This little guidebook would permit him to become an expert in marital double-talk in a few days.

For example, when a wife asks, after a party: "But did you think she was *really* pretty?", a husband is supposed to answer, "No, not really." What the wife means by this oblique question is that the woman under discussion is undeniably pretty, but her character is so loathesome that any clear-thinking, upstanding husband could see right through her "surface" prettiness.

Again, when a wife tries on an old frock and inquires wistfully: "I wonder if this dress still becomes me?", she is not asking about the dress, but about herself — has she put on too much weight, is her age beginning to show, has child-bearing done her in? The trained and seasoned husband will say nothing about the dress (she is going to buy a new one, anyway), but should concentrate on reassurances about youth, weight, and the ripening charms of women who have gone through parturition.

Men, poor simple creatures, are used to obvious questions and blunt, direct answers. But when they enter the cobweb of matrimony, they must be prepared for a whole new linguistic world, so subtle and shaded that only a Talleyrand would feel quite at home in it.

When a wife asks, in a particular tone of languor, "What should we have for dinner tonight? — I can't think of a thing that sounds appealing," the alert mate will immediately translate the question into the plaintive call "Let's go out for dinner tonight — I'm sick of menus," and will gallantly offer a night on the town before his wife is forced to drag the issue into the open.

For some obscure reason, a woman likes to believe that all these ideas come from the husband; if she is forced to state them directly, in plain declarative English, she feels she has lost even when she wins.

The female of the species is particularly fond of the lateral approach to basic decisions — she sidles up to questions by way of far left field, and before the man is aware of what is happening, a casual remark about Aunt Hattie's old trunk in the attic has suddenly been turned into a vigorous discussion of a trip to Honolulu next winter.

There are a lot of books on marital relations, most of them bad. But communication is still the key to a flourishing marriage, and it's time some shrewd semanticist provided young husbands with a Dictionary of Feminese.

People Don't Judge Man by His Wife

THIS IS a friendly tip to a young married man I observed not long ago at a large party: people don't judge a man by his wife as much as by the way he treats his wife.

This chap had evidently married a rather silly woman, but a sweet one, and instead of being pleased with her sweetness. he was ashamed of her silliness, and rebuked her for it in public.

Everyone's sympathy, of course, was with her; and the

young husband did himself considerable harm by his attitude. He is the victim of a fallacy common to bright and insecure young men.

He mistakenly believes that a wife's negative qualities somehow rub off on the husband. This is not, and never has been, true, from Socrates down to Lincoln. People may be sorry for a man with a silly or mean or vulgar wife; but they do not ascribe *her* characteristics to *him*.

Husbands who want their wives to shine in public, and feel let down when they do not, are really confessing their own weakness as individuals. They want the world to approve their choice of a mate — as though a poor choice somehow reflects discredit upon the chooser.

But the world knows better than this: great men have often picked deplorable wives, and fine women just as frequently find unsuitable mates. Character and intelligence have little to do with the area of the emotions, as anybody above voting age should know.

Indeed, those persons most admired (and rightly so) are the ones who are able to put up with defective partners gracefully and patiently. We rise, not sink, in the estimation of our friends when we surmount the handicap of a defective partner; just as a man with a twisted ankle is doubly applauded for finishing the race.

Ironically enough, in many cases, such as the young husband I observed, the wife is not at all defective, except by his own perfectionist standards. He simply wants her to be too many things at once, because he does not feel himself enough of a man. When a husband uses a wife for public support or decoration, it raises a well-founded suspicion that he feels frail and vulnerable without this marital armor.

The world may judge falsely, but it judges individually, not by blood ties or marriage ties; children who are "ashamed" of parents are just as foolish as husbands who are ashamed of wives. But the children's excuse is their age; and we can rightly infer that such husbands have not grown up, either.

Boredom, Not Vice, Ends Marriages

A STATEMENT that may be perfectly clear to the person who writes it may make no sense at all to the person who reads it. Today I received a letter from a woman in Michigan who asked for the meaning of a recent paragraph of mine, which said:

"A wife who is dissatisfied with a good husband is a thousand times unhappier than a wife who is dissatisfied with a bad husband."

For the benefit of any other readers who may have been puzzled by what I think is a quite obvious observation, let me expand the thought beyond the mere sentence I first gave it.

To be dissatisfied with a bad husband (or a bad wife, for that matter) is a commonplace experience. He is brutal, or drinks, or gambles, or neglects the children, or is faithless. The unhappy wife has a realistic handle to seize in cases of this sort; her misery has an objective basis in fact.

But what of the wife — and there are thousands of these — who can point to no such gross defects on the parts of their husbands? They are married to men who are considerate, and sober, and prudent, and faithful — and yet the wives are pathetically unhappy.

Such a wife is not only unhappy with her husband — she is also unhappy with herself. She feels guilty because she is bored or restless or resentful living with a man who does not provide her with an excuse for her unhappiness.

The wife of the drunkard or the gambler can make some kind of precarious adjustment, for there is something *outside herself* that she can blame for her discontent. And being able to blame some external cause often enables her to continue functioning and to find some substitute gratifications that keep the marriage alive, if not active.

But when we are unable to point to any realistic defect on the part of another; when our only feeling is one of a vague, gnawing dissatisfaction — then we are attacked by a sense of our own emptiness or unworthiness, which is much more intolerable than blaming another.

More marriages, I am convinced, dissolve because of boredom than because of vice; the relationship does not grow bad, it grows stale; the causes stated in the divorce petition are rarely the true causes, which lie deep in the unconscious mind of the complaining party.

To be dissatisfied with a bad husband is natural; to be dissatisfied with a good one is neurotic; and, paradoxically, the unhappiness that is not "real" is a thousand times more miserable than reality.

Why Opposites Attract in Marriage

SOME FRIENDS of mine have a son who is a college senior, about to get married. His parents are worried because the girl is unlike anything they expected him to choose.

"I know the old adage that opposites attract," the father said to me. "But *why* do opposites attract? I've never understood it."

My own theory may be too simple, but it is the only answer I can find. It seems to me that opposites attract because each of us finds in the opposite a buried part of his own nature which craves expression.

Why does the punctual person so often marry the person who has no sense of time, or the parsimonious person marry someone who is extravagantly loose with money? Why will the soft-spoken man wed a loud, aggressive woman, or vice versa?

Unconsciously, I think, the punctual person resents his compulsion to be on time, or ahead of time. Often, this compulsion is the result of strict early training — but a hidden part of him yearns to defy the strict censor implanted in him by his parents or by his own personality needs.

Each of us yearns to be a thoroughly well-balanced person, but few of us can succeed directly in this — because the particular curve of our formative years inclined us to one extreme or another.

The soft-spoken person, who simply cannot assert himself forcefully, finds great psychic relief in being married to a partner who freely expresses his feelings of anger or hostility. He is simply using the other person to act out his own hidden impulses.

Opposites attract because the opposite represents a part of us that has been long repressed. As an example, I know an extremely polite and gentle man married to a woman who backbites, criticizes all her friends, deprecates their children, and quarrels with the tradesmen.

People wonder "how he puts up with all this," but from close observation I have deduced that he is quietly delighted with her behavior — for, unconsciously, he is using her to express the aggressiveness he is not able to vent.

That rare well-balanced person, of course, does not require an opposite, because he gives proportionate representation to all the varied needs of his personality. But most of us, locked within a more or less rigid framework of personality, need and look for a mate who will pull strenuously in the direction of our buried impulses.

Loud Shirt Is Explained at Last

"WHAT ARE YOU wearing tonight," casually inquired the lady

with whom I lodge, as we were preparing to go out for the evening.

"Oh," I shrugged, just as casually, "I thought I'd wear my basic black. It's always in good taste, you know."

She smiled tightly. "Don't give me any of your smarty talk; I just wanted to know whether you're going to wear a suit, or slacks and that ghastly striped sports jacket you're so indecently fond of. I don't enjoy dressing and then learning that you're going out looking like a bowler in a beer ad."

I bowed deeply from the waist (no easy trick, when you're attired only in a bath towel), and promised to wear my mourning suit. With the dark maroon tie that hints discreetly of untold wealth and lofty status.

As I showered, I thought of the curious transformation that has taken place in the world of finery. Until modern times, it was the man (like the male of all lower animal species) who adorned himself in resplendent fashion — with satins and silks and lace and ribbons, and no one to call him effeminate for it, while he still carried a sword in his scabbard.

But the beginning of the Industrial Revolution signified the end of all that. Man in the Western World soon became as drab as the factories that were springing up in corn fields, and quickly he began to transfer his symbols of conspicuous wealth from his own person to that of his wife.

Today, of course, the bank president and the janitor look pretty much the same on Sundays — except that the janitor customarily pays more attention to his clothes. It is the wives of each who reflect their comparative wealth and social standing.

Regard the men at any party. Even if they are not wearing conventional black ties, they look as standardized and anonymous as background traffic in a movie. One dark suit is pretty much like another; there are distinctions in material and tailoring, but the net effect is scarcely dramatic to the eye. They all look like parts of the same man.

This modern repression, this break with the tradition of grandeur in male attire, has created its own unconscious resentments. Nothing else could explain the recent rise of the hideously flamboyant sports shirt, the vividly mottled tie, the odd jacket that would make a horse blanch with embarrassment.

Man is the naturally vainer of the two sexes, and when he put away his ribbons and his lace, he did not bury his dandyism, but simply shifted it to the golf course, the swimming pool and the backyard barbecue.

Gossiping Ranks Close to Peeping

"I THINK that men are viler than women," said the college girl. "After all, most men are Peeping Toms, in one degree or another. But have you ever heard of a Peeping Tomess?"

Frankly, I haven't. But I don't think this proves that the masculine interest in sex is more highly developed than the women's. I just think it takes a different form.

Men, on the whole, are visual-minded. Women are verbal-minded. That is, men achieve sensual enjoyment by looking, and women by talking. Gossip is the female equivalent of the man's picture magazine.

Most feminine gossip — at least, the most fascinating kind — revolves around the relations between the sexes. When two women are gossiping about a third, the juiciest morsels they dredge up are in the areas of romance or marriage.

On the whole, this can be a healthful activity — if it is done with a minimum of malice — just as a man's turning his neck to observe a pretty leg is a normal outlet for his sexual curiosity.

The Peeping Toms are shy, weak and withdrawn men, who cannot obtain gratification from a normal relationship. Most so-called "sex fiends" are impotent little creatures scared to death of women.

Gossip is a form of play, a discharge of energies — much like a young man's whistling at a shapely form passing down the street. I would be much more worried about a son who did not crane his neck at the girls than about one who did.

It is a discredited Victorian notion that men are "viler" than women about sex. First, it rests on the assumption that there is something inherently "vile" about sex, which is a damaging idea to hold. Nor is it even a good Christian idea, but is a vestige of the ancient dualism of the Manicheans, which St. Augustine fought so hard to defeat.

It is a sin to believe that the body is vile, and only the spirit is good. Children who grow up with this notion can have the most severe neurotic problems in later life. It is not sound psychology, it is not sound theology, and it is even not sound common sense.

Perspective is all: having a *right relationship* between the demands of the body and the demands of the spirit is the goal of human development — and a culture which degrades the body is as perverted as one which ignores the spirit.

Peeping Toms are mentally sick because they lack perspective; malicious gossips are morally sick because they lack charity; but each man and woman is a little of either, and only the excess is "vile."

More to Divorce than Meets the Eye

I ENJOY hearing gossip as much as the next person — although I sometimes pretend not to — but gossip about a broken marriage always exasperates me. Who really knows why any couple separate? All we know is what we see on the surface, and a marriage is like an iceberg, with most of its bulk submerged beneath the public view.

Even when we genuinely regret the breakup of couples we know and like, a little *frisson* of excitement and pleasure runs through us when we hear the bad news. There is a touch of malice in our sympathy, a fleck of superiority in our friendly headshaking.

He seemed rather brutal toward her; perhaps that was it. She failed to keep up with his growth; possibly that started the split. And, of course, there were money troubles . . . anyone could see that.

So the discussion goes, with a kind of half-baked psychiatric jargon: he wanted a mother, she was looking for a father figure, they were both ambivalent — a conversational mixture of ignorance and nonsense and truths ripped out of context and a smug sense that we are made of sterner, and more sensible, stuff than they.

We render verdicts on incomplete evidence, pass judgments on perjured testimony, draw morals that cannot be justified by any of the known facts, and sit back to bask in an atmosphere of self-satisfaction. If only people were more reasonable, if only they could see as clearly as we, if only . . .

And of the true inwardness we know nothing — as little as we know of our own deepest drives and motivations. Of the hidden forces inexorably moving toward the dissolution of a relationship, we are blandly unaware. For a good marriage is a grace as well as a fact in law, and who among·us can penetrate the mystery of grace?

Some, the loveliest and the best, have failed to win the hotly coveted chalice. Others — trivial, shallow and selfish — have somehow managed to find a kind of serenity and satisfaction with another soul equally trivial, shallow and selfish.

The rain falls on the just and the unjust alike. A happy life is a free gift from the blue, which nobody really deserves; this was the hard lesson that Job, that most virtuous and pious of men, had to learn, sitting in sackcloth, on his boils.

"He was too this, she was too that." All such words are noise devoid of meaning — and, worse than that, devoid of true charity.

What It Takes to Be a "He-Man"

A READER in Texas has written me a note asking: "Why do women belittle (at least, my wife does) a man's attempt to take to the deep woods and be the he-man?"

It's not as simple a question as it sounds, nor is the answer a simple one. Women belittle men for different reasons, good and bad; and men want to take to the woods for different reasons, good and bad.

What interests me, however, is my correspondent's implicit assumption that the one who takes to the deep woods is necessarily a "he-man." He may or may not be — but it is in his daily life, not in his forest flights, that he reveals his manhood or his boyhood.

In a book, *Courage,* that he wrote shortly after the war, General Slim, who commanded the Allied forces in Burma, said that his experience with soldiers and civilians and refugees had taught him that "moral courage is much higher and rarer than physical courage, and that women and civilians often exhibit more courage of this kind than the bravest combatants."

What it takes to be a real "he-man" in modern society is no longer the physical intrepidity of the soldier or frontiersman in the past.

What modern man is called upon to be and do requires

moral courage of a high order, tenacity, patience, a deep sense of responsibility, and the willingness to endure boredom, fatigue and tensions that can be only occasionally relieved.

The real he-man, it seems to me, is not the one who takes to the woods (except, perhaps, as a relaxing weekend off once in a while), but the one who feels a quiet and deep pride in taking care of his family as a man ought to.

Sitting home at night, reading a book, while the children are tucked in their beds, it can be immensely gratifying to reflect that the whole structure of their safety and welfare depends upon one man, his work, his reliability, his responsibility, his refusal to funk his obligations.

Being a man has little to do with stalking deer in a woods or shooting ducks in a blind; these are pleasant vestiges of boyhood, not tokens of manhood. But continuing to work when you are tired, assuming duties when you would rather loll, making sure that the nest is safe and warm and that the future holds promise of continuity and growth — these are the unrelenting demands modern society makes upon its grown men.

How well and how willingly we measure up to these demands — unheroic in a dramatic sense, but more difficult in many ways — is a more accurate criterion for separating the he-men from the he-boys.

Beware of Self-Styled Virtues

THE VERY TRAITS we pride ourselves on may be those that are most damaging to us. This far-from-original thought occurred to me recently, when I learned that a couple we knew slightly had not been invited to a party the wife ardently desired to attend.

The reason they were not invited would have been an unbelievable shock to the wife. She considers herself a scintil-

lating personality, always ready with a quip, and the life of
every party. On the other hand, she regards her husband as a
sweet, dull, stick-in-the-mud, whose social success depends
wholly upon her gaiety and aggressiveness.

Actually, people see them both in a quite different light.
The husband is liked and wanted — but the couple is frequently not invited to parties because hostesses can't stand
the wife.

He is shy, but quite bright and amusing in his own dry
way, with a hidden charm that repays digging for. He is also
supremely unconcerned with what others think of him, and
couldn't care less whether he is or isn't included on any guest
list.

The wife, however, is frantic with a need to seem popular.
As a result, she laughs too frequently and too loudly, is willing
to be malicious at the expense of others, and when she feels
she is failing to make an impression she will set out to shock
her audience with candid comments which she imagines are
cute, but which are only in poor taste.

"I just couldn't invite them," the hostess of the evening
confided to me, "because although I'm crazy about him, I
couldn't take a chance that she might offend some of my
guests."

I am sure that in the privacy of their own home, this wife
blames her husband for their sparse social life. She probably
is convinced that if she had only married a more vivacious
man she would by now have been the toast of society.

It is utterly impossible for her to see that what she calls
"gaiety" is only desperation; what she calls "wit" is only
hostility; what she calls "frankness" is only adolescent fence-
scribbling; what she calls "animation" is only an embarrassing
form of nervousness.

When our self-styled virtues are spoiling our lives, we ought to seriously consider cultivating what we think of as our "defects" — they might easily prove to be the best parts of us.

Making Marriage a Mockery

"How LONG do you think they'll stay married?" I overheard one woman saying to another, in discussing the Burton-Taylor affair. "I don't give them two years together after they're legally tied."

"I quite agree," nodded her friend. "People like that make a farce out of marriage. Why do they bother with it at all?"

A most sensible question; and the answer, I think, is to be found more in the cultural patterns of modern America than in the psychic or moral makeup of the celebrities on the marry-go-round.

There is a certain kind of person — in the arts or on the fringes of it — who cannot stand any permanent relationship. In more permissive cultures (and more realistic ones than ours), such persons do not marry, at least after the first time; they simply go through life as a series of liaisons.

In much of the rest of the world, society tolerates this mildly deviant behavior; nobody cares or bothers, so long as the couple live discreetly and quietly. In America, however, marriage is regarded as the norm for *everybody;* a man and his mistress living together openly are a scandal and an offense to the community.

These Hollywood couples, and those like them, make a mockery of marriage because our social attitudes force them to hypocritical conformity. And ours is a stupid attitude, which does more to harm the fabric of marriage in the eyes of impressionable young people than any capers or caprices of the Burtons and the Taylors.

In America, such people try to have their cake and eat it,

which simply cannot be done. They marry, buy a house, have children; but neither by intention or temperament is it a permanent alliance; so the marriage is dissolved, the house is sold, the children are scattered to governesses or boarding schools or stepparents.

In Europe, and elsewhere, such people generally do not have children, which is more honest and kind. They settle for the sort of life they want to lead, and realistically give up whatever else marriage implies. They accept their own limitations, and do not pretend that marriage is for them when it is not.

They do not make a farce out of marriage, because they never enter it; they never assume its obligations, and so they never violate them. Living outside the structure, they become incapable of damaging it by their destructive examples, as they do here. And, most of all, they do not hurt the children — which is the most painful result of our blind insistence on conjugal conformity.

Love Is Not Like Merchandise

A READER in Florida, apparently bruised by some personal experience, writes in to complain, "If I steal a nickel's worth of merchandise, I am a thief and punished; but if I steal the love of another's wife, I am free."

This is a prevalent misconception in many people's minds — that love, like merchandise, can be "stolen." Numerous states, in fact, have enacted laws allowing damages for "alienation of affections."

But love is not a commodity; the real thing cannot be bought, sold, traded, or stolen. It is an act of the will, a turning of the emotions, a change in the climate of the personality.

When a husband or wife is "stolen" by another person, that

husband or wife was already ripe for the stealing, was already predisposed toward a new partner. The "love bandit" was only taking what was waiting to be taken, what wanted to be taken.

We tend to treat persons like goods. We even speak of children "belonging" to their parents. But nobody "belongs" to anyone else. Each person belongs to himself, and to God. Children are entrusted to their parents, and if their parents do not treat them properly, the state has a right to remove them from the parents' trusteeship.

Most of us, when young, had the experience of a sweetheart being taken from us by somebody more attractive and more appealing. At the time, we may have resented this intruder — but as we grew older, we recognized that the sweetheart had never been ours to begin with. It was not the intruder that "caused" the break, but the lack of a real relationship.

On the surface, many marriages seem to break up because of a "third party." This is, however, a psychological illusion. The other woman or the other man merely serves as a pretext for dissolving a marriage that had already lost its essential integrity.

Nothing is more futile and more self-defeating than the bitterness of spurned love, the vengeful feeling that someone else has "come between" oneself and a beloved. This is always a distortion of reality, for people are not the captives or victims of others — they are free agents, working out their own destinies for good or for ill.

But the rejected lover or mate cannot afford to believe that his beloved has freely turned away from him — and so he ascribes sinister or magical properties to the interloper. He calls him a hypnotist, or a thief, or a home-breaker. In the vast majority of cases, however, when a home is broken, the breaking has begun long before any "third party" has appeared on the scene.

When a Woman Buys a Dress . . .

I BOUGHT a new suit last week. I walked into the shop, said to a salesman, "Let me see a gray suit in a medium weight." He brought out a gray suit in a medium weight, I tried it on, said, "It seems all right," and the tailor came out to make the necessary alterations.

This is how a man, on the whole, buys a suit. I had no illusion that it would do anything for me except hide my underwear and provide pockets for my notes, cigarettes and glasses.

When a woman buys a comparable garment, however, it is not mostly a material purchase. It is a moment of magic: what she is looking for is not something to *cover* her, but something to *change* her. The involved and protracted purchase of clothes by woman cannot be understood unless we know what she is really looking for.

Husbands who are impatient and derisive and superior about their wives' clothes-buying habits fail to appreciate perhaps the most fundamental difference between the male and the female. The male is idealistic in his beliefs, and practical in his conduct; the female is practical in her beliefs, and idealistic in her conduct.

Most of the abstractions that men believe in, and work for and fight for and sometimes die for, are thought to be nonsense by women. Abstract concepts of duty and honor and the dubious victories in conflict are considered as adolescent foolishness by women.

They are immensely practical and pragmatic and expedient and personal in their beliefs. It is in their conduct that idealism displays itself: and nowhere more so than in the purchase and wearing of clothes. Here, all practicality deserts them, and they become the victims of abstract delusions with no basis in fact.

What a woman wants in a new dress, or suit, or coat, is another facet to her personality. She clings to the irrational conviction that if only she had enough clothes, of various sorts, then somehow life would be different and better, new vistas would open, old problems be resolved, and her internal beauty would blossom for all the world to see.

This is a rather sweet and pathetic delusion, comparable to the male's delusion that if his party were only in office long enough, or his nation were solely supreme, then taxes would decrease, wars would cease, and profits would be limitless. There is little to choose between either of these forms of monomania — but the woman, at least, does not try to impose her delusions upon others. Her idealism is harmless, if expensive: man's is fatally dangerous and incalculable in cost.

5

OF PARENTS
AND CHILDREN

Reason and Irrational Impulses

THE MAN on the beach was talking to his teen-age son about "reason," and the need to follow the rule of reason in one's life. I could not help overhearing what he said; it was clear, simple, logical and true — as far as it went.

But it did not go far enough. As he spoke, I recollected a lovely line from one of Santayana's books, in which the philosopher said: "Reason in my philosophy is only a harmony among irrational impulses."

This is precisely what the father left out: "harmony among irrational impulses." The man was trying to be more reasonable than a human being can be — and that road leads only to tyranny (witness the French Revolution) or individual breakdown (an insane person is the most relentlessly reasonable of all, once you accept his first premise).

What is most valuable among Freud's discoveries — and ultimately much more so than the current overemphasis on sexuality — is his exposure to the light of our irrational impulses, of the blind and sometimes demonic forces that compel us to repeat our childhood patterns of relating to others and to ourselves.

Reason is not, as the ancients thought, the power to think logically while rigorously expelling all irrational feelings from one's mind. Rather, it is the rare ability to accept and understand such irrational feelings, and to make them work in harmony with one another, instead of in conflict.

This is the task of the mature human ego — to deal out even-handed justice both to the dictates of reality and to the infantile needs that persist within us. And the dangerous paradox of "reasonableness" is that, inevitably, it leads to severe repression of our instinctual needs and makes us wildly irrational in our defense of "reason."

Parents of this type most often fail to understand their children, because the parents have "grown up" in only one direction. They are responsible, prudent, rational, in terms of the social roles they play — but they have, at the same time, not grown up enough to reach a harmony among their irrational impulses. They push back and deny such impulses (except when they drink), and therefore resent them in their children.

To know that one is incomplete, imperfect, irrational, at times dominated by childishly wicked wishes, is to be truly rational. To pretend otherwise is the height of folly. It is no accident that the greatest tragedies of history have been committed by men who followed an utterly "reasonable" goal, which led them to the bloodiest depths of fanaticism. Denying the child within us is the surest path to monsterism.

Delinquency Could Be Worse

WE ARE CONCERNED, as we should be, about the delinquency problem. It is growing every year, and its prevalence and intensity threaten the whole fabric of society.

But it is also wise to keep in mind the words of Dr. Lauretta Bender of New York University. Dr. Bender said in a speech some years ago: "Far more children should be delinquent than actually are. They have an amazing capacity to tolerate bad parents, poor teachers, dreadful homes and communities."

As we look around at our disrupted social order, with its corruption, its fierce competitiveness, its nervous instability, its tremulous existence under the cloud of atomic catastrophe — it can then be seen, more coolly and clearly, that young people do have an astonishing tolerance for growing up under adverse conditions.

For how can we compare the world today with the world in which we experienced our childhood? Within one generation, the world has moved a thousand times faster than in all the previous generations since Adam. Most of the familiar landmarks have disappeared — not only the physical ones, but the psychological, social and moral landmarks as well.

It is hard to believe that when I was a little boy, forty years ago, there were virtually no automobiles, few telephones, the radio had barely been born, and the child's world was utterly divorced from the adult's world.

My playmates and I moved in a separate sphere; indeed, until the Great Depression of 1929, we were not aware of the adult world. Our diversions were different, the things we heard and saw were designed for children, the activities we engaged in were sharply marked off. There was no such thing as a "teen-ager" in my day.

Now of course, children are exposed to the adult world from the earliest age. The auto, the telephone, the television, impinge upon their senses from the time they can walk and talk. Crime, war, calamities of all sorts are now part of their natural environment. There is no longer a "world of children"; the ages have blurred together into one long continuum.

This fearful acceleration in the physical world has made for an equal acceleration in the emotional world: children become sophisticated before they become wise, cynical before they become knowing, jaded before they become satisfied, ambitious before they become able, and sometimes decadent before they become civilized. The real wonder and delight is that so many of them survive and flourish as decent human beings in the setting we have provided them.

Good Reason for Parental Pride

ONE OF the great joys of parenthood that I have never heard, or read, much about is the blossoming sense of "fairness" in the child.

There is a great deal of sentimental satisfaction when the young child takes his first step, or utters his first word, or exhibits any of the "cuteness" or "brightness" so endearing in little ones.

But what should be most celebrated by parents — if they know what a human being ought to be — in the beginning of a sense of justice and fair play in the child's mind and character.

That is a lovely thing to see, much more admirable and worthy of comment, encouragement and praise than the show-off antics we customarily give our approval to.

When the child first returns a toy to its proper owner, when he admits the blame for an action, when he wants no more than his fair share, when he absolves another from guilt, and when he displays the charity that goes beyond justice — then we have reason to be proud.

But this budding sense of fairness, this tender flower of humanity, is too often ignored or neglected by parents who lavish their praise on smart sayings or self-conscious precocity on the part of the child.

It is curious and depressing that proud parents will place so high an evaluation upon the child's mental or physical prowess but will pay little regard to his development of character. Yet in later life, as we know, if the character is stunted or twisted, not all the mental or physical skills can compensate for this poverty of soul.

It is interesting, too, that while parents pay so high a tribute to the child's "brightness," this brightness comes to be regarded with suspicion and resentment if it is continued into adolescence and young adulthood.

Most parents do not feel easy or comfortable with extremely bright children; and, indeed, our whole society views intellectual superiority with a sullen eye. Why, therefore, do we place so high a premium on the small child's "brightness," if we want to stifle it when he grows older?

I think the reason for this is that parents who excessively encourage smartness in their little child often do so at the expense of the child's general character. They would rather have the child be shrewd than fair, quick of tongue than warm of heart. Thus, many bright children grow up deficient in character traits, for these traits have not been nurtured in the family.

A "cute" child is a delight; but a fair-minded one is a blessing beyond all value, long after the cuteness has disappeared.

Anti-Smut Weapon: A Happy Home

IN ANY discussion about "pornographic" literature, the people who would censor it always make a last-ditch defense of their position by bringing up "our children."

"Even granted that adults should be able to choose their own reading material freely," they say, "would you allow your children to be exposed to such trash?"

I am quite honestly puzzled by their attitude. They seem to have such a low and nasty opinion of children, and to have little faith in the training and character of their offspring.

During my youth, all my schoolmates and myself were exposed to the most pornographic kinds of cards and pictures and illustrated jokes. We weren't amused, we weren't shocked, and we weren't corrupted; we were simply bored by the graphic dirtiness, after the initial curiosity wore off.

Children who are at all affected by that kind of thing are already the victims of a poor upbringing at home. If sex is portrayed as something dirty, or cruel, or contemptible, or unnatural, or shamefully furtive, then the children will respond to such attitudes by taking a pathological interest in the subject, pornography or not.

Of course, if any community wants to "protect" its children from smut, it has a perfect right to do so — but it should not be surprised if the results are negligible. Children reared in an atmosphere of love and trust and decent values are not "corrupted" by dirty books or pictures — and the others are going to wander into the ways of depravity no matter how vigilantly we may guard against it.

By the time a child is six years old, his basic attitudes have already been shaped. If these attitudes are not healthy and productive ones, he is going to look for other outlets, in sex violence, in lying or stealing or playing truant. No police power or censorship power can be a substitute for the moral function of the parent and the family.

The parents who are so angry and worried about pornography falling into the hands of their children are really expressing deep doubts or fears of their own effectiveness as parents. They feel they have failed in some way, and hope that some outside discipline will take up the slack for them.

We cannot ask the schools, courts and police to do our job for us. Character is built only at home. Let us keep the dirty books out of the children's hands, by all means, if we want to — but let us not imagine for a moment that the feverish fantasies of an unhappy or unstable child can be curbed by burning books or prosecuting peddlers of smut.

Split Families Breed Discontent

THE HIGH INCIDENCE of troubled youth in our time — of which juvenile delinquency is only one aspect — is caused by many combining factors, and it would be foolish to isolate one factor for special blame.

Yet it seems to me that, if society is a seamless garment (as I believe), the problem of the young is related to the problem of the old. In our society, in our time, both the young and the old are detached from the core of family life.

This pattern is distinctively new in the twentieth century. We live in the age of the "atomized family" — father, mother, and children revolving around the axis of a common income. The old-style "clan family" has all but been abolished, except in parts of Europe or in some rural communities.

I was the last of my family to have been born in a house that contained not only parents, but grandparents and uncles and aunts as well. I was born in a "three generation" house, but my children were not, nor will their children be. Each family constellation of parents and children is now its own separate galaxy.

As a result, there is isolation at both ends. The old people live alone, or in dreary nursing homes (except for the few who can afford otherwise), while the children grow up lacking that wider contact with the adult world that was formerly provided by clan living.

Whatever disadvantages may have inhered in the old system, I think that its breakdown has a significant relation to the widespread discontent among young people and the increasing sense of forsakenness by old people. Any feeling of continuity through the generations is lacking.

It is this continuity, this sympathy, that we still find (although diminishing) when we visit a country like Italy, where the generations intermingle freely within the same house and neighborhood. But America is predominantly the country of the young middle-aged: the children have their own world, and the old people are pushed into limbo as speedily and as decently as possible.

In the history of mankind, the truncated parent-and-child family is a social novelty and psychological burden. Discipline is harder, recreation becomes structured and external to family living, indifferent sitters take the place of grandparents or uncles and aunts; in short, the home turns into a launching pad and is no longer seen as a refuge. I have a strong conviction that we will not solve the "problem of the young" until we attack the "problem of the old" at the same time.

Parental Goals Can Be Unfair

THE BOY returned home from college for the Christmas holidays, and he seemed drawn and depressed. Somebody asked me why, and I said, "Too much pressure."

"Too much pressure of school work?" I shook my head. "No, too much pressure at home. A boy can't carry so big a burden."

The burden I referred to was the expectations of his parents. They are pinning too many hopes on his career; his success is too important to them. And he feels this keenly, and resents it without knowing why.

Even the burden of parental love is sometimes too heavy for a growing child to bear. He feels this warm, moist, concentrated affection pressing down upon him, almost suffocating in its intensity. But most young people eventually learn how to cope with that.

What is much harder to handle is the sense that you have to live up to the mark someone else has set for you. The grades become too important, the competition too frantic, the fear of disappointing those who believe in you turns into an overwhelming nightmare.

And it is desperately unfair to the boy. He cannot live his parents' lives over again for them. He cannot make up for their own lacks, their own unfulfillments. He cannot carry their torch — only his own.

I know boys who do not try — either in high school or in college — simply because their parents' standards are too high for them, and they are afraid of letting down the team.

If they do not try, the parents can always say, "He's very bright, he's very capable; if only he would try, he would do marvelously well." But the boy knows that no matter how hard he tries he will not do as well as his parents' expectations; and so by refusing to try, he is keeping his psychological cake and eating it too.

All this, sadly enough, is truer of the more educated, higher-income, professional families. It is here that the competition is the greatest, the expectations most elevated. If the boy would be happier as a telephone linesman or a Forest Ranger, he is in a hopeless bind. His goals have been set for him by his milieu, and he cannot be his own man; so he simply refuses to play the game. He "does not try."

A poor boy has difficult odds to struggle against; but at

least he sets the terms of his lifework. A child from a more affluent home is given the terms — doctor, lawyer, business chief — and the Lord help him if he wants to be an auto mechanic or a painter or some other occupation outside the prescribed limits of genteel activity.

As Warden Lawes once said of convicts, no man can be called a failure until he has tried something *he really likes*, and fails at it.

Why Do Pupils Lose Their Curiosity?

IF YOU VISIT a first-grade class, as I did recently, you will find that the children are bright-eyed and eager, warm and responsive, direct and spontaneous.

Then, if you visit a sixth-grade class, you will feel a distinct difference in the emotional and intellectual atmosphere. The students are wary; their reactions are calculated; their answers are based on what they think the teacher — and society generally — wants to hear, not on what they themselves think.

One of the real needs for educational research today — and one of the main objectives of a bill now in Congress for that purpose — is to discover how the teaching process actually works best, and how we can prevent it from freezing and formalizing pupils so that their natural curiosity and enthusiasm is not dampened and extinguished.

The whole process of communicating knowledge in the most effective way is still largely a closed book to us. All we can be sure of is that something happens to pupils between their kindergarten experiences and their emergence into high school — and what happens is too frequently a loss of intellectual tone, a cramping of imagination, a resistance to ideas.

I am absolutely convinced that this is not a natural development, but comes from some perversion in the teaching process.

All youngsters are normally interested in painting and music; they are fascinated with words and with numbers; they enjoy hearing about strange countries and ancient times. Indeed, the whole curriculum of education is a matter of delight to the inquiring young mind.

The most important thing in the whole learning process, it seems to me, is an emotional component: the continuing responsiveness of the child. And what is it precisely that turns a child from an eager receptor of knowledge to a dull-eyed reciter of facts he neither cares about nor will bother to remember after the class is over?

This is by no means an academic problem, but an increasingly vital one for modern society. For as knowledge becomes greater, and as the utilization of knowledge becomes more imperative in our national life, we find at the same time that more and more pupils look upon education as merely a tedious preamble to "real life," which means earning a living in the world.

The number of school drop-outs is alarmingly high, and rising. More than that, the number of students who are graduated from high school and even from college without a rudimentary education is depressingly high. Modern civilization, if it is to survive at all, calls exactly for those traits of imagination, creativity and curiosity which the schools seem to drain out of their students at an early age.

A College Need: A Clash of Minds

STEPHEN LEACOCK, who was a good college professor as well as a great humorist, once said that if he were asked to start a college with one room only, he would make it a lounge.

Then, if funds permitted, he would add a library. And only after these two would he build a classroom.

Having traveled and lectured extensively to colleges and

universities around the country, I heartily agree with his scale
of values. What most college students need, and desperately
lack, is an informal place to meet with each other and with
their teachers.

With their teachers, however, *as human beings*. The modern college lounge is elegant and comfortable, with hi-fi and
bridge tables and soothing decor — but there is no meeting
of minds, no clash of ideas.

What is missing in the modern college is a sense of reality,
a feeling of relevancy. The students read their texts and perform their assignments; the teachers are busy lecturing or
grading or doing administrative duties. All are operating more
or less in an academic vacuum.

Leacock understood that a dozen or more students sitting
around a room, smoking and talking to a teacher or two about
essential ideas and ways of life — this is the heart and soul of
education, as distinct from mere learning.

College students on every campus have said to me, "If it
weren't for Professor So-and-So, I'd have got nothing out of
college." And what they mean is not so much the professor's
classroom teaching as his personal radiance, his willingness to
come to grips with basic ideas in informal conversations over
coffee or beer or while pulling at a pipe.

Such *rapport* is usually lacking in large universities because
of their very size; but even smaller schools fail to promote an
atmosphere of discussion and debate, where young people
who are groping for belief can come in contact with warm
and balanced minds.

Some wise man once defined education as "what remains
with you after you have forgotten everything you learned,"
and this is in a large sense true. It is the bull session, not the
lecture hall, where we come fully alive to the fundamental
issues of human life.

So long as our colleges are run like huge industrial plants, so long as the personal equation is submerged in the testing and the grading — so long will our students feel that college is just a passport to a job, without a visa admitting them to the promised land of wisdom.

A New Approach to Delinquency

WHAT IS CALLED in some circles the "negative case" method is finally beginning to receive the attention it has long deserved. Perhaps it was too simple for academic minds to bother with.

How do we try to determine the "causes" of juvenile delinquency? Well, we do a statistical survey of 50 or 100 or 500 delinquents. We compare their educational backgrounds, their family life, their intelligence quotients, their personality structures.

Then we try to identify and isolate those traits and tendencies that are common to most of them — broken homes, or drunken fathers, or some such pattern.

Unfortunately, this kind of survey doesn't get us very far. The statistics are too easily manipulated and too glibly interpreted. In most cases, we are left pretty much where we started — for everyone already knows that certain general types of environment are more likely to breed delinquency than other types.

What the "negative case" method does is to try to find out why certain boys *don't* become delinquents, even when all the factors seem to be predisposing them toward it.

Hundreds of studies have been made of delinquent boys who come from broken homes, whose fathers are drunks, and whose mothers work — but scarcely any research has gone into the *nondelinquent* boy with this background.

Why has he not succumbed to his environment? What factor went into his makeup, or his early training, that prevented him from becoming a delinquent? What are the positive attributes that enabled him to resist the pull of his environment, what secret source of strength did he draw upon?

The answers to such questions are bound to be much more fruitful than the present method. And, of course, the technique applies to many more areas than delinquency. For instance, why don't the majority of cigarette smokers acquire lung cancer? Why do certain marriages, that seem doomed at the start, turn into good and permanent relationships? Why do some children seem relatively immune to virus diseases?

Instead of being so concerned with pathology, the social sciences should turn more of their attention to health, to a rigorous examination of those who have successfully resisted infection, even when heavily exposed to it. We can all see the multiple causes that result in the failure of a marriage; what is hard to detect is the cohesive factor that enables one to hold together. Only this kind of research can help us.

Another Kind of "Neglected Child"

THE PHRASE "neglected child" conjures up a picture of slums and broken families, of poverty and drunkenness and cruelty, in the familiar pattern of the social worker's case history.

I think another kind of neglect is even more widespread, and just as deleterious in its effects. I am thinking of the ordinarily intelligent middle-class child who is rarely, if ever, treated like a person by its parents, but only as a child.

A few weeks ago I was chatting with an eight-year-old girl of the most appalling ignorance. She didn't know her birthdate, what her father did for a living, how old her teen-age brother was (she guessed "thirty-seven"), or the most commonplace facts that any five-year-old should be aware of.

This was not a stupid child, but a profoundly neglected one, in the social and psychological senses. It was quite evident from our conversation (and I hasten to add that she was not shy, simply nescient) that her home life is utterly devoid of dialogue in any real way. This child was intellectually under-privileged, and many remain crippled by it for a lifetime.

As much as food and drink, love and companionship, a child needs some stimulation at home that can be got nowhere else in the early years. A child requires information, enlighten-ment, serious discourse at its own age level. More than this, a child desperately needs puns and word games, riddles and jokes, puzzles and poems.

These latter, contrary to popular thought, are not mere luxuries: they are the basic fabric out of which the adult personality is loomed. The parents of this eight-year-old girl will dutifully send her to college, even if they can't afford it, will give her a "good education" — but by then it will be too late. Education, as Justice Holmes said, begins in the womb, before the child is even born.

Like so many millions of others, she has little curiosity, no interest in words or the ideas they convey, no sense of the richness and diversity and wonder of the universe. The parents, perhaps, suppose that somehow she will get all this at school — which is a monstrous fallacy almost wrecking our entire educational system.

Parents, of course, should not push or lead too fast, or expect too much too soon. But for every one set of parents who do this, a thousand do nothing; they are content if the child has surface good manners, is "obedient," and keeps out of the way. They would be angry and horrified to be told that their home contains a well-fed, scrubbed "neglected child."

"Tribal Rites" on the Highway

WRITING about the young people riding around in their white convertible, as I did recently, reminded me of another incident on the eve of the Fourth of July holiday.

It was one-thirty in the morning, and I was parked in my car near the main intersection of the little town in which I spend my summers. I was waiting for a passenger due to arrive on an out-of-town bus.

During the half hour I sat there, dozens of automobiles whizzed by me. Almost all of them were filled with teen-age boys, circling the town noisily, cutting corners sharply, and pretending to themselves that they were having a wild time.

It called to mind what an American anthropologist said recently about the "rites of passage." In older times, young men were given opportunities to prove their manhood, their courage or skill, by performing certain difficult rituals that the elders of the tribe had prepared for them. If they "passed," they were declared to be men.

We have no such line of demarcation in our modern industrial society — and so the automobile has become, in its synthetic way, the symbol of the rites of passage. The boys whizzing around the corners, brakes screeching and rubber burning, were (in a wistful and unsatisfying way) trying to demonstrate their manhood.

As the anthropologist remarked, a good deal of what passes for "delinquency" in contemporary life is an ineffectual effort to create some rites of passage by the boys themselves. Society sets no tasks for them, so they try to make their own standards of virility.

But this does not, and cannot, gratify them in any deep, lasting and confirmatory way. It does not receive the approval of the "tribe," and, more important, it actually proves nothing

— for any idiot can drive a car with reckless abandon. In trying to prove their manhood in this false way, they actually become more juvenile than ever in the eyes of society.

The puberty rites and the rites of passage that obtained in less sophisticated societies served a very real purpose, both socially and psychologically. The boys had something to look forward to, and the tests were actually meaningful, for it took dexterity and courage and endurance to qualify. Most of all, it bound the youths to the manhood of the tribe.

Juvenile delinquency, in various forms, is spreading throughout the civilized world — even in countries which had no such phenomenon until the present generation. There is a vast resentment and rebellion against the canons of the adult world, and the teen-ager forms a subculture that is often threatening to the continuity and stability of the social order.

We are not tackling this problem in any sensible way; indeed, we do not even understand its dynamics. As Paul Goodman points out, in his book *Growing Up Absurd*, unless we give youngsters something meaningful to do, they will find a meaning in violence itself.

Education — Or Sausage Stuffing?

WHEN HEINE asked his coachman, "What are ideas?" the coachman pondered a moment and answered: "Ideas? . . . Ideas are the things they put into your head."

Even today, most people might answer as the coachman did, for our formal system of education seems to consist of things put into our heads — names and dates and battles and multiplication tables and the three principal sources of raw material in the Malayan Peninsula.

Of course, these are not ideas. Ideas are what *come out* of the head. Nobody can put them there, although a good education can stimulate them, organize them, and give them a solid basis in reason.

Education, if it means anything, is a *drawing out;* it is not a pushing in. The human mind is not a sausage casing into which we can stuff knowledge; and, usually, the harder we try to stuff, the more resistance we encounter. This is why so much formal education is a waste of time and energy.

A human being is a repository of ideas; the whole trick is to get these ideas out in the open, to test them against reality, to expose them to other ideas, and thus to sharpen and toughen them.

The greatest flaw in formal education, in my opinion, is that it has little respect for ideas and too much for information. Children can get easily bored with information, when it seems to have no relevance; but they are excited and interested in ideas.

I vividly remember how the subject of zoology was ruined for me in school by teachers who were concerned only with classification and memorization of insects and such. No attempt was made to relate the subject to the other links in the great chain of life. Any real curiosity was considered almost an impertinence. As a result, the bright students quickly lost interest, and only the dutiful parrots scored high marks.

Nor was this merely a defect in the teachers. It was, rather, their general attitude toward learning in my day; there is some evidence that it has improved a little, but still not enough. The "drop-out problem" is largely economic and social — but a part of it is also pedagogical, in that dead teaching turns students away from the classroom and toward more animated aspects of the human scene.

Every child's mind is teeming with ideas. Too often these ideas are systematically throttled or strangled in the school system, which looks only for the "right answers" that are in the back of the book. What is in the back of the head is rarely encouraged to move to the front.

Children Hit Back by Laughter

MOST PEOPLE, including parents, don't know much about a child's feelings until the child begins to cry; but much more is revealed by what the child laughs at.

I thought of this at the circus last week. Michael and Barbara found some of the clowns fairly amusing, but the one that convulsed them was dressed like a little baby, in a carriage.

The older people would come up and make a fuss over the "baby" — whereupon he would haul off and hit them with an inflated bladder right on their noses. Michael and Barbara howled with delight.

Finally, when he could no longer endure the attention of the fawning adults, the clown baby stuck a ferocious cigar in his mouth, lit it, and blew huge noxious fumes in their faces. Our kids died at that one.

What broke them up, of course, was this vivid enactment of their own repressed feelings. We tend to forget what small and helpless children are subjected to, in their prams and strollers — but they do not forget.

They are treated like Things: chucked under the chin, smacked by wet lips, tickled and turned and petted and prodded and put through their paces, quite irrespective of their own needs or desires.

We "mean well," of course, when we fuss over a baby or a small child; but there is still a basic violation of the child's individuality. We treat him like a little toy, designed for our amusement and edification, and the child feels somehow *used*, even though fondly.

The baby clown was doing exactly what Michael and Barbara, and all children, wanted to do when they were quite young — namely, to strike back at the fussing adults who regarded them as wind-up dolls whose "cuteness" could be turned on by a twist of the wrist.

It is a dangerous illusion to believe that a child who cannot walk or talk is somehow devoid of a sense of integrity. This is inborn in all of us. The infant, like the adult, resents performing upon demand, responding to moist affection when it is not in the mood, rolling over and being cuddly when it wants to sleep or sulk or suck its thumb.

Children laugh at aggressiveness not because they are young savages, but because this is the only way they can express their repressed urges to hit back at an adult world that is rarely content to leave them alone. They are trained, at an early age, to resist the impulse to strike; but no training can keep them from laughing uproariously when a Biggie falls on a banana peel or is bashed on the nose with a bladder. Laughter has always been the revenge of the weak upon the strong.

Let Him Pick His Own Career

I FANCY myself as being able to understand many different kinds of people, but the one sort I am frankly baffled by is the father who wants his son to follow a particular bent. Invariably, this is the father's bent, and not the son's.

Of course, it is common for us to try to work out our frustrations through our children — the hideous "stage mother" is the most flagrant example — but there is so much solid evidence of the damage inflicted by this that I am always surprised when I hear of a father who "insists" that his son become this or that.

Some years ago, a study of midshipmen discharged from the

U.S. Naval Academy at Annapolis showed that few wanted to go there in the first place. They did it either as a reluctant means of raising family prestige, or because their fathers desired it.

Incidentally, a similar study showed that suicide attempts in military service are more frequent among enlistees than draftees. Among the enlistees, presumably, are many young men who sign up for family reasons. Those who are drafted are resigned to their temporary fate; the enlistees, however, could not live with the decision they had made.

It seems to me the most cruel and stupid thing a father can do is to force his son, by threat or bribe, to embark upon a career he is not suited for or interested in, whether commercial or professional.

One reason the sons of great or powerful or influential men often turn out so badly is the dominating aspect of such fathers; being used to making decisions for others, they treat their sons like subordinates or employees, and think they are helping them when they are only hurting them. Such boys often gravitate to their mothers, with disastrous results to their sexuality in later life.

I have seen dozens of young bankers and brokers, lawyers and doctors, who should not have been in these occupations at all; but their social status, their family background, and most of all their father's position propelled them into jobs for which they had little aptitude. Many would have been happier and more productive as forest rangers or telephone linesmen.

Our society is lacking in good technicians and craftsmen because, among other reasons, many boys who are clever with their hands are diverted to white-collar work by parents who desire status, rather than satisfaction, for their sons. I would rather have my boys be first-rate auto mechanics than third-rate doctors. Lord Chesterfield's son became a bum precisely because his father tried so hard to make him into a gentleman.

Parents, Watch Your Language

I THINK it was James Thurber who once recalled an image he had, as a boy, of his father bound to the chair of his office desk, straining at the bonds, and unable to free himself from the knots until late.

For when his father did not show up for dinner some nights, his mother told young Thurber that "Daddy is tied up at the office." To a vividly fanciful mind such as his, Daddy was tied with heavy rope.

This recollection of Thurber's occurred to me the other evening, when my six-year-old daughter asked to see my "chains." I thought she meant for the tires on my car, and told her I have none.

"But you must have," she insisted. "I heard Mother tell someone you were a chain-smoker, and I've only seen you smoke cigarettes. Where do you keep the chains?"

We adults have very little notion of how the perfervid minds of children work overtime to construe (and often misconstrue) what they hear. Commonplace idioms and stale metaphors we take for granted and scarcely think about as we say them are sometimes taken as literal truths by children — who may worry secretly for years about their true meaning and import.

We forget that all children are natural worriers, for growing up is a fearful, as well as a joyous, process. The world is large, strange, changing, filled with seemingly capricious commandments and prohibitions, and permeated with a language that the child regards, in part, as mysterious and evasive.

When President Kennedy was shot, a little girl we know asked her mother who would take his place. She was told that the Vice-president had already assumed the office. "That's nice," said the little girl. "I think every child should have a vice-daddy in case she loses her own."

Through the oblique medium of the President's death, she was able to express her meaning of disaster and tragedy — a father was taken away. This is a fear (or sometimes a wish, or both together) that all children have, but are not able to convey verbally. When parents quarrel, and say thoughtlessly angry things to one another, the children quite often take such remarks literally, and brood about their fulfillment.

What is said in front of a child may have psychic repercussions the parents are wholly unaware of, for the child has an immense capacity for distorting reality, for treating the metaphor as real, for taking the word for the deed. Repressing memory of pain, we forget how the world can seem a labyrinth of arcane dangers to the mind of a child.

The Child Must Find Himself

TO THE FATUOUS question put by so many adults to little boys: "What are you going to be when you grow up?" the only sensible answer is, "I hope to be a man."

This is not as flippant or disrespectful as it may sound. One of the terrible perplexities of growing up today consists in the pressure to make premature decisions about "what to be."

Children, and especially boys, are often urged to think seriously about this by the time they enter high school, so that, four years later, they will have a definite goal when they enter college.

But, except for the rare personalities with exceptional and well-defined gifts that bubble to the surface at an early age, a child is not equipped — emotionally or intellectually — to know his true vocation in the adult world until he has exposed himself to life.

A young man who enters college today with the frank admission that he doesn't know what he "wants to be" is regarded as odd or indecisive or lazy or almost feeble-minded.

But college actually is the place to find out how to make up one's mind about such things.

Everybody pays effusive lip-service to the humanities and liberal arts, and to the idea of cultivating the "well-rounded" person; yet a lad who takes such a course is continually prodded to "think about a career," and made to feel as if he is dodging his responsibility as a student by simply opting for a "general education."

A university is not, primarily, a place in which to learn how to make a living; it is a place in which to learn how to be more fully a human being, how to draw upon one's resources, how to discipline the mind and expand the imagination; how to make some sense out of the big world we will shortly be thrown into.

Those who fail to do this in college almost never get to do it afterwards. They may acquire occupations and professions, but they remain narrowly locked within themselves. As they get older, indeed, they adopt what the French call *un déformation professionel* — that is, the occupation takes over the whole personality, constricts and deforms it, and the rest of the person is lost forever.

Ambitious parents cripple more sons than they inspire. Pressure to become this or that — or to make any unripe decision — turns college into a mere anteroom to life, rather than the laboratory it should be. If a child is not permitted to find himself, in his own time, nothing else he ever finds will satisfy his deepest needs.

Why Children Talk So Loudly

NOT LONG AGO, I took out nine seven-year-old boys for a birthday party given by my son. All the boys behaved well — but the din of their voices was deafening.

Why do young children, on the whole, talk so loudly, and seem incapable of communicating below the level of a shout? Part of it, of course, is due to the exuberance of youth, the superfluous energy that must be discharged in physical motions and exercise of the vocal cords.

But there is another, and perhaps larger, part. Young children are not used to being listened to by adults. They have to repeat and repeat, until finally they adopt the habit of shouting to be heard at all. Few adults really "listen" to what a child is trying to say.

I came home from work the other day tired and a little cross, and my boy accosted me enthusiastically with a report of some chemical experiment he had been making. I nodded absentmindedly as he told me about the chemicals he had used, and the results he had achieved. But I wasn't really listening — until he repeated it the third time, in shout-language. Then I told him not to be so loud.

Very little children, of two or three, are just learning to communicate. Their words are garbled and imprecise — but *they* know what they mean. If adults make little effort to understand this embryonic language, then the children sense a kind of "psychic deafness" in us and raise their voices to compensate.

We can see this mechanism working more clearly when we are addressing a foreigner in our language. If he doesn't grasp what we are saying, we speak more loudly — as if the physical volume alone will get the message through. Most of us address foreigners as if they were deaf and dumb, as if sheer force of tone will pierce their minds.

To children, all adults are foreigners of a sort, in that we do not readily grasp what they are trying to say, because we are tired or inattentive or worried or preoccupied with our own problems. And since they cannot speak our "language," they quickly learn to raise their voices to command attention, to repeat, and sometimes to whine.

Of the four essential human arts — reading, writing, speaking, and listening — the art of listening is surely the most rare and difficult. Even in business and the professions, the great majority of executives and doctors and lawyers do not know how to listen (with the "third ear") to their employees and patients and clients. Shouting is the way in which children criticize their parents for lazy listening.

An Honest Look at Parenthood

I HAPPENED to overhear three women at a luncheon table next to mine discussing a childless couple they knew. One of the women wondered why the couple hadn't had children, and the second woman suggested that perhaps they couldn't.

"And maybe they don't want to," chimed in the third. "Don't assume that every couple wants children — some couples shouldn't have them, and are smart enough to know it."

Her comment (with which I fully agreed) reminded me of a passage in a Robert Louis Stevenson story, in which a doctor is congratulating himself and his wife that their marital state has not been "marred" by the presence of children.

Looking up the passage later, I found that this was what the husband said to his wife: "I think of it more and more as the years go on, and with more and more gratitude toward the Powers that dispense such afflictions. Your health, my darling, my studious quiet, our little kitchen delicacies, how they would all have been sacrificed! And for what?

"Children," he went on, "are the last word of human imperfection; health flees before their face. They cry, my dear; they put vexatious questions; they demand to be fed, to be washed, to be educated; and then, when the time comes, they break our hearts, as I break this piece of sugar. A pair of professed egoists like you and me should avoid offspring like an infidelity."

How many other "professed egoists" are so candid and self-discerning? How many others of this type delude themselves that they want a child, when all they really want is the abstract idea of a child? How many have children because it seems the thing to do, but would be far happier without such encumbrances?

Many childless couples genuinely yearn for offspring and would be excellent parents; but just as many prefer their childless state, knowing — either consciously or unconsciously — that they lack the patience or the interest required for rearing a child properly.

The world is full of couples who should not have had children, who resent the obligations it imposes upon them, and who turn the resentment upon the children in obvious or subtle forms. How much more clean and honest to admit that two professed egoists have no room in their lives for another personality, and thus to spare themselves, the child and society from the damaging consequences of this twisted relationship.

Why Parents Must "Abdicate"

THE BEST THINGS work for their own reduction and elimination. If we understand this curious process, we can then judge the value and the direction of our efforts.

"Medicine," said Lord Bryce, "is the only profession that labors incessantly to destroy the reason for its own existence." The aim of the art of medicine — when it is not perverted by greed — is to put itself out of business.

The aim of parenthood, likewise, ought to be set the child

on its own feet and make the parents more and more superfluous. The aim of true education is to make the student less
and less dependent upon the teacher and the textbook.

In these three essential realms — the physical, the intellectual, and the emotional — the proper end of medicine, education and parenthood is the freedom of the object. Whatever
binds the object more tightly violates this end and damages the
object.

This is the only test we can apply to discover whether our
dedication and love are real or counterfeit — for the counterfeit always discloses itself by trying to *possess* the object rather
than *liberate* it.

Parental love, for instance, should be a ladder, leading the
child upward and outward; too often, however, it is a cage or
a chain or a corset of unyielding suffocation. Its aim is not
the child's liberation, but the parent's gratification.

We can see how this perverted process works most clearly
in education. The most badly miseducated person is the one
who must continually use references, appeal to authorities, and
substitute what has already been said by others for his own
thinking. His education has crippled him for creative thought
and made him totally dependent on "the books."

The readiness (however painful in part) to give up their
children is the most profound characteristic of genuine parental love. Just as the doctor aims at liberating the patient from
his physical ills, and the teacher aims at liberating the pupil
from his intellectual confinements, so the parent must aim at
freeing the child from its emotional dependencies.

And the end of this paradox is that only when the child is
thus free can he have the proper attachment to his parents;
only when we allow his independence can he then freely offer
us love and respect, without conflict and without resentment.
It is the hardest lesson to learn that the goal of parenthood is

not to reign forever but to abdicate gracefully at the right time.

Careful, the Children May Hear

PARENTS SIMPLY do not know how children hear them. The things husbands and wives say to one another in the presence of children sound quite different to the ears of the children than to the ears of adults.

This point was forcibly borne upon me a few Sundays ago, when my income tax man came over to help me prepare my returns. We spent a few hours closeted together, and when he left I walked into the kitchen for a badly needed cup of black coffee, and told my wife the grim news.

My eight-year-old was munching a cookie in the pantry and overheard my wailing of voice, my gnashing of teeth, my pulling of hair. He then quietly walked over to me and slipped a quarter in my shirt pocket.

"What's this for?" I asked in surprise. "It's all I've got left of my allowance for this week," he said. "If we're so poor, you'll need that to pay your taxes with."

I was much moved. "Now it isn't all that bad," I explained to him. "We're really not poor compared to many people, and actually I'm very grateful that we have what we have. It's just that income tax time makes most daddies feel broke and hard put-upon. Thanks, anyway."

What picture must a child get of adult reality after hearing a constant stream of complaints and recriminations and self-pity from one parent or the other? How is the child to know that this exaggerated verbal response is not a faithful portrait of conditions in adult life?

I was able to tell my boy about real poverty in the world — and not too many blocks away from us — with the assurance that we are an especially lucky family, and should thank God for our good fortune. This was a relatively easy matter to straighten out.

But I happen to know, for instance, a little girl whose mother is always complaining about a housewife's role — how hard it is, how thankless, how martyred she has become to home and husband and children. Most of the time, the woman does not even know she is whining — it is so much a part of her temperament.

The little girl, however, will take her life's cue from the mother. She will not accept her femininity, she will always feel cheated at not being a man, and will unconsciously resent men in later life. This kind of emotional crippling is much more common than we think.

The only permanent gifts we can give our children are courage and cheerfulness and an acceptance of difficulties. If parents constantly vocalize and exaggerate their resentments in the home, this becomes the child's inevitable concept of the world at large.

Another Kind of Relativity

IT IS A TRUISM by now that what we call "time" is relative to the position and speed of the observer. In handling children, we have to recognize also that "time" is relative to the age and experience of the observer. There is an important psychological dimension to time.

When a child promises to come in the house at the end of ten minutes, and is still out after an hour, this is usually not willful disobedience. Children cannot be judged on the same time scale as adults, for their reveries and dawdling are geared to a different clock from ours. Twenty minutes spent in tying a shoelace may pass like a second when the fantasy of the spaceship is more compelling than the reality of the school bus.

At the age of five, my boy wanted to know if I had lived in the era of the cavemen, and seemed disappointed that I had never met any personally. At the age of six, he knew that a great time gulf existed between the cavemen and me, but he still wanted to know if I had ever met Abraham Lincoln.

To a child, a father in his forties might as well be 150 years old. The difference between a father and a grandfather, which seems so pronounced to us, is nothing at all to a child.

Years, decades and centuries are all blurred in the short focus of the child's mind. What happened two years ago might have been yesterday, and next Friday is a million years away.

Understanding the relativity of time, in this psychological dimension, is absolutely essential if we are to cope with the world of children. It is a long and laborious process for them to acquire the time sense of adulthood — and some people, it is true, never seem to acquire it.

The habitually unprompt, the inept planners and last-minuters, are really clinging to emotional vestiges of their childhood, and are unconsciously reliving the past, reluctant to break with their fantasies.

On the other hand, those persons with an overacute sense of time (and I happen to be one of them) have perhaps relinquished too much of their childhood capacity for taking the present as it comes and enjoying it. They are forever planning ahead, living in the next hour, the next day, the next month, and the present is swallowed up by the future.

If the habitually unprompt are self-indulgent, the compulsively prompt are self-punishing; and it certainly seems to be true that the person who is late for an engagement is generally more charming than the one who gets there early. This is what makes the punctual person so angry: he feels that people who are late have no right to be so pleasant. Maybe this is what we resent in our dawdling children.

6

OF THE MIND
AND PASSIONS

Believe It — And It May Happen

THERE IS, in the field of the social sciences, something called "the theory of fulfilled expectations." It was illustrated with remarkable clarity some years ago by the late Robert Redfield, the anthropologist, in a talk he gave to members of the Chicago police force.

Suppose, he said, that red automobiles were generally believed to be more mechanically defective, more accident-prone, than cars of any other color.

"What then," he asked, "would be the responsibility of the officer who was trying to keep the traffic running smoothly? He would have to know that every time he saw a red automobile in a traffic difficulty he would anticipate a greater chance of accident.

"Now what," he continued, "would be the effect of these beliefs upon the drivers of red automobiles?" The effect of the belief, naturally enough, would make them nervous and apprehensive and they would tend to drive less steadily.

"Next," he went on, "people would come up with statistics showing that there are 28 percent more accidents with red automobiles than with any other color. And it would be so.

"But," he concluded the illustration, "the statistical proof would, of course, not really be proof that the cause of the accident lay in the color of the car. It would lie in the way people thought about the situation."

What he was pointing out was simply that beliefs are factors in changing reality, and that if we have expectations of a certain sort of behavior, our very attitude tends to make that behavior more probable. What we think about the Negro (the point he was getting at) both confirms and changes their response to any given social situation.

Perhaps we can see it more easily if we go from the tragic to the frivolous. Almost no wife drives the car as well when her husband is sitting beside her — if she knows he is critical and superior about his driving ability. One reason (perhaps the main reason) that women are "bad drivers" is the prevalent male view of them as drivers; it makes them nervous and insecure, and so they begin to drive badly.

It is extremely difficult for a woman to park a car in a tight spot if a man is watching her, because she knows he expects her to mess it up. And most of the time she *will* mess it up — but not if she is unobserved and feels unchallenged by male superiority. Those who expect more of people — of minorities, of women, of children — are generally gratified; those who expect less find exactly what they expect.

The Conditions of Maturity

A COLLEGE STUDENT in Kansas has written to ask me if I could define the word "maturity" for him. "The word is thrown around so loosely these days," he writes, "that it seems to mean everything to everybody."

I quite agree. In my time, when a girl threw a boy over, it was because he was a "jerk" or a "drip." Now she does it for the grand-sounding reason that he's "immature" — when she may be just as immature herself.

It reminds me of the comedian I recently heard who explained he divorced his wife because she was "immature" — "She'd come into the bathroom while I was taking a bath, and sink all my boats!"

I wouldn't care to try a one-sentence definition of the word "maturity," because the idea covers too much ground. Besides, it's important to recognize that nobody is wholly mature in every direction, and that it is a goal we should keep aiming at, rather than a pinnacle we can never attain.

But I do think it's possible to set down a list that will embrace the most important aspects of the word. And the first condition of maturity is to use this list for judging ourselves, rather than others.

If we can recognize, accept, and (most of the time) act upon the following nine maxims, I think we have a right to call ourselves grown-up:

1. Everything must be paid for, either in material or psychic coin.

2. The similarities between people are much greater than the differences; differences are accidental, similarities are essential.

3. The more we get to know someone, the harder it is to dislike him.

4. It is impossible to understand oneself without understanding others, and impossible to understand others without understanding oneself.

5. Nobody can cheat us as we cheat ourselves; nobody can deceive us as we deceive ourselves; nobody can defeat us as we defeat ourselves.

6. Everybody is more or less irrational, more or less infantile, more or less tied to the past with invisible chains; therefore, we must not be quick to judge or quick to blame.

7. The sins of the parents are handed down to the children; no law of heredity is more certain than this, or harder to accept.

8. What we call "intelligent self-interest" always fails in the end, for the more interest we show in the self, the less intelligent we become.

9. The means we use eventually change our ends; we become what we do.

"Performers" and "Personalities"

A WOMAN I know met a celebrated actor in New York recently, and was surprised and disappointed in his personality. "He was like an empty vessel just waiting to be filled with some liquid," she said. "The liquid being, of course, whatever role he is enacting at the time."

Actors (and actresses, too, of course) tend to come in only two shapes: the Performer and the Personality. She undoubtedly had met one of the Performers.

The difference between the two is quite readily seen by anyone who is personally acquainted with the theater: the Performer is nobody, and the Personality is nobody but himself.

There are some actors who are always themselves, no matter which role they are playing. Their talent may be large, but their capacity for subordinating themselves is small: it is they themselves, rather than their impersonations, that dominate the audience. These people are Personalities.

At the other end of the spectrum is the actor who can be anybody, and prefers to be. He himself has no "essence" or "aroma," and confesses that he feels empty when he is not impersonating a character.

Peter Sellers, perhaps the finest character actor of our time, has admitted in an interview, that "the real Sellers" eludes him. It is only when he is somebody else that he feels "most myself." A great many persons enter the theater profession- ally not to exhibit themselves, as is commonly supposed, but rather to escape from the nothingness of themselves into somebody else. Acting becomes "reality" to them, and reality is but a shadow.

We can see some evidence of this in the case of stutterers. It is generally known that stutterers forget their affliction when they are playing a part, either talking or singing. As long as the words belong to someone else, as long as they are *not themselves*, they can speak as swiftly as anyone. Several famous comedians stutter badly in private life who never show a trace of it in public performance.

The failure to distinguish between the Personality and the Performer has cost even experienced producers millions of dollars in Broadway flops. Needing a "big name" for a star- ring role, a producer will hire a famous Personality when the role calls for a Performer — and then it turns out that the Personality cannot subdue himself to the part, cannot make it believable, because he is too much himself.

The woman had no right to be disappointed in the actor. What is given to the public is what we would like to be; what is left over is what we have to be. For any artist, the best goes into his work.

Drinking Not Just an "Escape"

IT IS A COMMONPLACE these days to say that the alcoholic drinks so heavily as a means of "escaping" from himself. This is a seductive half-truth: drinking is surely a means of fleeing from oneself, but it is also something more than that.

Like most fundamental human problems, it is a paradox. Drinking is both an escape *from* reality, and a flight *into* reality. Only they are different kinds of reality.

What happens to a man when he drinks a great deal? Two things at once: first, his own identity becomes blurred and fragmented. He loses the "sense of himself." He is unable to see himself, to judge himself, to command or control himself. He relinquishes his internal reality.

Secondly, and just as important, he sees the world more sharply, more clearly, more cohesively. He is able to "pick up" things about other people that would never get through to him in sober moments. He can sense inner feelings, hidden attitudes, vibrations of meaning and relationships that are lost to him in his normal state.

In vino veritas, the Romans used to say — in wine there is truth. The truth apprehended by the drunk is not about himself, but about others. This is what makes it so gratifying to him.

For there is something in the makeup of the alcoholic (either chemical or psychological, or both) that does not hold these two realities in equilibrium. While sober, the reality of himself is overwhelming, and the reality of others is indistinct; drinking reverses this balance, and enables him to escape from himself and into others.

Unless we understand this, we will be making moral judgments about him and failing to grasp the *good thing* he is trying to do (however ineffectually) in his drinking. He wants to escape not into oblivion but into the world of external reality, of other people.

An unusually high percentage of alcoholics can be seen to be, in their normal state, shy, sweet, reserved people. But much of this shyness is the inability to project, to relate, to expand the confines of the ego beyond its shrunken boundaries. Drinking becomes the way of breaking out of this shell into the outer world.

It is slavery, but it is also, in a peculiarly pathological way, freedom. It is (temporary) emancipation from a self that looms too large and too threateningly. The alcoholic is not drinking to kill himself (as is popularly supposed), but to make himself come alive. This is the only way he knows how to do it; a tragically futile way. He is looking for fellowship, and can only obliterate himself to find it, or its sad and transient counterfeit.

Will Power Is Not a Cure-all

THERE is nobody I wish any harm, but there are some persons who almost deserve to break both their legs in an accident — and then have the bystanders say to them, "Use your will power, just stand up and walk!"

Exhorting the "will" to use its power is as silly and futile as exhorting a dead automobile battery to use its power. A charge must be put in before any power can be put out.

We will not come effectively to terms with the problem of mental illness in our nation (which is the largest medical problem today) until we recognize, for once and all, that a person with crippled emotions is no more able to behave normally than a person with broken legs is able to walk normally.

We can walk with a strain or even with a sprain; we grit our teeth, summon our inner resolve, and take painful steps. But not with a major break — and if we try, it only gets worse.

What obtuseness prevents most people from seeing that a fractured personality is as real, as painful and as disabling as a fractured femur?

A patient with deep emotional problems (I don't mean the ordinary kind we all have) is a slave bound in chains he has forged himself. He can no more break these chains by his own conscious volition than a prisoner can escape from a barred cell.

His "will power" can operate only after someone has cut the bars and shown the way out to freedom. To be locked within one's own distorted personality is the most cramping of solitary confinements.

Yet millions of decent, humane, well-meaning relatives and friends of such neurotic prisoners can offer them little more than the buck-up-and-take-a-grip-on-yourself treatment. And then these relatives and friends are resentful when this pathetic advice is not gratefully received and promptly acted upon.

The best of modern theologians — such as the Protestant Reinhold Niebuhr, the Catholic Jacques Maritain, the Jewish Martin Buber — have understood this and have written about it sympathetically; but the great mass of "religious" laymen still cling to the naïve belief that all a neurotic needs is "faith" or "courage" or "will power" to emerge from his dungeon into the sunlight of reality.

Each age has its own superstition, which it confuses with religion; and the superstition of our age is the stubborn conviction that a mental ailment can somehow be cured by moral means.

Good Deeds Can Be Misused

IF YOU'RE GOING to do something nice, be nice about it or don't do it. This is a simple and obvious thought — but it rarely seems to occur to certain types of people. I am referring to those who will go out of their way to do something nice — a favor, a chore, an extra kindness — and then silently demand repayment in terms of gratitude or appreciation.

These are what Dr. Edmund Bergler, the late psychiatrist, called "the injustice collectors." They go around in life collecting injustices. They do nice things to prove to themselves that other people do not appreciate them as much as they should. Then they sulk, or adopt a martyred pose, or take to their beds with some real or fancied ailment. And, in one way or another, they exact a high retribution for their "niceness." Finally, those around them begin to realize that it's not worth the price.

Many acts of generosity and self-sacrifice are not at all what they seem to be on the surface. Rather, they are techniques employed for neurotic ends; these "tyrants of goodness" would be better off — and so would their families — if they acted a little more selfishly (that is, a little more naturally) much of the time.

Self-pity is the leitmotiv in the lives of such personalities. They enjoy demonstrating, over and over again, that others do not appreciate them, that they are victims of the world's injustice, that the bread they cast on the waters is never served up to them as toast on a tray in bed on Sunday mornings.

What they utterly fail to understand is that nice things are done for our own sake, not for the sake of others. The pleasure must reside in the performance, not in the applause. Good deeds are, in a deeper psychological sense, *a favor to oneself*. If this is not grasped, then our whole sense of personal relationships becomes warped.

A kind act, a piece of generosity or self-sacrifice, must be its own reason for being, an end in itself, not part of a barter system. It must not be used later to reprove someone else with, or as a lever to pry up ancient grievances under a rock. Yet this is what the self-sacrificers tend to do.

They pile up their good deeds like misers stuffing bills in a mattress; hoard them, count them over at night, and recite their complaints. Eventually, with this hoard they try to purchase affection and admiration and gratitude — but it does not work that way. The injustice collectors only collect more injustices.

There are many people who should try to be a little better; but there are almost as many who should stop trying to be better than they can be. If their hidden feelings (hidden to themselves, if not to others) do not correspond to their generous acts, there can be nothing but bitter fruit in the end, for themselves and for those they are so "nice" to.

What True Education Should Do

WHEN most people think of the word "education," they think of a pupil as a sort of animate sausage casing. Into this empty casing, the teachers are supposed to stuff "education."

But genuine education, as Socrates knew more than two thousand years ago, is not inserting the stuffings of information *into* a person, but rather eliciting knowledge *from* him; it is the drawing out of what is in the mind.

"The most important part of education," once wrote William Ernest Hocking, the distinguished Harvard philosopher, "is this instruction of a man in what he has inside of him."

And, as Edith Hamilton has reminded us, Socrates never said, "I know, learn from me." He said, rather, "Look into your own selves and find the spark of truth that God has put into every heart, and that only you can kindle to a flame."

In the dialogue called the "Meno," Socrates takes an ignorant slave boy, without a day of schooling, and proves to the amazed observers that the boy really "knows" geometry — because the principles and axioms of geometry are already in his mind, waiting to be called out.

So many of the discussions and controversies about the content of education are futile and inconclusive because they are concerned with what should "go into" the student rather than with what should be taken out, and how this can best be done.

The college student who once said to me, after a lecture, "I spend so much time studying that I don't have a chance to learn anything," was succinctly expressing his dissatisfaction with the sausage-casing view of education.

He was being so stuffed with miscellaneous facts, with such an indigestible mass of material, that he had no time (and was given no encouragement) to draw on his own resources, to use his own mind for analyzing and synthesizing and evaluating this material.

Education, to have any meaning beyond the purpose of creating well-informed dunces, must elicit from the pupil what is latent in every human being — the rules of reason, the inner knowledge of what is proper for men to be and do, the ability to sift evidence and come to conclusions that can generally be assented to by all open minds and warm hearts.

Pupils are more like oysters than sausages. The job of teaching is not to stuff them and then seal them up, but to help them open and reveal the riches within. There are pearls in each of us, if only we knew how to cultivate them with ardor and persistence.

Crackpots Can't Tolerate Humor

THE MOST devastating critique that can be made against extremist movements is a very simple and yet deadly one: without exception, they lack a sense of humor.

Whatever the political, economic, or intellectual flaws in such doctrines as Communism and Fascism, the really telling charge against them is a kind of ferocious solemnity that is at bottom alien to the human spirit. No humor, no satire, no nonsense, can flourish in a country, or in a movement, that views life in black-and-white only.

A few weeks ago, for instance, the official Communist Party newspaper in Italy attacked the American comic strip, "Peanuts," for its depiction of characters ranging from the "suicidal" to the "stupid." One of the cartoon characters was even stigmatized as a "fascist."

And, of course, in Nazi Germany and Fascist Italy, no real humor was ever permitted. For genuine humor is the eternal enemy of all pomposity, all officialdom, all fanaticism, all the political creeds and doctrines and dogmas that strive to become, in one way or another, state religions.

We all know that artistic expression dries up in a totalitarian country; writers and painters and musicians, who are by nature rebels, cannot produce in response to official decrees. What is even more significant, however, is that the sense of humor atrophies in such an environment: people are afraid to be funny.

This is a worse enslavement than the economic injustices that Marx inveighed against. The slavery of the intellect, of the spontaneous emotions, is more killing than any of the capitalistic excesses of the nineteenth century. It is one of the wry paradoxes of Marxism that it made men "free" for more dullness and drabness and conformity than they had ever known before.

The most effective way to combat the extremists is with humor and satire and parody; and a democratic nation that begins to limit and censor its satirists has already fallen under the corrupting blight of totalitarian attitudes. Mocking self-criticism in a nation is a sign of health, not of sickness; the hand that salutes the flag must also be free to thumb its nose at those who wave the flag for venal or hypocritical reasons.

Freedom of speech must include the freedom to speak impertinently, or it means nothing; it must include the freedom to *laugh at*, the freedom to deflate the important, deride the orthodox, and dissect the "received wisdom" of the people. Otherwise, we lose the capacity, and the will, to correct our national stance when it slumps or sways.

The best method of testing the strength of a doctrine is by subjecting it to humor and irony and burlesque. The extremist movements invariably fail this test, for they are based on a grimly unyielding view of man's nature. Exposed to shafts of comedy, these doctrines turn nasty, brutish and violent. Which, of course, they always were in the beginning.

Two Ways of Playing the Game

IN NEW YORK, some time ago, I was invited by a friend to play bridge with him one afternoon at the Cavendish Club, where the masters make their home between tournaments. Afterwards, there was the customary gossip about various experts, their habits and peculiarities.

What interested me was the discussion about one particular master, who invariably wins at rubber bridge, even with the most mediocre partners. Other experts play just as well as he, but he knows best how to adjust himself to the flaws and deficiencies of his partner of the moment.

Most of his colleagues, I was told, do exactly the opposite. If they find themselves in a serious game partnered by a duffer, they make the partner "pay" for his ignorance and ineptitude. They punish him for being a poor player — even though he is their partner, and they suffer the same bad score for their behavior.

They make bids he cannot understand, place burdens upon

him that he cannot fulfill, and then heap withering scorn upon him for falling down on the hand — which scorn only makes him play worse, and adversely affects their own score as well.

This self-defeating attitude reminded me of marriages I have known, in which one of the partners is always excoriating the faults of the other, and would rather see the partnership become a dismal failure than forgo the bleak pleasures of criticism.

Cutting off one's nose to spite one's face is a much more common attitude than we realize. This attitude says, in effect, "If you're not going to fulfill my expectations, if I am to be saddled with your shortcomings, then I'll strain you to the limit and test you to the breaking point, as much as it may hurt me; because the satisfaction I get from feeling superior to you is greater than the cost of disaster."

But the winning player in bridge — where all the masters have about the same level of technical skill — is the one with the most flexible and adaptable temperament, the one who can bring out the best in his partner, the one who knows that the noose he draws around his partner's neck also hangs him.

When one reaches a certain high level of aptitude in any pursuit, the decisive differences are then emotional; the line that really separates winners and losers is not a technical or strategic superiority, but a psychological approach. In bridge, in tennis, in most other competitions, games are not so much won as lost — lost by those who are not in full command of their inmost natures.

Moral vs. Physical Courage

IN A RECENT issue of the *Atlantic Monthly*, I was interested in reading an interview with Stirling Moss, the pre-eminent racing driver of our time.

Among other things, Moss confessed that his great courage on the track does not extend to other activities; for instance, he would under no circumstances dive from a thirty-foot board into the water, even though he "knew" the water was deep enough and safe enough for the dive.

We tend to do with the word "courage" what we do with the word "intelligence" — we assume that it is indivisible, when actually there are many different kinds of courage and many different kinds of intelligence.

And those who possess one special kind of courage or intelligence tend to think that those who lack it (even though possessing some other kind) are wholly without the virtue.

Physical courage, for example, is most admired in our society; yet a good case could be made out that not only are there differing forms of physical courage, but also that there may be superior kinds of courage that make the physically brave man look like a coward.

I was impressed some years ago listening to the rebroadcast of a BBC talk given by General Sir William Slim, former commander in chief of the Allied Land Forces in Southeast Asia, in which he began by saying that "Moral courage is a higher and rarer virtue than physical courage."

He went on to point out that no other army has ever possessed "massed physical courage" as the Japanese did. The Japanese generals, he added, shared their men's physical bravery, but lacked moral courage. "Thus, we played on this weakness and destroyed their armies."

Moral courage must be taught, he said, because so few, if any, have it naturally, and "most men with moral courage learned it by precept and example in their youth." The outstanding impression of courage he carried away from the retreat from Burma in 1942 "was that of Indian women refugees, and not of the fighting man."

One man fears heights, another speed, and still another

water. One man will make the most heroic attack and then
faint if a hypodermic needle is plunged into his arm. Physical
bravery or cowardice are more a matter of childhood experiences than an indication of basic character.

Humanity has always respected physical courage, but high
moral courage usually meets with contempt or martyrdom —
in its own time. How many men have been "brave" in an
unjust war simply because they lacked the moral courage to
resist the force of public opinion?

Why Freud Was Not "Freudian"

PERHAPS the two most influential men of the twentieth century — in terms of changing the moral and intellectual climate
of our times — have been Einstein and Freud.

Yet, by the paradox that always accompanies their kind of
greatness, neither of them is really understood — by the
masses or even by the majority of educated people.

Of course, their technical theories need not be understood;
what I mean is that not even their basic premises are grasped
accurately and clearly. To most people, Einstein said, "Everything is relative," and Freud said, "Everything is sex."

Both these statements are totally false, and would have
horrified the men to whom they are ascribed. Leaving Einstein aside for the moment, let us consider the widespread
distortion of Freud's view into "Everything is sex."

Some psychiatrists in the past believed this. They were
known as "pan-sexualists." Freud fought these men vigor-
ously and relentlessly. But at the same time, he was fighting
conventional society, and forcing us to recognize that many
kinds of "nonsexual" behavior had deep sexual roots.

What we have forgotten — if we have ever known it — is
that Freud also demonstrated the opposite: that, in neurosis,

what often seems to be sexual conduct is not really sexual at all.

Take, for example, patterns of adultery and promiscuity. These certainly seem to be motivated by sexual drives. Yet, in many if not most cases, the sexual "acting out" is merely a symptom of other discontents and dissatisfactions.

Of the people who behave this way, relatively few are driven by genuinely sexual needs. They are unhappy in other ways, they are enslaved by infantile fears or conflicts never resolved within themselves — and their sexual misconduct is simply a symptom of their deeply unconscious problems.

Freud showed that many things we do not commonly think of as "sexual" are sexual in origin; but he also demonstrated the contrary — that "pseudo-sexuality" is one of the prime ways in which the disturbed or immature personality tries to come to terms (unsuccessfully, of course) with its conflicts. This is why, as he pointed out, there is no real joy or lasting satisfaction in such compulsive behavior.

The finest tribute humanity can pay its great men is to understand them. Instead, they are venerated or condemned, out of blind admiration or blind ignorance; which is why Freud said, "I am not a Freudian."

Prejudice Is Never "Reasonable"

THERE IS A story about a man who accosted a wealthier friend and asked for a loan of a hundred dollars. "Can't do it," said the friend, "because my mother-in-law is visiting us right now."

The man was puzzled. "What has that got to do with lending me the money?" he asked. "Nothing at all," replied the friend, "but when you don't want to do something, one excuse is as good as another."

I thought of this recently when I heard someone holding

forth on the reasons he doesn't care for Negroes — they are shiftless, they lack ambition, they won't accept responsibility, they commit many crimes, they don't even help one another, and they are simply unintelligent.

This same man, I happen to know, doesn't care much for Jews, either. And what do you suppose his "reasons" are? The Jews are too ambitious, they stick together and help each other too much, they are too clever and study too hard and get the best grades and run the big businesses and the most prosperous law offices and the most flourishing medical practices.

The very opposite traits that prejudice him against the Negro prejudice him against the Jews. One group reacts to discrimination in one way; another in another; and he objects to both reactions.

Many of the things that are said about Negroes and Jews are false; some of the things are true. But what is significant is that if you don't want to like and accept somebody, one excuse is as good as another. The objective facts don't matter, and the reasons are never as "reasonable" as we like to think they are.

It is interesting that, for a long time, the Americans as a group were talked about by Europeans just as we talk about our own minority groups. Even up to modern times, the educated elite among Europeans dismissed the Americans as arrogant, crude, barbarous, boastful, greedily materialistic, and vulgarly ostentatious in their habits and goals.

Many of these charges were true, but the Europeans failed to recognize the historical and cultural reasons for such behavior. All they knew was that the Americans were a different breed, and their very difference was an offense to Old World standards. They both resented and envied us, and so they used the same vituperation that older and more settled communities have always used against the newcomer and the outlander. The ancient Greeks said the same things about the Romans.

If you tell a child long enough that he is unattractive and undesirable, he comes to believe it despite himself, and begins to react in an extreme manner. The real tragedy of prejudice and discrimination is that the person (or the group) turns into a caricature of himself.

It's a Pity We Lose Our Candor

A SEVEN-YEAR-OLD BOY I know — know very well — left a note on his father's dresser just before Christmas, asking for an Eastern Ring-Necked Snake for a pet.

At the end of the exhaustive recital about the snake's virtues, its amiability, its well-bred feeding habits, and its all-round suitability as a member of the household, the boy appended a P.S. to the note.

"*I speld some words rong,*" he wrote, "*because I did not stop to think.*"

The boy didn't get the snake, I am sorry to report, owing to the horrified objections of his mother, a woman of overwhelming sensibility. But his father would have brought him a whole nest of (defanged) pythons as a reward for that wonderful Postscript.

"I did not stop to think." How many of us would ever say that? How many of us would exhibit the candor, the modesty, the blithe confession of thoughtlessness?

When I spell a word wrong in the column, and it happens to get into print, I blame the typesetter, or the proofreader, or even — if possible — the dictionary for betraying my literacy.

More importantly, when I make a mistake in judgment or taste or evaluation, it would not occur to me to say "I did not stop to think." Instead, I will usually find some defense, or explanation, or rationalization, that glibly shifts the blame from me to something outside me — I was given the wrong information, or I was misinterpreted, or I really meant it in another context.

What we lose as we grow older is the marvelous freshness and honesty of youth that is not afraid or ashamed to say "I did not stop to think." I have no doubt at all that this is what Jesus meant when he said that "a little child shall lead us." Because only this spirit, which dulls as we grow older, can show us the right road to our true selfhood.

Millions of words have been written on how and what children can learn from us; but little has been said about what we can learn from children. Yet the education that a parent with open eyes, ears and mind can get from a growing child is incomparably more important than the education a child can get from all its formal training.

What we get (if the child has not been damaged in early years) is a portrait of our lost Eden, of a land in which shame and vanity and self-deceit have barely begun to erect their bristling barricades. In a few years, of course, the child will become more like us; that is to say, he will be "educated" and skilled in orthodox hypocrisy.

Good and Bad Traits Are Entwined

I WAS having lunch with a magazine publisher from New York, in the course of which he mentioned a man we both knew. "Sam would make a fine editor," he said, "if only he would learn to give the other fellow a chance to speak up."

"Yes," I agreed, "but then he wouldn't be Sam any more; he would be somebody else."

One of the most frequent mistakes we make lies in assuming

that a personality is a collection of traits, or that a personality is merely the sum of its parts. Personality is a *way of organizing* these parts.

Sam's "bad trait" — his unwillingness to give others a chance to speak up — is directly related to his "good" traits. They are integrated in a complex structure, like a set of molecules, and removing or changing one would affect the whole nature of the structure.

If we look at persons dynamically, and not simply as a static set of traits, we can see that certain defects are the price they pay for their virtues, just as ulcer or migraine is the price some people pay for their perfectionism or their passivity or their aggressiveness.

This is why "pointing out" a bad trait to a colleague or a subordinate — even in a kindly and well-meaning way — usually does no good, and may even do some harm. It makes him feel worse, and does not enable him to act any better.

When we single out one trait or characteristic and ask the person to change it, we are really asking him to change the *organization* of his whole personality; and this is a formidable task for which most of us are not equipped — especially when it has taken us years of effort to achieve some success and equilibrium with this particular organization of our traits.

Perhaps we can see the problem more clearly if we conceive of the personality as a closely integrated team of acrobats who stand on one another's shoulders — three men below, then two on top of them, and finally one on the top. If we change the position of any one of the men, or take one away, the whole act is different. And, indeed, it may be the man on the bottom (whom we find "undesirable") that enables the top man to maintain his precarious balance.

Of course, people change, and modify their conduct, and learn from experience if they are open to it. But it is important to know that some "bad" traits make the good ones possible, just as the pathology in the oyster produces the pearl.

How We Defeat Ourselves

WATCHING the National Clay Courts tennis tournament recently, I saw a player come within one point of winning his match. He lost the crucial point, and his opponent finally came from far behind to win the match.

From where I sat, it seemed clear to me that the player who lost had really beaten himself. His game was at least as good as his opponent's: his strokes were clean, his footwork agile, his strategy sensible. But it was his own temperament that finally broke him.

When he lost a point, he blamed himself. On a close decision, he scowled darkly at the umpire. When the breaks went against him, he forgot that his opponent had bad breaks, too. He was an unattractive personality.

It has been my unwavering observation over the years that 90 percent of us beat ourselves. Nobody else does it to us. We beat ourselves in various ways — by too much confidence, or by too little; by blaming the other person, or by blaming ourselves; by too much pessimism when things look bad, and by too much optimism when things look good.

The one trait in common that all great and consistent winners have is an absence of the "blameworthy" sense. They do not pout when others are at fault, and they do not rage at themselves when they are at fault.

Occasionally, they may be beaten; but they never beat themselves. And over the long pull, they win more often than they lose — and they win, in many cases, by simply allowing their opponents to beat themselves.

Why Nature gives an equable temperament to some and

not to others is a mystery we can never solve. But I am convinced that it is temperament, more than talent or brains, that determines whether we are self-fulfilling or self-destroying. The difference between one champion and another may be trifling in terms of pure ability; it may be vast in terms of spirit.

We hear a great deal about the so-called "killer instinct" in champions; and that the reason one man failed to reach the ultimate goal was his lack of this killer instinct.

All this means, I think, is that in the ultimate crisis the real champion forgets himself entirely, and concentrates with passionate ferocity upon his object. In the familiar Zen term, "the archer, the arrow and the target are one." The "near-champion" never forgets himself, never subdues himself to the object, never truly subordinates himself to the game.

It is not the instinct to kill, or even to conquer, but the instinct for perfection — a perfection so exquisite in itself that it obliterates the man who is achieving it. He is beyond praise, beyond blame, beyond all our sublunary ambitions. He does not beat himself, for he does not fight himself; rather, he forgets himself in an almost holy manner.

An Institution Is More than Men

"AN INSTITUTION," wrote Emerson, "is the lengthened shadow of a man." Like much of Emerson, this is a brilliant half-truth that obscures the other half.

An institution is also greater than the sum of the men who make it up. Add together, Smith, Jones and Robinson, and you get the SJR Company — but you also get a sum larger than the individuals.

Failing to recognize this fact has puzzled many workers in successful institutions. They look around them and wonder how the company does so well — Smith drinks, Jones is not precisely truthful, and Robinson spends half the day at the club.

Nobody seems to be very wise, or very knowing, or terribly efficient; and yet the firm prospers, the doors open every morning, the books balance, the dividends are paid, and the stockholders rejoice.

There is in chemistry a thing called *synergism*. This rule states that the combined action of several elements, taken together, is greater than the sum of all of them taken separately.

If, for instance, you swallow the ingredients of a cough mixture at half-hour intervals, you lose the potency that is present in the mixture itself. Two and two add up to much more than four.

This rule also holds true in the chemistry of human interactions. The combination of Smith, Jones and Robinson produces a result that could not be predicted if you simply analyzed each of these men as an individual.

Young people, for instance, are often critical of the workings of the institutions employing them. The president seems a dolt, the vice-president a popinjay, the office manager a dreary robot. It appears nothing less than a miracle that the company staggers along from day to day.

Yet, even when these harsh judgments are true (and young impatient minds tend to exaggerate the stupidities of their elders), the dolt and the popinjay and the robot work synergistically together, and the daily product is a magical piece of human alchemy, transforming lead into gold.

Of course, the perils of an institution are many — mustiness, red-tape, massive unfairness to subordinates, a clumsy chain of command. But the defects should not blind us to the possible virtues, and to the knowledge that an institution can have a vitality and a stability and a creativeness that give it a supernal life of its own.

Only a Conflict of Body and Mind

EVERY five years or so, I visit the eye doctor for a checkup — mostly to make sure that the glasses I keep in my pocket (and rarely take out) are still suitable for my vision.

On a recent visit, I told the doctor that from time to time I experience a slight giddiness, and wondered if it could be my eyes. He found nothing wrong.

I asked him the possible reason, and he shrugged. "It may be circulatory, but who knows? I've been having blinding headaches for thirty years, and I can't find out the cause of them!"

This from one of the foremost ophthalmologists in the country. He can't find the cause of his headaches, nor can any of his medical colleagues. So he simply accepts them as a fact of nature.

This is not to say that symptoms should be ignored. To the contrary, they should be investigated at once, and by as competent a man as you can find. But it *is* to say that many people waste time, energy and money in consulting a series of "specialists" for their symptoms when all the tests show that nothing is organically wrong.

Most of these fears come from an outdated conception of the human body — a conception handed down to us by nineteenth century biology, and still perpetuated in most of the textbooks.

Thus convention holds that the body is a "machine." When something goes wrong with the machine, you take it to a mechanic, who fixes or replaces the defective part.

But the human body — as twentieth century medicine

knows — is a *process*, not a *mechanism*. It is not merely a system of wheels and pulleys and feed lines to be straightened and adjusted and cleaned.

Sometimes, of course, a mechanism *does* go awry: a gland fails to work properly, or a joint becomes inflamed. These are relatively simple cases to diagnose, and to remedy or to ease.

The blinding headaches, though, and the giddiness, and the vague stomach pains, and the difficulty in breathing, and all the thousand and one other vexing symptoms that attack the body — these, more often than not, have little to do with the *machinery* of the system, but represent some deep conflict in the marriage between mind and body.

My eye doctor honestly admitted this in the case of his blinding headaches. The time is ripe for more of his colleagues to practice the same candor with their giddy patients.

"Gratitude" Isn't Just a Payoff

AT DINNER the other night, someone was telling about a famous artist who, when poor and struggling, had borrowed money from a rich friend. Many years later, he told his friend: "I have repaid the debt — not by returning the money to you, but by passing it on to a young artist who is now where I was then."

This anecdote reminded me of a true and touching observation on that much-abused word "gratitude" made a long time ago by the French writer Frédéric Paulhan. He said:

*

The obligations of gratitude, like all approved obligations, are a low form of morality. Real gratitude does not consist

in loving a person who does us a service and in doing him a
service in return.

Gratitude consists in profiting by the service that has been
done so that we can act as well as possible toward the whole
of humankind, and not only toward the individual to whom
we are grateful.

*

Parents often made the calamitous mistake of expecting their children to be "grateful" for sacrifices or advantages; but a child's gratitude does not have to go back to his parents — it should be passed down to his own children.

If we do things for the child in the hope of winning his gratitude, we are really engaging in what Paulhan properly calls "a low form of morality." The higher form consists in wanting the child to behave as decently, as fairly, as kindly, to all people as we do to him.

Artists, after they become affluent and famous, may be grateful to their patrons for having given them the initial push; but how many of them express their gratitude by offering the same help to struggling novices? This kind of gratitude is much rarer, and much more valuable. Sadly enough, only a handful of composers, authors and painters have been noted for their willingness to give a hand to the newcomer, whom they commonly regard as a threat.

It is easy to feel grateful toward someone who has done us a considerable service, but the debt is not discharged when we pay him off. It is not discharged at all unless his kindness has started a chain reaction, and we do for someone else what he has done for us.

Illness is catching, but health is not. In the same way, ill feelings seem to travel from person to person, like a contagion, but good feelings usually remain static; they do not radiate outward as they would if we really understood the nature of gratitude and love and the other positive emotions. For most of us, like King Lear, want to get back what we have given, want to balance our emotional books, and cannot stand to be in the red.

Why Sammy Continues to Run

"WHY DOES he want more money?" said my friend at lunch, about a third man we both know. "He's got far more than he needs, and he'll just kill himself trying to double his fortune."

This is a commonplace enough situation. And, of course, it is obvious to anyone that money itself is not what the man wants: it is the "game," the "thrill," the gratification of "winning" that makes Sammy keep running long after he has any need to.

What I think is less understood, however, is that a chase of this sort is essentially a *substitute experience*. And a substitute is always something that we can never have enough of.

The man is really looking for self-esteem, and he seeks to find it by winning the esteem of others. In our society, the fastest and surest way to do this is by amassing a great deal of money. So the money becomes a substitute, a symbol, for the esteem.

But in the deep chemistry of the psyche, things do not work out this way. Getting the esteem of others does not give us self-esteem; worthiness comes from the inside, never from the outside. This is why a substitute experience always leaves us hungry for more.

Money is only one example. Sex, of course, is another. The man who chases women (like the one who chases money) can never have enough, can never be satisfied, can never settle down to one possession. The compulsive Lothario is perpetually as insatiable as the compulsive driver in the market-place.

For the same motives operate in this area. When sex becomes a substitute for love, it can never be gratified, but must go on from dizzying triumph to dizzying triumph (and each triumph ends in a kind of internal exhaustion and defeat, convalescence and continuation). The libertine can never find what he thinks he is looking for, any more than the acquisitive man can never have "enough" money.

Our genuine needs are self-confidence, self-esteem, self-sacrifice. These can be achieved only by giving, not by getting. When something in the psyche blocks us from expressing and gratifying these genuine needs, we turn to substitute ones. But no liquid can quench our thirst except water itself.

Not only can the substitute not satisfy us; it also contains its own law of diminishing returns — like the dope addict who needs more and more of a "shot" in order to maintain the same level of euphoria. Finally, he needs massive doses simply to keep alive, to keep reality at arm's length. Sammy runs because if he ever stopped, he would drop dead at the mere confrontation of his real needs.

Reversing the Spool of Thought

IF YOU ARE NORMALLY a right-handed person, try a little experiment for a half hour or so: do with your left hand everything that you usually do with your right.

The most simple and obvious acts will become complicated and cumbersome. You will hardly be able to write or cut or eat your food; and you will quickly become baffled, frustrated and exasperated.

Now imagine this lopsided process intensified a thousandfold, and you may have some idea of how painful and difficult it is to think "with the left hand" — that is, to reverse our customary process of thought.

Why has science made such enormous strides in knowledge and development, while human affairs still remain largely as they were in the days of the Assyrian Empire? Largely because every advance in science is gained by reversing the spool of thought — by thinking in a way that is opposite of the traditional and customary ways.

Of all the habits of mankind, the habits of thought are the most persistent, the most tenacious, the most enslaving. We put on an idea in the morning as we put on a shoe, left or right first, unconsciously and without ever varying the procedure by a fraction.

And our resistance against changing our habits of thought is immense and unrelenting. If we try, briefly, we find it as vexing and unrewarding as writing a letter with the left hand. What we are used to is comfortable; what is comfortable is good; and what is good is right — this is the unspoken belief of almost all people everywhere.

When a scientist, however, tackles a problem that has hitherto seemed insoluble, he abandons all his preconceptions, and all the preconceptions of the past. Only when he begins to question the basic assumptions he has always held can he make an utterly fresh start, unencumbered by the intellectual baggage of the past.

I am not suggesting that a knowledge of the past is not useful, or that history and tradition have little to offer us — but they must be used as tools, not as points of departure. Our thinking about them must involve a painful re-evaluation of our most cherished ideas and ideals.

Not one person in a thousand is willing — although many are able — to think left-handed for more than a few minutes at a time. Yet every important discovery has been made in this way, from Harvey on circulation of the blood to Freud on the role of the unconscious. And we know what derision and abuse such men were subjected to for daring to violate the right-handedness of their times.

"Good" Things Don't Quite Satisfy

IN HIS recent book, *On Knowing,* which I unreservedly recommend, Jerome Bruner, professor of psychology at Harvard, observes that "In time, and as one comes to benefit from experience, one learns that things will turn out neither as well as one hoped for nor as badly as one feared."

We can learn fairly early in life that our fears are generally exaggerated — the "bad" things that happen to us are not nearly so bad after they happen as they seemed in anxious expectation of them. There is some compensation in almost every loss; the mind takes care of that.

What is much harder to learn, however, and what is usually not learned until quite late in life (unless we are possessed of exceptional maturity) is that the "good" things that happen to us are not quite as fully satisfying, do not solve our problems, as we had hoped.

Every gain seems larger before we have it than after we have achieved it: the raise that looked so considerable a year ago has added to our expenses without substantially increasing our savings; the woman who fitted our needs so exquisitely during the engagement is a moon whose "dark side" we begin to glimpse only after the marrriage.

Unless we are able to hold our fears and our hopes in a more or less sophisticated equilibrium, we are continually in danger of losing our emotional balance, of pinning too much on the Big Break or shrinking away too fearfully from the specter of failure and disaster.

If we look back upon our childhood, we can plainly see how obvious this is: neither the catastrophes nor the triumphs were as meaningful or decisive as we had imagined. Yet the time ahead of us is not much different from the time past — it is the same psychological game, played on a larger scale, for larger stakes, but still not as consequential to our souls as we still, half childishly, imagine.

The public is baffled, and a little contemptuous, toward those celebrities (usually in the entertainment world) who despite fame, fortune, extraordinary good looks and all the other desiderata we so ardently yearn for, nevertheless are disgruntled, unhappy, confused, and sometimes embittered to the point of suicide.

Such personalities cannot be understood unless we recognize that they have been *betrayed by their hope coming true.* They delusively believed that things would be well once fame and fortune were theirs; and all their fanatical striving for success was directed toward this end. When their infantile wishes were gratified, however, they quickly found that some basic satisfaction had eluded them. They had climbed to the peak — but the top of the mountain is cold, windy, and lonesome.

Hope, of course, is a better comrade-in-arms than fear, if we must make a choice. But both attitudes must be tempered by the calm recognition that neither leads us to heaven or to hell.

A Writer Must "Have the Call"

IN NEW YORK recently, I was introduced to a young man who had just resigned his position in a brokerage firm in order to become a writer. We chatted for a half hour about his new life, and I was tempted to ask him: "What is it that you have to say?"

For it seemed perfectly plain to me that this affable, not unintelligent young man was singularly devoid of any ideas or views that cried out to be heard. He wanted to say something, but he seemed to have nothing of special importance to say.

There is a widespread mistaken notion that "writing" is a talent that exists in a void — a sense of words and phrases, a style, a gift of expression and arrangement. But this is only the hollow form of writing; it needs to be filled with substance.

Nine-tenths of all writers, including many of the established ones, have very little to say. Their world-view is either banal, unformed, or nonexistent. They are a mass of feelings and inchoate ideas, but these have never been enough to give shape and point and direction to literary works.

Good writing — as distinct from mere "style" — is first of all sound thinking. A writer needs a prehensile mind, one that can grasp an idea and hold it in the round, firmly and forcibly, using it as a tool. I don't even mean that these ideas need necessarily be conscious ones — but they must be present, driving the engine and providing its motive power.

The young man in New York, like so many of his kind, feels that the urge to "express himself" is a valid enough reason. It is not. The writer does not express "himself" — he expresses his view of the world, refracted through his own unique personality. Unless he can objectify himself — which takes study, patience, and the right shape of mind to begin with — he would do better to express himself by taking up flower arranging or finger painting or some other therapeutic craft.

The subjectivism that is running wild in the modern world tends to make everyone think that all he requires is the urge and a few technical pointers in order to become a creative artist. Nothing could be further from the truth. Writing, like the other arts, is a *vocation* — and a vocation implies a call, a summons, to a certain way of life, of thinking and feeling. The Church wisely rejects those probationers who, despite their feelings, do not truly have the call; how much anguish would be spared if these would-be writers had a bishop to turn to.

Too Many Words and Voices

A MAN I know was talking at lunch about a widely known columnist who specializes in humor and whimsy. "Why doesn't he ever write about serious and important things?" he asked me. "Certainly he's amusing, but there are more substantial matters in the world to write about."

I disagreed with this point of view. "Each person should do what he does best," I suggested. "And this columnist is excellent as a light entertainer. He fills a need, does no harm, and gives people pleasure. Why ask more of him?"

The man at lunch was a victim of what I call mock-seriousness. He wants everyone in the public prints to focus on the important issues, and he ignores the obvious fact that some writers are not equipped to comment on matters beyond their immediate perceptions.

The columnist in question is modestly aware of his limitations. He has a keen eye for foibles, a deft way with language, and a puckish sense of humor. If he tried to do more, he would end up doing considerably less; like Sir Arthur Sullivan forsaking the blithe Savoyard operettas for ponderous "serious" music that is mostly unlistenable-to today.

I would make precisely the opposite criticism: that there are too many commentators who are floundering beyond their depths, who lack the background, the intellectual stature, and the analytic powers to convey more than a superficial (and thus distorted) picture of what is happening and what it means.

There are many who deplore the fact that so witty and saturnine a sports writer as Westbrook Pegler, for instance, decided to cover the larger arena of world events, for which nothing in his background had prepared him. Overwhelmed by the complexity of his subject, his humor turned corrosive and his perspective became warped.

Many people, it is true, do not live up to their potential; but just as many, it seems to me, are trying to live beyond theirs. The air is filled with voices pontificating on everything from birth control to bomb-testing, and the voice of the reformed disk jockey is often louder than that of the man who has devoted a lifetime to studying such matters. Too much is said about everything, and not enough of it has any meaning.

The puckish columnist is to be commended for working within his severe, but admirable, limitations, and refusing to become an oracle. What he does is small, but craftsmanlike, and it is a real pleasure among so many pundits whose volume is equaled only by their vacuity.

The Warm and Moist vs. the Dry and Cool

THE WARM, moist people always feel cheated or let down by the dry, cool people. And the dry, cool people always feel embarrassed by the warm, moist people.

I have a friend in the West who is a fine person, but warm and moist. He is full of feelings, very big on Friendship, on

Letters, on Photos of the family. He goes for "Real Human Beings."

My own temperament tends more toward the dry and cool. I write no letters, carry no photos, find any effusiveness rather sticky. This has nothing to do with my feelings, only with my way of expressing them.

This bothers the warm, moist people. They feel that their friendship is not adequately returned. They want you to be as demonstrative as they are. Their ideal of true companionship is sitting around a campfire, holding hands in a circle, and singing old songs.

It is hard to get them to understand that one can be a true friend without saying so every half hour, without writing long, chatty letters, without celebrating the fraternal rites. Their sensitivity is so acute that every omission seems a snub, every understatement seems a rebuff. They interpret a difference of temperament as a personal affront to their own code of living relationships.

Some of them, indeed, are so excessive in their unremitting desire to prove their friendship that they remind me of what Talleyrand said about Mme. de Staël: "She is such a good friend that she would throw all her acquaintances into the water for the pleasure of fishing them out."

And, no doubt, we dry, cool personalities are just as vexing and trying to them. We must seem singularly unresponsive, changeable, uncommunicative, and frightfully offhand about the sacred bond of friendship. They must wonder if we have any "real feelings" at all.

Laissez-faire may or may not be a good economic philosophy; it is certainly the best emotional philosophy. Live and let live, each in his own way, working out his own life-style — this is the only sensible attitude to take toward those around us, close or not.

But it is devilishly hard for many people to do. Parents, especially, become infuriated if their children differ temperamentally from themselves; they look upon it almost as a rejection or repudiation — which, indeed, in some cases it may be. A warm, moist parent tends to breed a cooler and drier child, as an inevitable reaction to all that steam.

There is no right or wrong in matters of this sort; personalities are as different as fingerprints. And if we are ever going to learn to love our enemies, the best way to start is by tolerating our friends a little better, and not trying to change them.

"Dear Sir: You Really Goofed"

Looking through the spring issue of the *Antioch Review*, I ran across a reference in one article to "what name Ulysses assumed when he went among the women."

Upon reading this, I promptly inserted a sheet of paper in my typewriter and addressed a brisk admonitory note to the editor of the magazine, informing him that it was Achilles, rather than Ulysses, that the author meant. I mailed the letter off just as promptly.

Shortly afterwards, the unpleasant thought occurred to me that this was exactly the kind of reaction I most dislike in many of my own readers. They will write: "I have enjoyed your column for many years, but in the issue of so-and-so you quoted Montaigne when you meant Pascal . . ."

Certainly, errors should be called to one's attention — but did I ever take pen in hand to tell the editor of the *Antioch Review* how much I enjoyed the essay on positivistic philosophy, or existential fiction, or the short story I read with much pleasure?

No, I did not. I patiently waited until I caught a hasty

author and a careless editor in a minor error — and then I pounced with my superior knowledge, to make them feel that here was a reader who could not be found napping.

That we are motivated by negative rather than by positive forces is one of the most discouraging aspects of the human animal. We will not lift a pen to praise a writer who has gratified us for years, but the moment we disagree, or are rubbed the wrong way, or detect an error of fact (which may very well be typographical), we rush pell-mell to the desk and send off a snide little note, as I did to the magazine editor.

The pleasure of putting someone else down is one we are enormously reluctant to relinquish. Some personalities are so distorted, in fact, that they can identify themselves only in terms of what they dislike and feel superior to: all bigotry, at bottom, is a way of pushing some group into the muck and exclaiming how dirty they are!

Appreciation, freely given, is one of the outstanding marks of a generous character. I am not talking about compliments, which are social in nature and exist on a *quid pro quo* basis — but about a voluntary expression of gratitude for pleasures we normally take for granted. Only when the pleasure stops for a moment, or reverses itself, are we prompted to react in a negative manner.

Whether it was Ulysses or Achilles or Ajax made absolutely no difference to the author's point. What made a difference was my alacrity in pointing the finger of blame, and my inertia in penning the praiseful note I should have written many months ago.

Contradiction Is Not Enough

"To do the opposite," remarked a German wit two centuries ago, "is also a form of imitation."

I was reminded of this comment at a college recently, when I was approached by an angry young student writer with a sheaf of manuscripts. He asked me to look through and evaluate his work.

As kindly as possible, I tried to point out to him that everything he showed me was written in the spirit of contradiction. And contradiction, which seems to be independence, is always a form of subservience.

He was puzzled by this seeming paradox. Yet it is absolutely true that the writer or thinker whose aim is to be "unlike others" is really getting his cue from them: he lets popularity decide which attitude he will take — and to be always against the popular is as much an enslavement as to be always with the popular.

Aristotle said that both the master and the slave are tied to different ends of the same chain — and so it is with the chronic contradictor: mass taste determines what he will be against, and he cannot be original because he is only reacting to other people. What he mistakes for his "independence" is really a great dependence on society.

Somewhere in his fine book of reflections, published more than thirty years ago, *Life and the Student*, Charles Horton Cooley observes: "It is the mark of a rarely stable mind that antagonism cannot drive it to extremes."

The angry young writer, antagonized by what he conceives as the stupidity or hypocrisy or apathy of the social order around him, is driven to the extreme of contradicting everything, of disagreeing with all — which makes his position as ridiculous as that of the most placid conformist. Any philosophy based on a negative, on being the opposite, has given up its essential freedom.

Real changes are effected in society not by the contradictors and opposers, but by those who are able to synthesize what is best out of the old and the new. A revolution that simply turns over the past is doomed to make the same terrible mistakes, only in an upside-down position. (And what was uniquely remarkable about the American Revolution was its willingness to retain the positive aspects of English common law and merely modify the traditions it broke with politically.)

Most of us define ourselves by what we are against — the banker no less than the beatnik. And thus we are, in a way, the captives of our antagonists. Only great men are truly free, for they alone define themselves by eternal standards, and not by social ones.

To Persuade, You Must Teach

A CONSIDERABLE portion of my daily mail comes from the crackpot contingent — those fluent, passionate and persistent men who are perpetually writing long letters, diatribes, broadsides, manifestos and denunciations of everything from world affairs to water supply.

All these people desperately want to persuade their readers — but they lack the faintest idea of the persuasive process. Even when they happen to be right (as I think some of them are), they defeat their own purpose by their manner of expression.

They blame the world for turning a deaf ear to their proposals and protests; but the fault is theirs, for failing to understand people and the nature of education itself.

All persuasion is a form of teaching, and teaching is the highest and rarest of arts. In his new book, *Guide to Thomas Aquinas*, Josef Pieper, the German scholar, points out that "teaching in the real sense takes place only when the hearer is reached — not by dint of some personal magnetism or verbal magic, but rather, when the truth of what is said reaches the hearer as truth."

Teaching presupposes, Pieper says, "that the hearer is sought where he is to be found." This means that the teacher has to understand the condition and disposition of the hearer, that he "must proceed from what is valid in the opinions of the hearer to the fuller and purer truth as he, the teacher, understands it."

The crackpots do not move toward the hearers; they expect the hearers to come to them. They do not appreciate the counterarguments, they do not take seriously the elements of truth in the opposite position — for, as Pieper reminds us, "there are no entirely false opinions."

What the good teacher does is to start not from his own position but from the position of his audience. Then he tries to move them from where they are to where he thinks they ought to go. The bad teacher starts from his own position, and pull and prod though he may, he cannot move others.

Truth, as Socrates never tired of showing, develops only in dialogue, in conversation, in the give-and-take of opinions. The teacher, the persuader, must always be willing (as Aquinas was willing) to make out a better case for his opponent than his opponent could make out for himself — and only then to advance his own position.

The crackpots are not ignored because they are ahead of their time or because they are wrong. They are ignored because they do not want to persuade — they want to proclaim themselves right, and all others wrong.

Are You "Round" or "Angular"?

"Do you know so-and-so?" I am sometimes asked, and when I answer that I do, the second question is commonly, "What is he (or she) really like?"

To give a true and honest answer to this second question,

I have learned that it is necessary for us to divide the people we know into "round" and "angular" characters.

The round characters are the easiest to define and describe. They are the people — which includes the majority — who present a rounded appearance to all who know them. With minor variations, they are the same viewed from any angle of vision — like a circle.

Ask a dozen different acquaintances about them, and you will receive a unanimity of opinions: Joe is a good scout, Sam is a well-meaning blowhard, Ernie is tough and slippery, Mike wouldn't hurt a fly.

Where most of us go wrong, however, is in our estimate of the angular characters, in failing to recognize their angularity. These are the people who are many-faceted — depending upon the angle of acquaintance, they assume different shapes, sizes and textures.

With an angular character, one cannot say "This is what he is really like"; all one can say is "This is how he reacts to me, and I to him."

The angular personality is viewed in one way by his wife, in another by his business colleagues, in yet another by his subordinates, and in still another by his close friends. His personality glints with different lights, refracting the atmosphere he happens to be in at the time.

Of him, one person may say "He is terribly conceited," and another that "He is really very modest"; one may call him "aloof and superior," and another describe him as "friendly and humorous." And these are no contradictions — for the angular character is all these things, depending on the stimulus he receives from his environment.

None of us can know what he is "really" like, for his essence is determined by the particular mode of existence we see him in. Work brings out one side of him, family life another; at one kind of party he is shy and stiff, at another he is relaxed and vivacious.

When two acquaintances disagree about the nature of a third, it is hard for them to believe that *both* may be right — for they are discussing an angular character in terms of a round one, and are much in the position of the blind men touching different parts of the elephant.

In a deeper sense, we cannot even know what the round characters are "really" like, for they are likely to surprise us in moments of crisis; but we can at least agree on their basic elements. When it comes to the angular people, all we can say is "From where I stand . . ."

Are Stupid People Happiest?

ARE STUPID people "happier" than intelligent ones? This seems to be the general opinion among laymen, who are fond of pointing to some stupid acquaintance and saying, "He doesn't have enough sense to let things bother him — he's just like an animal grazing in the field."

I would tend to take issue completely with this judgment. Not only do I disagree with the opinion that stupid people are "happier" than more intelligent ones; I also happen to think that much of what seems to be "stupidity" is a form of neurosis in itself.

The way some people retreat from their problems is by becoming more stupid than they really are, by dulling their senses and blunting their responses to life. This reaction itself is a symptom of unhappiness that can cope only by withdrawing in a bovine way.

We can see it beginning more clearly in a child: when a certain type of child is emotionally troubled, he will act stupid. He will shake his head at simple questions, he will seem thick and uncomprehending, and will retreat into a shell that seems to be stupidity, if we did not know him better. If persistent, this emotional upset can turn the child into a stupid-seeming adult.

It is axiomatic in the field of psychotherapy that, all things being fairly equal, the intelligent patient will recover faster and more fully than the less intelligent.

An intelligent person *seems* to be unhappier because he can articulate his discontent, and because he is more obviously sensitive to his environment; but this very sensitivity is what enables him to change, to grow, and to heal the psychic wounds.

I happen to believe firmly that most people are much more intelligent than they give evidence of being; that a great deal of what we call stupidity is really an emotional defense against pain; it is simply the way a particular kind of personality handles its problems.

In an article on Sonny Liston in a sports magazine a few weeks ago, the writer shrewdly observed, during an interview with the fighter, that Liston was smarter than the public impression he has given in the past. The writer went on to observe that "Liston is not stupid, but his insights are impeded by his neuroses. Emotionally he is a child — stubborn, obdurate, and completely lacking in flexibility."

Given his dreadful background, this is perhaps the only way the boy could have developed. And what is true of him is true of millions of others who live angrily behind the iron curtain of the mind.

Perpetual Cheer Masks Troubles

OUR TEXT today, dear friends, is taken from the Old Testament, Proverbs 27:14 — "He that blesseth his friend with a loud voice, rising early in the morning, it shall be counted a curse to him."

I have in mind a particular woman — though her name is legion — who strides through our village on summer mornings, dispensing hearty good will to all the inhabitants. She is so resolutely cheerful that she makes the birds seem glum and downcast by contrast.

To me, there has always been something hysterical in the nature of such determined cheerfulness; I find it quite as offensive as the chronic grumpiness of the village malcontent.

Clinically speaking, in fact, the person who rises with the dawn and sets forth to inflict his high spirits upon the multitude is much more likely to crack up than the old grouch who asks merely to be let alone in his encrusted way of life.

There is a certain kind of loud laughter that often presages a plunge into deep and permanent melancholy; a certain kind of isn't-everything-just-marvelous attitude that is perched precariously on the edge of mania.

It was no accident that the most sturdily optimistic writer of the twentieth century — H. G. Wells — turned into a raving misanthrope some time before he died. In scores of books, Wells had been a propagator of the faith that man could rise by his own powers, by reason, by education, by political action, by sharing the ideas and principles of H. G. Wells.

When however, mankind was plunged into the fierce barbarity of Hitlerism and the Second World War; when all the bright and "rational" values Wells had defended were swept into the discard of civilization — then he simply collapsed, and wrote a final book of such venom, such hate, such disappointment, such lunatic rage as no long-standing pessimist could ever equal.

The thousands of cases of acute depression, the suicides,

the fleers from life in one form or another — these are almost
always those who broke under the dreadful burden of their
perpetual cheerfulness. For such high spirits, with their
desperate need to rise early in the morning and bless us with
a loud voice, conceal more than they express.

What they conceal, of course, is the normal anger, the
doubt, the fear, the aggression that is bottled up in all of us,
and that must be allowed to trickle out in safe and steady
form. The woman striding through the village may cut her
throat some fine morning — or her husband's.

A Strong Man Knows His Weaknesses

A YOUNG MAN I know who is doing a study on "executive
power" for his doctoral dissertation, told me at lunch the
other day about some of the interesting psychological conclusions he has arrived at.

He has been studying the "strong man" and the "weak
man" in executive situations, to try to find out some of their
principal differences in temperament and attitudes.

"There's a real paradox at the heart of the matter," he said.
"The strong man is one who knows his weaknesses consciously, accepts them, comes to terms with them, and knows
how to cope with them. In a funny way, his knowledge
serves to give him more strength.

"The weak man," he continued, "is unconsciously aware
of his weaknesses, but cannot admit them to himself or to
anyone else. He has not worked out his own inner problems
— the chief one being self-acceptance, and so he cannot really
accept anyone else in a normal, natural way.

"As a result," he went on, "the weak executive adopts
pseudo strength. He is afraid to be kind, because it might
be construed as a sort of weakness on his part; and he is afraid

to be open, because it might disclose too much of his real self to others."

"What about the man who's kind and pleasant, but simply incompetent?" I asked.

"That's not the 'weak personality' I'm investigating," he explained. "Men like that come and go; they're just mistakes, and they don't pose any problems. But it's the weak man who employs pseudo strength to attain and maintain his position who creates most of the mischief in executive capacities.

"What I've learned so far," he amplified, "indicates that generosity in judgment, a certain flexibility, and most of all, a degree of tolerance toward the weaknesses in others are the marks of real strength in an executive. We can afford the emotional luxury of such tolerance only when we feel genuinely strong within ourselves.

"For instance," he added, "it is fatal for anyone to reveal a weakness to a weak man. He will either take advantage of it, or despise you for it — because the weak man unconsciously despises his own weakness and therefore cannot stand it in others. But it is safe to reveal it to a strong man — because, having come to terms with his own problems, he doesn't have to project any self-contempt toward others.

"We have some peculiar ideas in our society," he concluded, "about what constitutes strength and weakness in men. Much of what we respect is simply pseudo strength. To that extent, we are a weak and immature people."

The Trouble With Serious Bridge

A GAME should mean itself, and nothing else. It should not be an excuse for social contacts, on the one hand, or a substitute for life activity on the other.

Yet it is my impression that the great majority of people

who play games, of whatever type, do not treat the game as an end in itself — do not, in fact, truly respect it, and therefore cannot get the maximum enjoyment out of it.

I was thinking of this while playing in a duplicate tournament a few weeks ago. My objection to most "social" bridge games is that they are merely an excuse for conversation and drinks, for chatter and canapés and "paying back" the Joneses.

But my objection to serious tournament bridge is even more severe: these players are using the game as an outlet for their failures, their frustrations, their personal lacks and resentments. It is a substitute — almost, one might say, a narcotic — for the pleasures one should be receiving from reality.

This is not true of all tournament players, of course; but a distressingly high percentage of them *use* the game as a weapon, and not as a recreation of a high, subtle and stimulating order.

Few people, in any social endeavor, are able to treat it as an *object*, deserving its own degree of respect and attention, without making it something more or something less than it actually is. The social bridge players demean the game, by giving it no relevance, while the tournament players pervert the game by giving it a relevance totally beyond its worth.

A game, to be worthwhile, must be an end in itself; in this sense, it shares a characteristic with the arts. And what is offensive about so many tournament bridge players is that (quite unconsciously, no doubt) they are transferring to the table their own personal dissatisfactions and disenchantments, their pent-up hostilities and angers and envies.

Perhaps the same is true of all the little worlds within the big world — the horse world and the dog world and stamp world — but in a directly competitive activity such as bridge, one can see more clearly the murky motivations behind the rudeness and the ruthlessness.

People who play bridge without taking it seriously are insulting a pleasurable pastime; but an even greater sin against the game is to use it as camouflage for one's own retaliatory slaps against the world. A game that begins to mean something else, and more, than itself is slowly but surely a corruptor of character.

Those "Boys in the Band" Are Men

A LABOR DISPUTE is generally regarded as an "economic" issue — as a matter of dollars-and-cents, of pensions and fringe benefits — but this is only where labor disputes end. It is not where they begin.

They begin, almost invariably, with bad communications. They begin in the area of the psychological, and then degenerate into bitter economic wrangles — much like a divorce, which ends in court with a fight over money when money was not the real issue at all, to begin with.

During the recent battle, for instance, between the players in the Chicago Symphony Orchestra and the Orchestral Association, I could not accept the statement that it was a "bread-and-butter" dispute involving the financial facts. Certainly, there were monetary issues involved; but they would not have loomed so large if there had not already been a breakdown in communication.

This is true of dock workers or truck drivers; it is even truer of artists. The men who play in symphony orchestras are highly trained specialists; they expect to be, and should be, treated with dignity and respect. As professionals with extraordinary talents, they are in no way inferior to the trustees, the governing board, or the donors.

Yet, living in a commercial culture as we do, they are customarily considered as "the boys in the band." While great honor is given to prominent conductors and notable soloists, the everyday musician is looked upon as a hired hand of little individual consequence. It is this general attitude that breeds resentment on his part — and that erupts into "labor trouble."

Moreover, the dominant businessman mentality of our time considers the artist as little more than a "child" — naïve, irresponsible, unworldly. Ironically enough, the very fact that the serious artist is willing to make economic sacrifices for his art downgrades him in the eyes of the more "practical." If he is so good, why isn't he making more?

It was symptomatic of this attitude that when President Eisenhower appointed fifteen trustees from the public for the National Cultural Center a few years ago, they were all businessmen, bankers, diplomats and society leaders. There were no writers, painters or musicians on the list. The management and operation of cultural institutions in this country is very much a closed club — to the detriment of all, in the long run.

To most of us, an artist is important only if he has achieved the dubious distinction of being a "celebrity," which puts a commercial value on a cultural product, and debases the whole nature of the artistic pursuit. A conductor is worth $50,000 a year, but a piccolo player scarcely rates a locker of his own.

Tennis Is in Head, Not Feet

FROM TIME to time, readers write in to accuse me of being too "psychological" in my approach to problems. I was beginning to wonder whether or not this might be true — until I took a few corrective tennis lessons last week.

Now, tennis is an extremely physical game: a game of

stance and motion, of stroking and footwork. I have been playing the game, in my own fashion, for more than thirty years, and thought it was time I learned something about the fundamentals.

To my vast surprise (and also to my delight), the tennis pro spent more time on my head than he did on my feet or my arms. His approach to this "physical" game was as "psychological" as could be.

Most of my playing faults, it turns out, are mental in origin, and cannot be corrected merely by changing my posture or my timing of shots. I have an anticipation of failure, I am ashamed to look awkward swinging at a ball, and, most of all, I suffer from middle-age inertia — which is a state of mind rather than of body.

In a narrow technical sense, my strokes are good. But what is basically wrong with my game is my attitude toward it. I wait for the "ideal" ball to come along, and if it doesn't, I make only a halfhearted attempt to hit it properly.

Again, like most players below the expert class, I am afraid both of hitting the net and of hitting the ball out of the court — and these two fears operate to make me hit many more balls into the net and out of the court than I otherwise would.

Of course, what is true of my tennis game is true of your golf game and his swimming prowess and her skiing — and anybody's attempts to master some "physical" activity requiring skill and coordination. The merely physical part is the easiest to learn, as a kind of automatic reflex action.

When big-league baseball players fall into a batting slump, or when crack golfers return to a pro for some remedial lessons, they are really trying to overcome a mental block in their playing — and overcoming a mental block means to stop thinking consciously and to begin acting instinctively, in a free and natural manner.

The lessons have improved my tennis; more than that, they have reaffirmed my conviction that the psychological approach is fruitful not only in the realm of ideas and feelings, but also in what we wrongly think of as purely physical activity.

Guilt Gives Rise to Double Talk

"HYPOCRISY," said La Rochefoucauld a long time ago, "is the homage that vice pays to virtue." And so it is with language — for those groups which are the most ruthless in their acts are also the most devious in their speech.

Totalitarian governments do not "kill" dissenters and heretics; they "liquidate" them. Goering did not speak of "gassing" the German Jews; he spoke of "the final solution" to the Jewish problem.

The fine art of double-talk has been raised to the ultimate degree by modern Communist and Fascist governments; and the more vicious their policies, the more they seem to feel the need to use the soft word.

If one carefully examines a speech by a totalitarian official, it will be filled with words like "truth," "peace," "liberty," and "the will of the people." And all these words, on further examination, turn out to mean something quite different, and much uglier, than their accepted definitions.

"Truth" means the dogma of the ruling clique; "peace" means acquiescence in the party line; "liberty" means the right to stir up sedition; "the will of the people" means exactly nothing.

In a sense, such euphemisms are customary in all diplomatic and political expressions; but the unconscious sense of guilt that seems to haunt the totalitarians compels them to find the most tortuous and abstract phrasing to conceal their grim and single-minded intent.

We find this same psychological tendency among criminals: the more heinous the crime, the more reluctant they are to call it by its proper name. A thief will cheerfully admit he is a thief — a burglar, a pickpocket, a safe-cracker.

But a killer is never called a killer, by himself or by his confederates. There are a dozen euphemisms for this, the currently most popular being "hit." A man who is murdered is "hit" by a "hitter." Some nagging vestigial conscience prevents even the professional murderer from uttering the true name of his occupation.

The worse the deed, the more the need to dress it in taffeta phrases. An aggressor never goes to "war"; he "defends the boundaries of the fatherland," or he "takes preventive action." Likewise, it is the awful enemy who "brainwash" our soldiers; what we do is "indoctrinate" theirs.

The more a person has to conceal and the more he is ashamed of — whether he is aware of his shame or not — the more pressing becomes his need to find another word for the right one, the plain one, the true one. Simplicity of speech is always the enemy of injustice.

The Critics and Their Heroes

WE SPEAK about the "attraction of opposites" in marriage and other relationships, but I have never seen anything written about the same kind of attraction in the literary and artistic field.

It has fascinated me for years that so many of the men who become "experts" on a certain writer are diametrically opposed to the writer, in temperament and taste and outlook. This may explain some of their weird interpretations.

I have met men who are experts on such literary figures as D. H. Lawrence, James Joyce and Dylan Thomas. Almost without exception, these men would not have been given the right time of day by the writers they have chosen to "interpret" to the world.

The Thomas expert is a prissy soul, at whose pretensions Thomas would have hooted in derision. The Joyce expert would not have been looked at twice by Joyce. The D. H. Lawrence expert would have been dusted off by Lawrence in a few moments of conversation.

What attracts such dry, dreary and pompous scholars to such vital and iridescent writers is the familiar moth-and-flame syndrome, so common in love and in letters. These drab little literary insects love to singe their wings around a glow they can never possess.

It is also possible, if we may dip into the Freudian armory for reinforcements, that a lusty, gusty and unconventional author appeals to the repressed parts of their own nature. They secretly yearn to be as iconoclastic as Joyce, as uninhibited as Thomas, as pre-emptive as Lawrence — but the only way they can achieve such postures is in the vicarious thrill of writing about these men.

Someone of the stature of T. S. Eliot, whatever his other failings, never falls into this psychological error when he is writing about other authors. In discussing Shakespeare, for instance, he has said bluntly at the start: "I do not imagine for a moment that Shakespeare was anything at all like me."

Most commentators on Shakespeare go so far off the track because they do assume, implicitly or openly, that Shakespeare was very like them, and that therefore they have a special insight into his nature. Ninety percent that is written about him is nonsense — and it is nonsense precisely because it begins at a false psychological angle.

So much literary biography and criticism consists of the meek writing about the bold, the bland writing about the sharp, the smug writing about the vulnerable, the ineffectual writing about the ineffable — little wonder that our great artists remain mysteries for hundreds of years after they have bared their minds and hearts.

Friends Are to Be "Put Up" With

A COUPLE I know slightly stopped seeing another couple who were their closest friends. It seems that the second couple turned up two hours late to an important dinner the first couple were giving.

"You simply don't treat good friends that way," said the hostess, who was filled with wrongous indignation. "I won't put up with that sort of thing."

But this is exactly what good friends are for — to put up with. Friendship, of the true sort, means accepting another person, not for his good points, but in spite of his bad points.

And that is the beautiful thing about friendship: we can take liberties, we can show our frailer side, we can afford the vast luxury of giving away to our boredom when we are bored, our anger when we are angry, our peckishness when we feel downhearted.

This does not mean, of course, that friendship will stand any amount of abuse. It must be based on genuine respect of the other personality; but once this exchange of respects has been firmly rooted, a true friendship is meant to stand a great deal of tension.

Many marriages falter, it seems to me, not because the couples are out of love, but because they have never been friends as much as lovers. They may love each other, in a vaporously romantic way, but they do not really *like* each other as individual personalities.

You can treat a good friend almost any way — short of basic disloyalty — because he understands the springs of your motivation, and knows that beneath your temporary bad behavior you are a decent sort with generous instincts and a desire to do well by your fellow men.

When a person won't "put up" with the rude or capricious antics of a friend, I suspect that such a person has never begun to have a real friendship.

After all, it is easy to like someone who is always polite and considerate and gay; the virtue in friendship consists of liking someone whose finest qualities may be hidden beneath a craggy exterior.

There are an appalling number of friendless people in the world. I have seen many among the most influential and famous of our time, and they all have one thing in common — a desperate need to be treated well at all times.

When they are disappointed in this, they break off a "friendship," never knowing that friends were made to endure mutual disappointments.

Logic Won't Reach the Unconvincible

It isn't until late in life — if ever — that most of us learn not to argue with the Unconvincibles. In Grandma's famous phrase, we might as well save our breath to cool our porridge.

The Unconvincibles are the people who are not amenable to reason of any sort. Their minds are not only closed, but bolted and hermetically sealed.

In most cases, their beliefs congealed at any early age; by the time they left their teens, they were encased in a rigid framework of thought and feeling, which no evidence or argument can penetrate.

"It is impossible," observed Dean Swift a long time ago, "to reason a man out of something he has not been reasoned into." A succinct and admirable statement about the Unconvincibles; for, having acquired their beliefs on an emotional level, they cannot be persuaded out of them on a rational level.

And it only makes matters worse to argue with them. They become more and more passionately partisan, more extremist, more defensive about their position. In the end, you are just exchanging invectives.

The moment I realize that I am engaged in a controversial discussion with an Unconvincible, I shift the subject to the weather, the crops, the T-formation, or the relative merits of the new automobiles. It has kept my blood pressure at a happily low level these many years.

How can one detect an Unconvincible before the discussion has gone beyond the point of no return? There are several gambits they all use, which should alert us to the presence of an Immovable Object.

They are, for instance, fond of quoting texts, which they have learned by heart. They may have memorized portions of the Bible — roughly torn out of context — to bolster their position. Or they may cite historical statistics, which they have at their fingertips. Or they tell you some long, rambling personal experience they have undergone — and then generalize outrageously from this one instance.

Logic, of course, is utterly useless against them. They will not define their terms, and they commit every fallacy in the book. If pushed to the wall, they will bitterly counterattack by impugning your ancestry, your mental condition, your patriotism, your solvency, your moral character, your very motives themselves.

And the surest sign of an Unconvincible is the description he immediately uses about himself. He thinks of himself as Broad-Minded.

Adults Need Some Infantile Outlet

"AREN'T they infantile," said my high-domed friend as we were having dinner in a restaurant. He was referring to a group of men seated near the bar, who were engaging in low jests and buffoonery.

A dozen years ago I might have agreed with him. But I have learned not to look down on the "infantile" antics of others; my own antics may be more subtle and sophisticated, but no less babyish at heart.

Everybody has a residue of childishness in his nature, and this residue must be expressed in some way, if we are not to grow rigid and sterile and repressed.

Those who are more mentally limited will express their infantile needs in a more obvious fashion; but even the severely intellectual personality will release his childish energies in some way.

And those who cannot, or will not, express the infantile part of themselves in jests or buffoonery or poker or bowling or harmless flirting — those who feel they must always be earnest and serious and adult — are the very ones who become most petulantly childish at home with their families.

The baby that remains in us demands some sort of outlet. Sports and vinous conviviality and aimless pastimes all tend to discharge such feelings and prepare us to meet once again the rigors of the "real" world. Men who sometimes act like little boys are really charging their emotional batteries for the resumption of their manhood when the hour of play is over.

A distinguished social historian, Huizinga, once wrote a book defining mankind as *Homo Ludens* — the playing creature. And play is, indeed, one of the distinguishing marks of humanity. Its instinctual roots go deeper than cultures and civilizations. Art is perhaps its noblest product; war is its most frightful perversion.

It is no accident that the one type of person universally detested (even though he may have brains and character and ability) is the humorless personality, the man who will not play, the unbending prig who has "no time for that kind of nonsense."

Life must be a hell on earth for such a man's wife and children. For, in his unwillingness to relax among his peers, he misdirects his infantile drives and becomes a perfectionist and petty dictator in the home. The baby in us will get out somehow — if not in the affable atmosphere of the poker table, then in the tense and tyrannous atmosphere of the dinner table.

Social Minorities Rule the Majority

SOCIAL LIFE is ruled by minorities, not by majorities; and it is a constant source of wonderment to me how minorities manage to dominate and even tyrannize the will of the majority.

I was thinking of this at a dinner party for twelve not long ago. Four of the couples wanted desperately to have dinner; two of the couples were in a corner calling for another round of drinks.

The hostess had no choice but to hold off dinner for another half hour, even though we had gathered at eight o'clock and it was now ten o'clock. Nor could the other guests murmur their disapproval of the heavy drinkers; it would have been "rude."

At the beach, one person loudly playing a portable radio drowns a dozen others in the vicinity — and our social sense in American life is so perverted that nobody cares to rebuke the offender, for fear of being thought a "crank."

In an argument, the loudest one subdues the others, or else the others are forced to raise their voices to his pitch. This is what has happened in advertising: if one advertiser screams extravagant claims for his product, the competitors have little choice but to scream also.

An aggressive and inconsiderate minority can almost always have its way — and, more than that, can often change the ways of a passive majority. A brawl at a sporting event, for instance, is usually begun by only a handful of hooligans; but hostility soon spreads throughout the whole crowd. The worse tend to drag down the good; the good are rarely able to lift up the worse.

If a dozen men are sitting in a room, and one of them is bellowing at the top of his lungs, the others cannot whisper and be heard; they, too, must bellow, or silence the offender. In most cases (as in advertising) they have no power or desire to silence the offender, so they too become raucous. Sin spreads by osmosis more than by deliberate imitation.

A small core of corrupt policemen can undermine the morale of an entire city force. The majority simply will not take effective steps in time, until the cancer is so rampant that an outside surgeon has to be called in. Ours is a society of late cures rather than of early preventions.

We can see it clearly beginning with adolescents, where one wild boy with a car can influence a half-dozen other youngsters, against their better judgment, to submit to a perilous midnight ride whose destination is fatality. But we have no right to blame the children, as long as our patterns of adult living are shot through with the same catastrophic weakness.

We Want Agreement, Not Advice

A HUNDRED years ago, Josh Billings, the American humorist, wrote: "When a man comes to me for advice, I find out the kind of advice he wants, and I give it to him."

I thought of his remark the other night, when I was chatting at a party in the corner with a small group of men, who included an advertising executive, a surgeon, and a lawyer.

"Not long ago," said the ad man, "I lost an account because I told a client that, in my opinion, he shouldn't advertise one of his products at that time. He switched the account to another agency because, as he told me later, he didn't think I had 'confidence' in advertising."

"That happens to me all the time," said the surgeon. "Most of my patients are divided into two groups — those who don't want operations and those who do. The ones who don't want them need them, and the ones who want them generally don't need them. When I advise the latter group not to have surgery, they quickly change to some doctor who agrees to cut."

"Exactly my experience," chimed in the lawyer. "If a client makes up his mind to sue, and I counsel him against it, he'll simply find a new lawyer. Most clients don't want legal advice — they want confirmation of their own attitudes."

"Ever since I lost that account," continued the ad man, "I've just stopped being honest in my advice to the companies which hire me. If they're determined to have an ad campaign, and I don't think they're ready for it, I simply go along and do the best I can. Otherwise, they'll look for some other agency that agrees with them."

"A doctor can't do that," the surgeon said, "although I'm afraid some of them do. If I don't think surgery is indicated, I'll refuse to take it on, and so will most of my colleagues. This is why thousands of patients are 'shopping' for new doctors every year. They make their own diagnoses, and they won't rest until they find a doctor to humor them."

"Most laymen think attorneys are always looking for court action," the lawyer added, "but that isn't true. We'd much rather settle matters out of court, wherever possible, because most cases aren't worth the money and effort involved. But

I've given up trying to persuade clients of this. They want to sue for emotional reasons that have nothing to do with equity or the facts of the law — and if I don't handle their case, they can always find some seedy counselor who is more than willing to."

The ad man turned to me. "How do you think we should handle this?" he asked. I shrugged. "Don't ask me," I said. "I never give advice. Besides, what makes you think you'd be more willing to accept my advice than your clients are willing to accept yours?"

Wrong Love Worse than Hate

"THE WHOLE trouble," said my friend, who is fond of generalizations that not only sweep but also soar, "is that there's too much hate in the world."

"That's not my view at all," I demurred. "It seems to me that there is very little real hate in the world — what causes most of the trouble is the wrong kind of love."

To start at the simplest level, what is ruinous for a child? It is not hate (which he rarely gets from his parents, and could learn to withstand), but a love that is either too possessive, too stupid to comprehend the child's needs, or too full of vanity and fear and unconscious resentment at having to make sacrifices for the child.

What is wrong with so much "religious feeling" is not hate against other sects, but a perverted love that shuts out the nonbelievers and disbelievers, that worships a tribal god and not the God of all mankind. This is why religious wars have been the bitterest and most prolonged in history. If we love our Deity in the wrong way, as an exclusive property, we soon begin to hate those who do not share these devotions.

The same is true with patriotism, which has become the

modern religion. True patriotism loves its country and wishes the best for it; but for every one person who has the right sort of love for his country, there are a hundred who love it as the bad parent loves the child — for vanity, for greed, for display, and for the material rewards it may offer.

All these corrupt forms of love — filial, religious, patriotic — tend to separate man from man, rather than to unite man to man, which is the ultimate purpose of all love. There is a profound difference between the ardent patriot who is willing to die for his country, and the bitter nationalist who wants to kill others for his country.

Hate is always a by-product of the wrong kind of love. It is generated by people who cannot truly give themselves to the object, who can find unity only by opposition — by the Germans, for instance, who could love Germany only by hating France; by the Crusaders who could love Christendom only by hating the Saracens; by the Communists who could love the proletariat only by hating the bourgeoisie.

Calls for the abolition of hate are futile, for hate is not a positive thing, but a negative — an absence of the ability to love creatively, productively, maturely, acceptingly. The human race will never rid itself of fratricidal hate until it learns that much of what passes for "love" is its deadly counterfeit.

Our Nation Is Beset by Violence

THE MOST violent people on earth are not the "savage" tribes in the African Congo, or the "primitive" inhabitants of the Australian bush. For no other nation on earth has a worse record than the United States for murder, manslaughter, rape, armed robbery, sluggings, muggings, carnage on the highways and assorted forms of violence.

In no city of Europe — at least those I have visited — is an adult afraid to walk home alone after dark. Here we are afraid — not merely in the "worst" neighborhoods but in the "best" as well.

There are more killings annually in the city of Houston, Texas, than in all of England. And large cities like New York and Chicago have a higher homicide total than most European countries.

What odd combination of elements has created in us this throbbing need for violence? We speak about human life being "cheap" in such countries as China — but no nation which slaughters almost forty thousand of its own men, women and children annually on the highways can be said to hold human life dear.

Nor can we put the blame upon our "youthfulness" as a nation. Fifty years ago Oscar Wilde remarked that "America's youthfulness is its oldest tradition — it has been going on for three hundred years." We are not all that young, although we may still be emotionally infantile.

In many ways, we are a gentle, generous, peaceable people; our virtues are many and profound. Yet, at the same time, we have somehow bred a national character — or a lack of national character — in which violence seems to be the dominant motif.

It is not the poverty of our masses; the rest of the world has much more poverty, much more glaring contrast between rich and poor. It is not our slums, for slums are prevalent throughout the world, and ours are by no means the worst.

Our lack of respect for human life, our raw violence, is to me a more sinister aspect of our nation's development than any of the political or economic changes that are so deplored by professional deplorers. We cannot see it in ourselves, of course; but nations, like individuals, can never see themselves as they appear to others.

Is there some tremendous hidden rage in us, some vast unconscious rebellion against the social organism, some mounting tension that could easily turn into blood lust? Our cities are becoming jungles, and our highways are charnel houses. Our crimes of violence have doubled since the end of World War II.

Perhaps it is time we stopped looking at ourselves as a "peace-loving" people. Our statistics of sudden death suggest we are involved in a civil war, in the towns, in the woods, on the roads.

Advice on How to Aid the Mentally Ill

HALF the hospital beds in the country, as we know, are occupied by mental patients; and one out of ten persons walking the streets today will have a mental breakdown of some sort.

Given these blunt facts, it is time we were also given some blunt advice on the handling of such cases by families, relatives and friends. And the first and best piece of advice is — stop moralizing.

There is no relationship between the moral and the mental structure: the mental patient does not have free will — that is why he is in trouble.

Don't advise him or her to "use will power," which is a dangerous, arrogant and ignorant thing to say.

Don't ask him or her to "pull yourself together" — for people in serious difficulties are beyond pulling.

Don't offer such fatuous remedies as "get a hobby," or "keep your chin up," or "think on the bright side," or "count your blessings." This is as infuriating (and as futile) as urging a man with two broken legs to go down a ski slide.

Don't suggest "a change of scenery" — for the mental patient takes his own scenery with him wherever he goes.

Don't urge "if you'd only try a little harder" — for this is like imploring a hunchback to straighten up a little.

Don't say "If you really loved me . . ." for the mental patient is beyond love, which is an act of the will.

Don't invoke "faith" or any religious inspiration, because religious feeling must be rooted in mental health, not in illness.

Don't imagine for a moment that a new job, or a new mate, or a new setting, will clear up the ailment — for the problems come from within the patient, not from without.

Don't preach, don't beg, don't give peptalks, don't threaten, don't bribe, don't do anything that assumes the patient could change if he only *would*.

In a positive sense, be sympathetic but not sentimental; cool but not hard; attentive but not oversolicitous; concerned but not frightened; and, most of all, keep in mind at all times that most saving thought of all: "There but for the grace of God go I."

None of this is easy; some of it is impossibly hard. The least we can do, however, is respect the illness and not expect the patient to stand up and walk with the equivalent of two broken legs. We cannot make him better; but we should not make him feel worse.

We're Often Blind to Mental Illness

It's NOT merely that so many mentally sick people are walking around the streets; it's that so many of them perform mentally sick acts for so long without calling any public attention to themselves.

The most striking and tragic recent example of this, of course, was the Florida fishing-boat captain whose craft capsized, presumably drowning all aboard. When a little girl passenger was found alive, however, the captain killed himself before the true story could come out.

Only then was it discovered that he had a long history of this sort of "mishap," that his personal and professional careers were blotched with dreadful "accidents," including the death of one of his wives and her mother while he was driving the car.

In his fascinating book *Asylums* (now available in a paperback), Erving Goffman cites several psychological surveys as showing that the public believes "mental patients" are those locked up in mental hospitals, as opposed to those who are not.

In the same way, the white-collar class looks upon "criminals" as only those in prison, while everyone else walking the streets is considered a member of the noncriminal class.

What is astonishing to those trained in the discipline of psychology is the public's blindness to blatant and prolonged displays of mental illness on the part of persons who are not committed to institutions.

Until such persons actually perform some outrageously illegal, or obviously insane act, they are permitted to breeze right along by friends and relatives. This indifference or ignorance, of course, is no kindness — for mental illness, like any other sort of illness, gets worse unless it is curbed and treated.

The fishing-boat captain is only a gross and shocking example of unbalanced behavior that persists for years, until the final incredible blowup. Only then, the friends and relatives begin to put the pieces together, to recall strange incidents and curious omissions.

We tend to think in tight little categories: there, behind bars, are the criminals; there, in hospitals, are the psychotic; and here are the rest of us, honest and sane, just walking around, minding our own business. We take the uniform for the person, the status for the state.

But there are more of us just walking around who need help than are in all the mental hospitals and clinics and psychiatrists' offices. Like delinquency, such behavior must be caught early to do much good. The more we ignore it in those close to us, the less right we have to reproach its prevalence in society as a whole.

Here Comes That Old Wish-Doctor

WE WERE trudging through the museum Saturday morning when Barbara halted before a case of Indian models and asked, "What's that man doing?"

Without giving me a chance to reply, Michael told her contemptuously, "Can't you see? They're a bunch of Indians having a dance, and the one in front is a wish-doctor."

"What's a wish-doctor?" she wanted to know. "You tell him your wishes, and he tries to make them come true," Michael explained loftily.

I said nothing, because a "wish-doctor" is much more to the point than a witch-doctor. Again, out of the mouths of babes and sucklings we are treated to an unconscious vision of the truth.

For is this not what most people want — the so-called sophisticated as well as the primitive — a medicine man who will grant their wishes, a magician who simply by his presence, by the knowing eye and the cool laying on of hands, will make their illnesses and infirmities vanish into thin air?

Medicine aims more and more at being a science, but at bottom it remains an art, and a dark art at that. For the personality of the doctor is often the imponderable element making the difference between recovery and regression.

Not long ago, in a lecture at the University of Chicago, Dr. George Engel of the Rochester School of Medicine made the same point in a more learned fashion. He said:

"That the physician can exercise a healing effect without the exhibition of any specific treatment has been known and exploited by physicians throughout the ages. Indeed, so striking are the effects of physician on patient that one might wonder how much this contributed to the survival of medicine as a profession, since what we know as *scientific medicine* is hardly one hundred years old and even now the number of specific curative remedies are few and far between.

"From time immemorial," he went on, "human beings have sought, found and used healers, and it is this need of the suffering and ill which has kept medicine as a profession alive through its millennia of dark ages and into its present scientific infancy."

There is, I am sure, some profound psychobiological process which works between doctor and patient, not on the level of potions and pills, but on the level of sympathy and understanding, confidence and good will. In some obscure but very real ways, wishes *are* granted by healers, and Michael's verbal confusion was closer to the truth than he knew.

Dull People Are Made — Not Born

"He's just basically dull," someone said to me about a mutual acquaintance. I nodded in agreement, because it is the sort of statement all of us make from time to time.

Thinking it over later, however, I wondered if anybody is "basically" dull. Are some infants born "duller" than others? I am not speaking here of mental equipment, which of course varies, but of personality itself.

Most of the small children I have observed have been anything but dull personalities, unless they have been severely repressed from birth. They are, with few exceptions, warm, outgoing, responsive, and merry.

What changes these charming creatures into drab adults? What combination of factors transforms a fun-loving child into a grownup who displays no imagination or verve or sense of the delightful unexpectedness of life?

No doubt the psychiatrists have an answer yet many psychiatric answers tend to be oversimplifications. Victorian children, for example, grew up in an extremely repressed atmosphere, and yet out of that generation came a great deal of whimsy, eccentricity and high spirits. (And also, it must be added, some of the greatest bores the world has ever known.)

Whenever I chance to meet a pompous and pretentious man, I try to imagine what he was like as a child. At one time, he must have been curious and comical and mischievous; how did all that get squeezed out of him, so that little was left except the dry husk of a personality?

This, perhaps, is the greatest injury that a poor family environment commits against a child — this draining away of his vital juices, so that no matter how much success or eminence he achieves in later life, he is not capable of giving genuine personal pleasure to others.

Is it possible to revive and restore the basic personality — which I am convinced is not dull — without the most radical kind of psychotherapy? And would even that do it? With our present limitations of knowledge, we simply cannot say. Psychoanalysis is still in its infancy.

I suspect that as few persons are "basically" dull as are "basically" bad; that dullness is a kind of pathology of the ego, perhaps a protective device to shield us from possible hurt; that humor and gaiety and whimsicality are coursing through everybody's veins, but some are suffering from an enormous "blot clot" which began in the early years.

It may be that life itself, that growing up, is a traumatic experience for some personalities, who retreat into dullness as a means of warding off the perils of an unpredictable universe.

The Worst Brings Out Best in Us

IT IS a great disappointment to learn that there is probably no life anywhere else in our whole solar system. What this world needs more than anything else, is the threat of invasion from another planet — nothing short of that will unite the human race.

The central problem of society is an emotional one: How to arouse and sustain feeling of affection and loyalty in constructive situations, and not merely in destructive ones.

Only when we are threatened by some external peril do we feel free to display what Gordon Allport, the social psychologist, calls "our affiliative tendencies."

We affiliate only under pressure from the outside. A war brings us closer together; so does a disaster of any kind. With all the fear, Britishers felt a real thrill of communion huddling together in the bomb shelters; strangers were kind to one another; everyone behaved in such an emergency as we should behave all the time.

War, curiously enough, brings out more love than hate. A study of U.S. soldiers in combat disclosed that fewer than one-third were motivated by "hate for the enemy," while more than two-thirds were motivated by loyalty and "not letting my buddies down."

Everyone has remarked on the deep satisfaction that is felt, for instance, in being trapped in a snowstorm. There is a common foe to fight; rivalries relax; generosity and self-sacri-

fice spring up spontaneously. People almost seem to be
yearning for some drastic situation which will permit them
to display their better selves.

Thus far, the human race has not been able to exploit this
emotion in a constructive situation, but only when disaster
faces us. It seems as if we can only be united *against*, and not
united *for*. It takes the worst to bring out the best in us —
this is the bitter paradox at the heart of the human condition.

I am sure that nothing less than fear of invasion from another planet would unite the peoples of the world — even
though it is plain to most scientists and students of public affairs that unless we unite we shall all perish, or near enough as
makes no difference.

More than a half-century ago, William James acutely observed that the prime task of mankind "is to find some moral
equivalent for war" — that is, to find some positive, creative
goal that will motivate our loyalty, generosity and affection,
without at the same time directing hate toward any other
group. It remains mankind's prime task, and time is running
out on us.

Inner Space Is Harder to Conquer

THE RINGING phrase we hear all about us these days is "Conquest of Outer Space." The prospect may excite you, but it
depresses me — for I think it takes our minds off the Conquest of Inner Space.

It is the inner relations between man and man that desperately require exploration. Between two persons living in the
same room may be a thousand light-years of space that can
and must be bridged.

It may be interesting, and perhaps useful, to learn what the
other side of the moon looks like; but it is much more essen-

tial to learn what our fellow men are thinking and feeling and desiring.

This inner space has scarcely begun to be investigated. We spend billions for rockets and satellites, but hardly a dribble for the tools that would permit us to explore the hates and hostilities and misunderstandings that may soon blow us all higher than Betelgeuse.

We are still a mystery to ourselves. There are no 200-inch telescopes to probe into the secret places of the heart and mind, no richly endowed observatories for charting the eccentric orbit of the human personality.

A few tentative explorers, such as Freud, have been dismissed or derided or distorted out of context. In a few months, we can build a projectile to outer space — but it has taken fifty years for his insights to make even a crack in the rigid armor of our self-esteem.

Yet the agony and bloodshed we call "human misery" is caused more by the inner space that separates us from self-knowledge, and from knowledge of one another, than by any of the political, social or scientific devices we so blithely blame for our troubles.

Our research into the intellect and the emotions, the will and the appetites, the lusts and fears and fantasies that lurk on the other side of each person's private moon — our research into these has merely chipped away an inch or two of surface in a half century.

If any platitude is true it is that man cannot control Nature until he has learned to control himself; that the more he is able to manipulate the dark forces of science, the more terror he will not loose on the earth, unless he has first attained the goals of moral sanity and emotional stability.

Let us hear no more of the Conquest of Outer Space by men who will soar a million miles to transplant the same old raging passions to another planet.

Fears of Mind Can Be Real, Too

"Don't be afraid — it's only in your mind." We hear this admonition every day. "Only" in the mind; as if the mind were something not quite real.

Actually, the fears that exist in the mind are stronger than the fears that are in the body alone. A child's physical fear of the water (which is reasonable) can be reasonably overcome; his mental fear of the dark (which is unreasonable) may persist throughout life.

It is never the physical fears that are crucial. The man who is afraid of dogs knows that not one dog out of a thousand will bite. The man who is afraid of heights knows that he will not fall while peering over a precipice.

Soldiers who have faced death gallantly in battle have been known to faint at the sight of a hypodermic needle about to be plunged into their arms. Mothers who have stoically suffered the pangs of childbirth become hysterical at the sight of a mouse or a spider.

The vital fears are precisely those fears we cannot rationalize or justify. The child who panics in a dark room is not afraid of something as realistic as burglars, but of something as irrational as ghosts.

It is cold comfort (and stupid, besides) to tell a person that a fear exists "only in the mind" — as though this makes it less terrifying. But nothing is more terrifying than a fear we cannot explain.

Millions of men who secretly thought they were cowards have learned in battle that they were as brave as the next man; and in shipwrecks, and in fires, and in all the physical catastrophes that are real and tangible, they rise to a courage that they thought was beyond them.

The core of terror — that nameless terror that may grip us

in a deep pit or on the edge of a gaping crevice or in a tiny elevator — is deeper than the quite sensible fear of battle or shipwreck or fire. These things are *facts;* but crucial fear is not founded on facts.

To be afraid of high places, for instance, is a common reaction among ordinary people who may otherwise be brave. They are ashamed of it, but they cannot control it. And they cannot control it because the root of their fear is buried beneath layers of consciousness.

What they really fear is some repressed impulse within themselves, which has nothing to do with the precipice, or the pit, or the elevator, or the spider.

Until they can drag this fear into the light, and understand its true significance, the dark terrors of the mind remain more real to them than the statistics on biting dogs.

7

Purely Personal

Prejudices

PEOPLE who frequently feel they are being "insulted" are highly insultable — they unconsciously provoke situations in which they can feel rebuffed and rejected, in order to justify their deep sense of grievance against the human race.

*

Nothing in the world is as useless as a moral generalization that everybody believes: its very unanimity allows us to give it complete verbal assent without bothering to put it into practice.

*

The happiest marriages are those between a husband who knows how to listen and a wife who knows when not to talk.

*

Those discontented souls who are perpetually searching for someone to "understand" them would be most discomfited if truly understood; what they are really looking for is someone to misunderstand them in a way they find acceptable to the ego.

*

Animals react to our tone of voice, not to our words; and so do children, who rightly pay more attention to the way we say things than to what we say.

*

It is a singular fact that obscene literature arises only in highly civilized societies, and would be incomprehensible to primitive societies; rather than a vice, obscenity is a disease of cultural old age.

*

Much jewelry on a woman always seems to exaggerate what she has or hasn't, or what she is or isn't; it makes a thin woman look thinner, a fat woman look fatter, a young one look pathetically vulnerable, and an old one look grotesquely ancient.

*

It is the magnitude of a fatal catastrophe that shocks and impresses us, so that our sympathy becomes statistical, and in the end it is only the "really big" hurricane or plane crash that moves us; but mortality is not cumulative, and the death rate is the same everywhere — one to a person.

*

More criminals are apprehended because of other criminals than because of the police; for when a man determines to lead an anti-social life, the tortured logic of his position forces him to become eventually anti-social toward his own confederates and associates.

*

A journalist is that odd sort of writer who begins to write badly as soon as he is given time to write well.

*

The things we say bear little resemblance to what is on our minds; for instance, the important questions we ask usually conceal some other question we are too ashamed (or too unaware) to formulate in words; and this is why the answers we get rarely satisfy us — because they do not answer the hidden question, only the verbal one.

*

Many more people would commit suicide if they weren't afraid of what the neighbors might say; what inhibits them is fear of scandal more than fear of death.

*

The chief difference between art and entertainment is the *demand* that each makes upon us; entertainment permits us to remain passive, while art requests that we meet it at least halfway; it should be no wonder, therefore, that the great majority should always take the line of least resistance, and prefer the passive receptivity to the active approach.

*

Some languages can be learned, and others only imitated; I am convinced that French cannot be truly learned after the age of ten, but only poorly imitated, because the lips, the tongue and even the nose are uniquely positioned in speaking the language properly.

*

Seeing a revival of a Eugene O'Neill play reminds one how much our psychological grasp has expanded in the last thirty years: half of what he says is already commonplace knowledge, and the rest has been discarded as obsolete.

*

Love and justice are impossible at the same time toward the same object; if we know an object with love, we cannot help bestowing upon it more than justice.

*

Male authors who write about women in a patronizing or critical tone are generally those who have been unsuccessful in their personal relations with women, and turn a temperamental flaw into a philosophical position; even so profound a talent as Nietzsche's was not exempt from this unconscious perversion.

*

Even though America may have the highest level of medical care in the world, not more than 10 percent of the population at most is receiving the most advanced and sophisticated treatment known to medical science — and this small percentage is concentrated in three or four large cities.

*

Those who end their letters with the phrase, "as ever," are giving reassurance that they have not changed, to people who perhaps wish they would.

*

The most awful and lacerating relationships are not between men and women who do not love each other, but between those who, in some desperately perverted way, love each other but do not like each other.

*

When a man writes a book to demonstrate that life has no essential meaning, one wonders what meaning he can attach to such a book that he gave so many months of hard work to its composition.

*

Arguments turn truths into dogmas: as soon as something we believe to be true is disputed, our attitude hardens and we claim much more for it than we otherwise would.

*

Every great monarch used to keep a Fool at court, not so much to make him laugh as to remind him of the wry paradoxes and inconsistencies of life that no one else would dare to utter; and it is a severe loss in our time that those invested with high power do not have a privileged Fool to mock their pretensions and ridicule their decisions.

*

A woman who cannot forget that she is wearing a beautiful dress simply calls attention to the fact that she does not feel up to it.

*

If a man said about himself what he says about his country, he would be considered the most arrogant boaster and megalomaniac; yet is not a country the multiplied version of one man, pounding his chest and bragging to all about his demonstrable superiority over other men?

*

We do not miss what we lack nearly so much as what we are deprived of: nobody misses an eye at the back of his head, but everyone would feel deprived if he lost one eye in front; it is the *taking away* that upsets us more than the *not having* in the first place.

*

There is an optimum point in compassion — it is a sentiment rarely felt by those who have not suffered at all, and never felt by those who have suffered too much; for the absence of suffering makes men think they are gods, and the excess of it turns them into beasts.

*

The boy who receives a "good" education in a protected environment, with only his own kind around him, pays the possible price of never becoming a man; whereas the boy who grows up in a more barbarous and diverse and threatening environment pays the possible price of becoming a man too soon — another form of immaturity that is just as crippling to the personality. The former learns nothing of the real world until too late; the latter learns it too early; and the basic task of modern society is to create an atmosphere for children in which a *creative tension* is maintained between the dangerous and the protected.

*

To the often asked question, "Which part of medicine is a science and which part as an art?" it is tempting to answer that treating the patient is a science, and keeping him from going to someone else is an art.

*

More can be told about a nation from its advertisements than from any other aspect of its high or popular culture; what we *think* about ourselves is one matter; which stimuli we *respond* to give a much truer index of our motivations, desires, and the kind of magic we believe in.

*

The *raison d'être* of every war, whatever its surface reasons, has always been to protect the future for our descendants, if not for ourselves; but what sense is a war that annihilates the future for everyone's descendants — and does this not render modern warfare a contradiction in terms?

*

Nothing is easier than to be proudly humble, passionately chaste, and dogmatically skeptical; when one pursues a virtue to its extreme, it becomes at last a contradiction in terms.

*

What is important in history is not so much "what happened," but what people made of it, how they thought about it and used it, for noble or perverted reasons of their own; and any history that is not interlarded with some social psychology is nearly useless for study.

*

Barbarous societies punish their satirists by imprisoning, exiling or killing them; but civilized societies, approaching decadence, punish their satirists much more effectively by laughing, lazily agreeing, and simply ignoring the truth behind the shafts.

*

The most dangerous man is not the bad man: it is the one with just enough good in him to appeal to our sense of justice, and just enough evil to appeal to our instinct for revenge.

*

Once the dancer has leaped higher than ever before, we quickly become discontented with such leaps, and demand that they be ever higher and higher; thus audiences inevitably bribe and blackmail art into acrobatics, trickery, showiness and a competition for setting meaningless records.

*

Some personalities make a lifelong career out of being disappointed in people, which enables them to satisfy two disparate desires at once — to feel superior, and at the same time to rationalize their continual failures in personal relationships.

*

One of the most ominous signs of disturbance in modern American society is that wives, by and large, are more mature and less content than their husbands; and a social order can flourish only when the men are mature and the women are content.

*

The kind of joke a person cannot take about himself is a surer index of his character than the kind of joke he relishes about others; what he does not find "funny" about himself is always the weakest part of his nature.

*

The man who has too high a respect for women is as despised by them as the man who has not enough.

*

One of the great unsolved riddles of restaurant eating is that the customer usually gets faster service when the restaurant is crowded than when it is half empty; it seems that the less the staff has to do, the slower they do it.

*

Nowhere is it more important to "hate the sin, but love the sinner" than in rebuking or punishing a child; his action may be labeled "bad," but he himself must never be called "bad," and we must enable him to distinguish between *behavior* and *character*, so that his self-confidence is not broken down.

*

What we call "brute force" can be mental as well as physical: The person who tries to overwhelm another by assailing him with verbal arguments is just as much a bully as one who uses physical force.

*

Most criticism is a form of egotism: The more different kinds of people a man does not like, the more right we have to suspect that he wholly approves only of those who are precisely like him. (But the neurotic inconsistency in such a critical person is that, if we probe deeply enough, it will be found that he doesn't like himself very much at bottom.)

*

Most "veils of secrecy" over governmental operations conceal nothing more mysterious than administrative incompetence; what is called "security" is too often simply the insecurity of those running the operation.

*

If you are looking for a hair in your soup, you can always find one, merely by shaking your head dolefully as the plate is put before you; and there are people who go through life never understanding why this always happens to them.

*

It is not in our power to like or dislike, but it is in our power to be kind or unkind; the first is a matter of feelings, the second a matter of will; and much of the world's trouble springs from a confusion between our private emotions and our social obligations.

*

The profound irony of people going to war for "ideological" reasons is that the people get killed, but the ideologies manage to survive.

*

Apart from all other considerations, the deep psychological reason that we need someone to love us is that we can freely confess our faults and our defects only to someone who acknowledges our lovability.

*

When people flee tyranny and persecution, and set up a community of their own, they do not permit any more freedom to their own dissidents than they themselves had been permitted in the past; with one exception, the religious settlers in the New World were just as harsh and tyrannical toward their heretics as the despots they fled from. What most people want is not freedom, but orthodoxy of their own sort.

*

The layman's idea of rigorous proof is to say, "For example . . ." and then proceed to cite some case so exceptional and dramatic that it proves nothing of a general nature.

*

A woman who does not know how to keep quiet when she is in the right quickly forfeits her moral advantage; as her rightness degenerates into self-righteousness, she loses her superiority and permits the man to counterattack; for silence on the part of the woman is a much more effective weapon of domestic combat than haranguing.

*

Speaking of the sexes, secret lovers give themselves away more by avoidance than by engagement; as Bruyère observed a long time ago: "A woman with eyes only for one person, or with eyes always averted from him, creates exactly the same impression."

*

The two rarest public types in the world of politics are the liberal who knows what requires to be changed and the conservative who knows which things are worth conserving — but these are only one out of a thousand, in both camps.

*

Small children instinctively feel more at home with animals than with adults; and this natural affinity, I think, is simply that animals do not pretend to be, or feel, what they are not.

*

When we say that someone has "independent means," we usually mean precisely the opposite — that he or she has inherited or married money and is dependent upon the legacy achieved through another's efforts. Such "independence" most often exacts a high price.

*

Watching a beautifully groomed and skillfully made-up woman in an elevator keep patting her hair with her fingers and adjusting her coat collar, it occurred to me that if a woman lacks repose all her contrived appeal turns to ashes in the beholders' eyes; and a woman who is overly conscious of being well turned out, and preoccupied with the impression she is creating, utterly destroys what she is trying to achieve.

*

To achieve self-honesty, we should approach with mistrust all those "principles" we uphold that coincide so neatly with our profit and self-interest; it is only when we hold to a principle that does not benefit us (and may, indeed, injure us in a material way) that we may feel reasonably confident of its truth.

*

No laborer works as hard for his necessities as the executive does for his luxuries; and this is the irony of modern-day affluence, as compared with the poverty of bygone eras — that what used to be called the "leisure class" is now the coronary class.

*

Men of similar vices band together, not for company but for camouflage; for when the birds are all of a feather, the peculiar striping of each does not stand out so much.

*

The conscious search for serenity is one of the main sources of continual agitation and perpetual unfulfillment.

*

The real reason that it is profoundly immoral to live by the rule that "the ends justify the means" is that nobody can know what the ends will be (so often are they contrary to our best intentions), and all we can regulate are the means we use; and if these are cruel or evil, they in themselves pervert and deflect the ends we aim at.

*

The author who sits down to write a certain book or play, and knows exactly what he intends to say in it, and keeps unswervingly to this original purpose — such a man cannot write a genuinely imaginative or creative work, for unless the creation takes over and guides the author to a purpose and in a direction he did not conceive in the beginning, his work will be stillborn.

*

When a person says with great finality, "I know my own mind," what he commonly means is that his feelings have ordered his mind to stop thinking on the subject.

*

Why the country life is called "the simple life" has always baffled me — in terms of the diverse number of things one needs to know, and the multifarious activities one needs to engage in, the country life is the most complex of all; but its very complexity provides a personal satisfaction not found in the automatism of urban living.

*

It is easy for us to believe, with Donne, that no man is an island; but each of us privately believes, at the same time, that he ought to be a peninsula, jutting out ahead of the rest of the mainland.

*

No person has a right to scorn the pomp of the world until he has tasted it and rejected it; the premature cynicism of the young is so unattractive because it has not yet been exposed to the temptations it dismisses with such arrogant idealism.

*

The only trouble with "enlightened self-interest" as a guiding rule of personal conduct is that in any real crisis the self-interest extinguishes the enlightenment.

*

How blessed are the comfortable bromides of the ignorant after listening to the strident pronouncements of the half educated!

*

The older I get, the more I become convinced that everybody is either an egg or a chicken — that is, the world is divided into those who are still encased in the shell they were born in, and those who have painfully pecked their way out and look at the world with their own eyes, unblurred by the ancestral casing.

*

The real danger of our technological age is not so much that machines will begin to think like men, but that men will begin to think like machines — that machine-oriented thinking will dominate us, to the exclusion of morality, of conscience, of value judgments.

*

Those who refuse to modify a system argue that modification is likely to produce disorder; but since conditions in any system are always changing, it may very well turn out that the refusal to modify the system is itself a "modification" which may produce disorder. (This is the paradox inherent in the conservative position, which so often loses everything because it is unwilling to change anything.)

*

The only time most people are aware of their conscience is when they can say, with more than a touch of smugness, "I have a clear conscience about that." When is their conscience unclear?

*

Sometimes we remain faithful to a cause only because its opponents are so stupid and obnoxious; in this way, blind opposition generates more fervor on the other side, even when faith is lagging.

*

The most dangerous lunatics in society are those who are not committable: those who would pass any psychiatric tests for insanity, but who nevertheless suffer from grandiosity, delusions of persecution, and enter public life to expose some "plot" that is "threatening" all of us. Both Hitler and Stalin were crazy in this way; and yet both were "sane" by ordinary medico-legal standards. Private lunacy gets a padded cell; this form of public lunacy too often wins a throne seat.

*

Some words are never used except by those who lack the quality: just as a gentleman never mentions the word "gentleman," so the word "cultured" is used only by those without it, the word "refined" used only by those lacking it, and the phrase "gracious living" implies its precise opposite the moment it is spoken.

*

Lovers' quarrels are a way of testing their love, not repudiating it; they are a means of renewing love from the doubts, the apprehensions and the fears that are attendant upon passion; and unless the quarrels are too frequent or too fierce, they possess a self-healing quality.

*

It is always easy to tell when a man is too small for his job — he gives his subordinates a great deal of responsibility, but no authority, so that he can take credit for the right decisions, and blame them for the wrong ones.

*

The money one gets for selling one's soul is always spent in deadening the conscience, so that the net gain at the end of a lifetime is no greater than if the diabolic bargain had not been made.

*

Most parents of any affluence give their children too many lessons too early — skating lessons, swimming lessons, dancing lessons, riding lessons, piano lessons — which merely rob the children of initiative and turn out "well rounded" mediocrities who can do many things fairly well but lack the passion and drive to do any one thing supremely well.

*

It takes a husband a long time to learn that it is useless to argue with a woman — for if she is right, she will overwhelm you with facts, and if she is wrong, she will undermine you with feelings.

*

For every evil that is perpetrated out of vice, a hundred are committed out of boredom; most viciousness is not so much an act of the will as a lack of will, a restless uncreativity, a negative rather than a positive gesture toward the world.

*

Biographies of geniuses are always at bottom unsatisfactory, because truly great men cannot be understood; they can only be admired. This is why it is easier to write a convincing biography of a rascal than of a genius — we share the limitations of the former, but lack the "x factor" of the latter.

*

A woman gets mighty restless unless, from time to time, she can find something to "forgive" a man for.

*

The phrase "United Nations" is as big a contradiction as "civilized warfare"; for as long as the concept of nation remains pre-eminent, the unity will last only when it serves the self-interest of each.

*

It seems to me that when a woman nags her husband it is not because she wants to dominate him, but because he has been unable to dominate her — nagging is usually an expression of the woman's unsatisfied need to be dependent.

The surest sign of a writer with a tin ear is that he records "very" as "veddy" when spoken by an upper-class Englishman; most attempts to transcribe Briticisms in American writing are as ludicrously false and outdated as the British attempts to record American speech.

*

With most people, their religion is a substitute for religion, just as their sexuality is a substitute for sexuality; on both the spiritual and the physical planes, authenticity of feeling and expression is much rarer than we think — otherwise, how explain the perversions committed in the name of religion, and the dissatisfactions recurring in the pursuit of sex?

*

There is only one thing inevitable in history: that men and nations will persist in following their short-term interest, to the profound detriment of their long-term welfare.

*

The life of a lie resembles infant mortality: it either dies in the first year, or continues to grow to a lusty old age, sometimes for centuries; there is no such thing as a middle-aged lie.

*

The first murder was an act of impulse, not of premeditation, and impulse is what mankind must perpetually guard against; after all, as Buber has pointed out, Cain knew nothing of murder or death, or even that if one hits a man hard enough and often enough he will die. Thus, the moral of the Cain and Abel story is plain enough — man understands good and evil, but he does not understand the consequences of his impulses.

*

It is an irony of our nature that we cannot punish a bad man, we can only hurt him; in order to be punished, a man must have enough sense of virtue in himself to appreciate the justice of the penalty.

*

In the middle ages it might truly be said, with Bacon, that "knowledge is power"; in modern times, however, it is truer to say that power buys knowledge, and uses it for its own ends.

*

Some people are incapable of assuaging their own secret doubts until they have persuaded others; in the very act of zealous conversion, they are stifling their own uncertainties while kindling the beliefs of others.

*

When the Corporation speaks to the Employee, it customarily says the things that *it* would like to hear, and not what the Employee would necessarily like to hear; thus the failure of so much official communication designed to improve morale, increase loyalty, and promote better understanding.

*

"In the final analysis" is a phrase only young men should use; men of middle age and over should know that there is no final analysis.

*

It seems to be the essential irony of the human condition that we have been given just enough intelligence to manufacture the tools for our dominance of the earth, but not quite enough intelligence to prevent us using these tools to oppress, exploit and exterminate one another.

*

In past generations, it used to be hard to be the child of a clergyman, and have to live up to the neighbors' expectations;

today, the hardest role, I suspect, is being the child of a psychiatrist and under the neighbors' continual scrutiny for signs of gross maladjustment.

*

A woman may be candid enough to tell you her age, but she is still vain enough to be annoyed if you do not pretend to feel surprise at the discrepancy between her years and her appearance.

*

Speeches should have three well-balanced dimensions: breadth, depth, and length; and it is only when a speech lacks the first two, that it over compensates in the third.

*

Parents who think they love their own children, but find other people's children annoying or deficient or blameworthy, don't really love their own, except as possessions or as extensions of their ego; for a person who genuinely loves trees might especially favor a tree growing on his front lawn, but would find all trees interesting and attractive, no matter where they grow.

*

The dullest people have the greatest faith in education; but the fact remains that when a bore acquires a new subject, it does not liberate his mind or spirit, but simply gives him another area to be boring about.

*

A high degree of poise is that quality which every woman desires in herself, and resents in other women.

*

When the worm turns, it's still a worm, just going in another direction, isn't it?

*

Most of our problems arise from reacting when we should meditate, and from meditating when we should react; divested of the instincts that serve other creatures so infallibly, mankind suffers from a perpetual confusion between his reason and his reflexes.

*

Every nation wants peace, and every nation wants its own way; but while nations are ready to risk a great deal to get their own way, they are willing to risk very little to obtain peace.

*

Whenever I meet a man who seems *guarded*, I feel that his spirit is not at one with itself; for the guarded attitude does not so much imply suspicion toward others as it does lack of confidence in one's own strength.

*

Real "equality of the sexes" is impossible as long as it remains a fact that any man, whatever his handicaps, can find a woman who will marry him, while numerous women cannot find mates; this matrimonial law of supply and demand will always ensure a buyers' market, in the man's favor.

*

What one sees in a mirror is not one's face as visible to others, but a version profoundly distorted in the mind's eye; as evidence, if you were to meet yourself walking down the corridor today, you would not have the slightest shock of recognition.

*

Of all parental virtues, *patience* is the most important for the child's development; to be impatient with a child is only to prolong his confusion, his frustration and his resistance — yet many educated, intelligent parents fail to realize what every farm animal instinctively knows about its young.

*

Much that passes for "modesty" comes from a supersensitive self that is unwilling to submit its inner features to the scrutiny of the world.

*

The art of living successfully consists largely in being able to hold two opposite ideas in tension at the same time: first, to make long-term plans as if we were going to live forever; and, second, to conduct ourselves daily as if we were going to die tomorrow.

*

Men used to expect virtue in women; now the most they ask for is discretion.

*

Every discontented person I have ever met has been discontented because, at bottom, he has been trying to be someone he is not.

*

When a woman aggressively adopts the role of mistress of ceremonies, we may be reasonably certain that is the only thing she is mistress of.

*

The phrase "vital statistics," used to mean something related to the life of a person; now, in modern journalese, it just means the bust, waist and hip measurements of some blank-eyed wench.

Nobody can make an American feel as inferior as a well-trained British upper servant, who knows his place — and knows yours, too.

*

It is significant that there is a high correlation between viciousness and illiteracy — most of the obscene and insulting letters that a newspaper receives are from persons who can barely write.

*

The man who shouts, "Deeds, not words!" is usually the same man who, when his deeds turn out badly, has to hire a man with words to explain what went wrong.

*

Many parents never learn the fundamental lesson that sometimes the best way to convince a child he is wrong is to let him have his own way.

*

We eagerly go to listen to speakers who appeal to our higher nature; and, having made this gracious curtsy to virtue, we then feel free to frolic with those who appeal to our lower nature. This sort of self-bribery is the most insidious, and most prevalent, form of spiritual corruption.

*

Whenever a man says to me, "I agree with you in principle . . ." I know he is going to act against his principles.

*

It is one of the world's perpetual tragedies that a stupid man can always find a clever man to do his work for him; this is why the common run of mankind are so suspicious of intelligence — they know it is too rarely allied with virtue.

*

Why is it that the American male, who is obsessed with pictures and statistics of bosoms, is invariably shocked or embarrassed if a foreign woman begins breast-feeding her baby in a public place? Our culture is fantastically pro-breast — except when it is being used for the purpose God intended.

*

The thoughtless bromide that "Marriage is a 50–50 affair" does more harm than good; 50–50 is not enough — every marriage must be a 60–40 affair, with each partner willing to give more than half; otherwise, the seam will rip apart at the first pull of difference; for a marriage must be an *overlapping*, rather than a mere *meeting*, of personalities.

*

Can't the dreadful phrase "mental hygiene" be replaced with something more human-sounding and less like a chapter heading in a social worker's casebook?

*

A lecturer who starts off with a "funny" story and then switches to the "serious part" of his talk reveals that he has no basic sense of humor; for humor is an interweaving of form and substance, and not just a piece of decoration. (And this is why so many "funny" stories fall flat in an otherwise dull talk.)

*

One of the most unfeminine remarks a woman can make is "My feet are killing me!"

*

Nobody should criticize his own work except on a clear morning after a good breakfast; the self-criticism of a tired mind is fatal to any constructive project.

*

We feel nothing but scorn for a husband who runs off and deserts his wife — but many a wife has deserted her husband, in spirit and service, and the world hears nothing of it, so long as she continues to inhabit the same house.

*

By the time a woman says to her confidante on the telephone, "I don't want to mention any names," they both understand whom she is going to talk about.

*

I've never yet met a "sharp operator" who didn't eventually decapitate himself on the edge of his own cunning, in one way or another.

*

When a politician calls a proposal "unthinkable," you may be sure that a great many people are thinking of it.

*

The hardest kind of tact to possess — and it must be an inborn gift — is the tact required to be efficient without seeming obnoxious.

*

We look with mingled pity and amusement at the hypochondriac who imagines himself ill much of the time, but much more deserving of pity is the *nosophobe* who is so frightened of illness that he dare not admit any weakness and would rather run the risk of total collapse than admit to any early symptoms of illness.

*

It is the unfailing mark of mediocrity to condemn what is beyond it; a certain type of mind must always call "fraudulent" what it finds incomprehensible, and "artificial" what it finds unnatural to itself.

*

Quarrelsome marriages are not nearly so likely to explode as politely silent ones; and every marriage chamber should have a framed copy of Nietzsche's observation: "All unuttered truths become poisonous."

*

Most charity deals with symptoms, not with causes; and we are willing to pay a great deal to alleviate the symptoms so long as we do not have to trouble ourselves about the causes.

*

Man is the only animal who is frustrated when his desires are not realized, and bored when they are.

*

The world of creative fiction seems to be divided into serious novelists who can't tell a story, and talented storytellers who have nothing to say worth saying.

*

Nothing is so distorted and unreliable as memory — a fact we cannot fully believe until we have revisited our birthplace after a long absence.

*

One trouble with education is that it so often *perpetuates* the errors of the past, rather than rectifying them; it teaches us what others have known, but it does not instruct us in discerning their fallacies and wrong turnings — which is why the world periodically requires its geniuses, to turn the conventional wisdom upside down, as Einstein did in physics and as Freud did in psychology.

*

What we call "a sense of humor" is simply a way of contemplating the immediate from the point of view of the ultimate, of observing the personal from the point of view of the cosmic.

*

Those who mistakenly compare the breeding of people with the breeding of dogs or horses should be informed that the only "purebred" people known to the modern world, the Tasmanians, are the only ones who became wholly extinct.

*

What a young person thinks of as "pain" is often merely the absence of pleasure; while what an old person thinks of as "pleasure" is often the absence of pain.

*

Misfortune, at first, makes our friends sorry for us — but if it continues, it makes them impatient with us, and finally fearful lest the "disease" be catching.

*

The liberal accuses the conservative of "wanting to turn the clock back," but maybe the clock should be turned back in some respects; the conservative accuses the liberal of "wanting to go too far too fast," but maybe we should go faster and farther in some things; when will both camps tire of repeating such meaningless slogans and start thinking?

*

Evidence that women are more critical of one another than men are lies in the fact that many women have a great deal of pity for other women's husbands, but few men have any pity for other men's wives.

*

The child who replied "My memory is the thing I forget with," was expressing a deeper Freudian truth than most adults are willing to accept.

*

The most severe punishment is the impossibility of calling back the past and changing it; and the irreversibility of time is so final that capital punishment seems redundant, as well as immoral.

*

There comes a time in life when we have to retreat in order to advance; when we have to retrace part of our path in order to find the right turning we missed — and those who cannot go back are doomed to travel in circles.

*

Most of the so-called "incompatibility" in marriages springs from the fact that to most men, sex is an *act;* while to all women, it is an *emotion.* And this difference in attitude can be bridged only by love.

*

Nobody is harder to pity than the self-pitier — which is something he never learns his whole life long.

*

The road to Hell is paved with inattentions; surely more sins are committed through neglect than through calculated purpose.

*

We make positive judgments about men, and negative judgments about women, in the sense that a good man is known by what he does, but a good woman is known by what she doesn't do.

*

The blending of opposites is usually the best course for the body politic, as it is for the body physical, but the hardest to achieve; yet we can see its value in medicine where, if we require radical surgery, we put ourselves into the hands of a conservative surgeon.

*

What a woman really wants is a man who is sturdy, self-reliant, independent, courageous, dominating — and will obey her slightest whim.

*

We have not passed that subtle line between childhood and adulthood until we move from the passive voice to the active voice — that is, until we have stopped saying "It got lost," and say, "I lost it."

*

The most common way of committing suicide is not by violence, but by inertia; not by shooting or stabbing oneself suddenly, but by stunning oneself over a long period.

*

A university should more properly be called a "multiversity" — because instead of trying to unify and coordinate human knowledge, it splits it into a hundred subjects, each filled with specialists who know little, if anything, about the relationship of their subject to others.

*

The most productive research has always come from investigating things people consider so well known that they aren't worth investigating; all basic revolutions in knowledge have come from scrutinizing the "obvious."

*

The uncouth can be made couth, the barbarous can be civilized — but those who move in an atmosphere of false refinement are incorrigible.

*

If some people didn't suffer, they wouldn't know they're alive; the organism of their personality quivers only in response to pain.

*

It is a mistake to believe that a "happy marriage" is one in which the husband and wife see eye to eye — it is, rather, one in which the husband and wife see things differently, but are able to interpret and communicate these differences to one another, thus achieving an added angle of vision to life.

*

After men finish fighting furiously for freedom, they begin just as furiously enacting laws to take it away from themselves.

*

Love is a kind of homeopathic disease: the only way to get over the ill effects of an unsuccessful love affair is by finding another.

*

When a man occupies a place he cannot fill, he creates turbulence simply by striking out at the empty air around him.

*

Wives who tell their husbands everything that happened to them before they were married are neither candid nor honest, but simply foolish; for a husband does not readily forgive a wife for having committed those transgressions he would have urged upon her had he been with her at the time.

*

"Freedom" is the most futile and meaningless slogan for any group to campaign under, for everybody believes in freedom — the despot most of all, who loves freedom so much that he wants every bit of it for himself, with none left over for the rest.

*

Men in their thirties who are still "pursuing" their studies will never overtake them.

*

Those who insist that they can forgive, but they can't forget, fail to grasp that the essential end in forgiving consists in the forgetting.

*

The chief argument against a coeducational college is that it forces the women to adopt the intellectual attitudes of the men — and a woman's mind cannot, and should not, work the same way as a man's.

*

What society calls a "sex fiend" is, in nine cases out of ten, some pathetic creature who is incapable of sex at all.

*

I am convinced that heart attacks are much more common among men than among women not because men are more constitutionally predisposed toward them but because women provide each other with therapy by their mutual confessions of weakness and worry, while men bottle up their deepest concerns until the cork finally blows out.

*

Ninety percent of what passes for "conversation" is not *communication* as much as *medication* — it is used to make the speaker feel better, either by depreciating others or by inflating oneself.

*

Youth is most attractive when its basic mood is humorous impatience; and old age is most attractive when its basic mood is humorous resignation; while least attractive of all is youth whose impatience is sullen, and old age whose resignation is bitter.

*

A man will do more to preserve his image of himself — no matter how distorted — than for his country, his religion, or his family.

*

The secret of all reformers is really "Let's find out what people unlike me are doing, and stop them!"

*

The most constant and prevalent of all human traits is that of overestimating something we want and do not have, and then underestimating it after we have obtained possession; the laws of emotional perspective are the opposite of physical perspective — things distant seem large, and things near by seem small.

*

Skepticism, as Diderot said, is the first step on the road to philosophy; he should have added, however, that many never take a further step, and become as much enslaved to their skepticism as others are to their credulity.

*

People who are inordinately proud of their "common sense" usually have little else to be proud of.

*

The most wonderfully peculiar talent of a woman is her unfailing ability to redress the balance of nature: she can immediately perceive the flaws in a bright man and the virtues in a fool — perhaps because this is the only way she could comfortably live with either.

*

There is no use in going for advice to a man who has not had your kind of troubles, for he will inevitably translate them into his kind of troubles, and give you highly inappropriate advice.

*

"Logic" is what we appeal to when the facts are on our side; "intuition" is what we appeal to when the facts are against us.

*

More persons have perished by persevering too long at the wrong things than by quitting too soon; there are so many maxims about the value of perseverance, and so few about the necessity for ruthless self-scrutiny.

*

A woman can forgive a man for his infidelities much more easily than she could forgive him for being indifferent to her own.

*

Why is it that the person who can't keep a secret always expects you to?

*

Most people who talk about "conscience" don't realize that conscience is a *capacity*, and not a *standard*; the cannibal's conscience, for instance, tells him it is "immoral" not to devour his enemy after battle.

*

A person who feels compelled to tell others about his past sins is still a little bit infatuated with them; confession can be as much a matter of pride as of penitence.

*

It is fruitless to look back upon our parents and grandparents and exclaim that they got along better in marriage than we do today; they got along better because they expected less, and we live in an age of "rising expectations," not only economically, but emotionally as well.

*

When the reader pauses to notice and admire a writer's style, it is a sure sign that the writing has failed to communicate its purpose; for a writer's style should be an integral part of his personality, not an adornment which distracts us from the total impact of the creation.

*

Lovers who make vows to each other are already aware, however unconsciously, that their love is beginning to falter; a promissory note in love changes the relationship from a romance to a contract.

*

The commonest way to cheat an employer is not by stealing his money or loafing on the job, but by refusing to disagree when you feel he is wrong— if he is paying you for your brains, and not just for your body, an employee has an obligation to dissent from decisions he thinks wrong.

*

Everything we have, including life itself, is simply on loan to us; and the greatest mistake, creating the greatest misery, is to regard such as permanent possessions "belonging" to us by right — for not even our children "belong" to us, as possessive parents quickly discover.

*

There is no such thing as "freedom" for the individual; freedom is a social good, not a personal one, consisting of a right relationship between persons; Robinson Crusoe had no freedom.

*

The hypochondriac, contrary to popular belief, is not somebody who wants to be ill, but somebody who wants to be well; and he is continually testing his health to reassure himself that his physical integrity has not been impaired — like the driver who keeps racing his motor at stops, to make sure it is working properly.

*

There are two kinds of envy: envying the good fortune of others, which most of us can repress; and feeling a little pleased about the bad fortune of others which most of us secretly do; and when someone says, "I'm not an envious person," he is talking about the former and not the latter.

*

There is a great difference between the politeness that comes from strength and the politeness that comes from weakness; the former is a virtue, while the latter is only a strategy.

*

No common universe exists for all of us: the dishonest man lives in a world of sharpers, the gloomy man lives in a world of shadows, the anxious man lives in a world of accidents;

each of us is the center of his own solar system which he has created and set in motion. And it is this conquest of false "space" between person and person that is the ultimate task of humanity.

*

Almost everything said about money, both pro and con, is true and not true; for money has a dark side, like the moon, which no one can see without going there.

*

The way a man traditionally maintains his self-respect is by doing a difficult job and doing it well; and the widespread loss of self-respect in the modern world is largely owing to the increasing number of jobs that can be done simply, perfunctorily, mechanically, uselessly, and under no compulsion to be done well.

*

Marriage has been called a "tie," but it is more like a belt, which cannot be too tight (or it binds) and cannot be too loose (or it falls); and marriages that fail are those which have only one notch in the belt, so that it cannot be loosened or tightened to adjust to the changing weights and pressures of the relationship.

*

Before we are proud of controlling our passions, it might do well to ask ourselves whether our control is so strong or our passions so weak.

*

The next time, before you blame your child for "not listening to reason," take a look around the world and count the number of adults who habitually listen to reason.

*

Speaking of that uncommon trait, might we not define an "unreasonable" husband as one who wants his wife to look lovely without taking the time that loveliness requires?

*

A venal police force is a greater threat to liberty in a society than a nest of subversives; subversives can be dealt with by the law, but who is to deal with the law?

*

The line between discretion and cowardice is exceedingly fine; and man's worst sin is the negative one of failing to speak up for justice when it cries out for support. Nothing we do is half as bad as what we do not do.

*

What young people fail to realize is that candor without kindness invariably defeats itself, for no one will take to heart any criticism that seems inspired by malice; "telling the truth" with ill will is only telling part of the truth, and most ineffectively.

*

To marry without physical attraction is a crime against the body; to marry for physical attraction alone is a crime against the spirit; and both crimes eventually exact a heavy punishment, of different sorts.

*

Those who profess to despise pleasure often do so because they obtain more pleasure from despising than they would from enjoying.

*

An ideal parent is one who knows when the child wants to be forced to do something against his will.

*

The same quality that attracts us to a mate is often the very quality that eventually repels us: a woman marries a man because she thinks he is dominating and then learns he is merely domineering; a man marries a woman because she is fluffy and then learns she is merely pulpy.

*

It is a vast oversimplification to suggest that poverty "creates" crime; what would be truer to say is that the man with the least to lose is most likely to take the greatest risks, in any direction. It is so-called "respectability," rather than honesty, that keeps the bulk of people from taking to illegal pursuits.

*

All of us are believers in free will when we are successful, and believers in determinism when we fail; success makes us overestimate our own powers, and failure makes us overestimate the blind forces of fate.

*

Speaking of success and failure, isn't it this polarity which determines whether we refer to someone as a "slight acquaintance" or an "old school friend"?

*

Impatient romantics should be cautioned that a daydream that comes true before we are ready for it can seem like a nightmare; to meet one's heart's desire before one is big enough or strong enough or steady enough to handle it maturely is the most devastating experience.

*

Talking with a strange woman who had come with her fiancé to a party, I was suddenly asked by her, "What do you think of him?" and could only blurt out the too candid reply, "If you have to ask a stranger, you're not ready to marry him."

*

Treachery is almost always a matter of weakness rather than a deliberation; for every one person who conspires in deceit, a dozen others fall into it through mere lack of moral energy.

*

An administrator is too often someone who begins worrying about the "morale" of the staff only when it is so low that nothing but a change of administrators can help it.

*

It's a curious paradox that so many men who passionately believe in *laissez-faire* in their business lives violate this precept every day in their personal lives, and are the most domineering of husbands and the most interfering of fathers; they believe in the open conflict of goods and profits, but not in the free competition of personalities and ways of life.

*

When we are young, everything familiar is boring and only the exotic attracts; when we are old, we begin to experience the odd reversal that everything exotic is boring, and only the familiar is attractive.

*

The men who succeed in their own lifetime are generally those who know how to play upon the weaknesses of other men; but those who achieve immortality are the ones who know how to call upon the strengths of other men, not merely for their own time, but for centuries to come.

*

Once we assuage our conscience by calling something a "necessary evil," it soon begins to look more and more necessary and less and less evil— thus do societies, in every age, justify anything from slavery to atomic-bomb tests.

*

The shortest excuse is always the best and most manliest; the first time my boy said, "I goofed," rather than giving some elaborate explanation, he had taken a giant step toward manhood.

*

Everything seems to rub up against a sore finger; and the same is true of a wounded personality, which blames its own rawness on the abrasive nature of the world.

*

The armchair philosopher who tells you that "everything is relative" would be baffled if you responded that his remark was only "relatively true."

*

The alcoholism of the rich consists in compulsive traveling; the poor man can alter his environment only internally, by narcotizing himself through liquor; while the more affluent are able to alter their environment externally, by constantly traveling for no purpose except release from reality.

*

Most moralists think they are following "God's will" — but what they are really saying, in their strictures to society, is "This is how God would have made the world if He had taken my advice."

*

All of us suffer, in some degree, from what I call the "delusion of magnitude"; that is, the false belief that because a thing may be good in small measure, it is even better in larger measure; if one vitamin pill will make up for a dietary deficiency, then three pills at once will have us bursting with health and vitality. This is almost our national disease.

*

Many people accept what they call the "inevitability" of this trend or that movement or the other destiny not out of any deep philosophical conviction, but simply because such an attitude frees them from the embarrassment of choice.

*

The paradox of thought is that as knowledge increases, ignorance increases; to one using his naked eye the sky at night seems fixed and limited, the stars countable; but to an astronomer using the most powerful telescope, space is infinite, galaxies innumerable, and the cosmos is a mystery constantly receding before us.

*

Equally obnoxious is the man who is assertively proud of his healthiness and the woman who is (with a fine air of martyrdom and self-sacrifice) proud of her sickliness.

*

Some men apparently feel that the great commandment, "Love thy neighbor," is too perfectionist for them to meet; therefore, they have modified it and scaled it down to the modern level—"Love thy neighbor's wife."

*

Whenever I hear one person say of another, "Well, he grows on you," I always envision a personality somewhat like a fungus.

*

Suicides are usually committed not by those who are disappointed with life, but by those who are disappointed with themselves; not by those who feel that life has failed them, but by those who feel that they have failed life; and thus their act is not a rejection of the world but a repudiation of self, not so much a sin against God (which always involves pride) but a sickness of the soul (which involves a pathetic loss of self-respect).

*

Some unhappy wives take their revenge on a husband by being promiscuous, but the more subtle ones take their revenge by remaining tenaciously faithful.

*

What the ardent alumnus apparently wants most of all is to get his son admitted to the same college he went to, where he will presumably learn as little as his father did.

*

Outside of a handful of large cities in America, a small town that contains a good college with a bad football team is the best place to live.

*

Speaking of places to live, when will communities learn that putting censorship in the hands of policemen is as dangerously absurd as putting professors of literature on the Homicide Squad?

*

Is there a wife who doesn't believe, either secretly or overtly, that her husband had terrible taste in women — until he met her?

*

Unlike men, by the way, most women have two "telephone voices" — the first is an artificial one that is used in answering the phone, and the second depends on who the caller is.

*

It is the vanity of fearing that others might think one was not invited that prompts many persons to attend parties they might otherwise forgo.

*

More people believe in religion than believe in God; they regard religion as a therapeutic process, and they hypostatize God as a kind of cosmic masseur.

*

Whenever we cannot make a person "good" — in the way in which we think he or she should be good — we proceed to make him or her miserable; for no matter what our political and economic views, no one really practices *laissez-faire* in his personal relations.

*

It is only a generation after a war that the ordinary people begin to admit that it was a futile, foolish and unnecessary war — which is something the prophets, poets and philosophers were nearly stoned for saying just before it began.

*

The nagging wife deludes herself with the thought that with a different kind of husband she would not be a nag; but she ignores the fact that she chose the sort of man she could nag, and that her nagging gratifies even while it upsets her.

*

If everyone were given, tomorrow morning, his or her prime desire in complete fulfillment — the morning after that, the germ of another prime desire would begin to form itself and would come to full growth before a year was out. The range of human desires is infinite and insatiable — and thus happiness can come only by rigorously limiting our wishes, not by relentlessly pursuing them.

*

A woman who is proud of her chastity is like a man who is proud of his honesty — in both cases, the sin of pride can be more damaging to the character than the vices they reject.

*

"Unreciprocated love" is a meaningless phrase; it is as impossible as clapping with one hand.

*

Most of our so-called beliefs are negative, not positive; we can say with vigor and precision exactly what we are *against*; but when asked to profess our positive beliefs, we are vague, general, confused and self-contradictory.

*

Not one person in a thousand knows how to live properly in the present, with a decent respect for the past and an intelligent anticipation of the future; most of us are either captives of the past or ransomed to the future — so that our joy in the present is clouded by memory or brushed aside by expectation.

*

Every company must give its responsible executives the right to be wrong — not wrong most of the time, or disastrously wrong, but a certain leeway of wrongness; for when an executive is afraid to be wrong, he sinks into passivity and conformity, and then is worth nothing to his company or to himself. "Don't rock the boat" is a slogan that will eventually capsize any corporate craft.

*

People whose philosophy of life is always to "look on the bright side" must view the crucifixion, and Jesus' real anguish, as a piece of capricious morbidity on God's part.

*

Unpunctuality may be, as they say, a feminine trait; but it is worth noting that it is rarely the homely woman who is late for an engagement.

*

When a man tells a woman that he wants her to "listen to reason," what he customarily means is that he wants her to be unreasonable in a male way rather than unreasonable in a female way.

*

It is a mistake to believe that the "spoiled child" is one who is given too much, for a child cannot be given too much of the right things; a spoiled child, rather, is one who is given too many other things as *substitutes* for affection, attention, understanding, respect and joy. It is not the magnitude of giving that spoils the child, but the symbolic meaning of the gifts.

*

No person has room for more than one "major theme" in his emotional life; for example, if someone has remarried and still bears active hate and resentment for the former partner, the new marriage is not a happy one — if it were, the happiness would drive out the ancient grudge.

*

Most people use charity not as an enhancement of justice, but as a substitute for it; they are willing to help the afflicted and the unfortunate after the event, but remain supremely indifferent to the causes of suffering and the prompt taking of preventive measures.

*

Pious people invariably assume that God has no sense of humor — when all one has to do is to regard the panda, the lobster, the kangaroo and the operatic tenor to see the sense of comedy involved in His creation.

*

The men who crack most easily are those who are afraid to expose what they consider a "weakness" — who feel they must always seem strong and decisive and self-assured, even when the occasion calls for doubt and deliberation. To be really strong means having the surplus strength to admit a weakness — just as the truly brave man frankly confronts his fear.

*

A person who insists that he listens "to both sides of the question" fails to add that he listens to each side in a quite different manner: with his ears critically cocked to the side he tends against, and with his ears flopping pleasurably to the side he tends to favor.

*

Everybody is against selfishness — usually for the most selfish reasons.

*

The man who mutters that "ninety percent of modern art is trash" forgets that 90 percent of old art was trash, too, but time has winnowed out the bulk of it; indeed, it might justly be said that 90 percent of all art (whether painting, writing, or music) is trash and eventually forgotten.

*

Worries cannot be willed away by consciously refusing to acknowledge them — they must be pulled up by the roots and examined in the light, not pushed down deeper into the unconscious, where they only do darker mischief by disguising themselves in some bizarre manner.

*

As the striking power of both sides increases in this cold war, it becomes more likely that the war will turn hot; for, as the British physicist and Nobel Prize winner P. M. S. Blackett has observed: "Once a nation pledges its safety to an absolute weapon, it becomes emotionally essential to believe in an absolute enemy."

*

The people who know what they want are able to travel in a straight line and either achieve or miss their goal; the people who don't know what they want are able to drift aimlessly through their lives; but it is the people who want opposite and irreconcilable things at the same time who can never be satisfied with fate. (This, by the way, is why most public performers are perpetually discontented: they want both notoriety and privacy in equal measure.)

*

If you don't return home from a foreign trip with the feeling that your own country has some odd habits and peculiar customs, then the trip has not "broadened" you — it has merely flattened you.

*

Whenever we have an argument with ourselves, the side that usually loses is the one that shouts, "You shouldn't!" and the side that usually wins is the one that whispers, "You deserve it."

*

Not to suggest that soft-voiced people cannot be stupid, but it is generally true that the louder the voice the lower the level of intellect.

*

Husbands who tend to be extremely critical of their wives in public are often quite dependent upon them in private; and the public treatment is simply a way of expressing resentment of the private dependence.

*

The ordinary people are duped by their simplicity, and the extraordinary people are duped by their sophistication; each type falls in the direction of its own special weakness, which it thinks to be a strength.

*

Women are unjustly accused of babbling a great deal, but that is how the feminine process of logic works; unlike a man, a woman cannot tell what she thinks until she hears what she says. The female mind is an exquisitely engineered "feedback" system.

*

From birth until twenty-five or so, we shape our lives; from twenty-five to fifty or so, our lives shape us; and we spend the years from fifty until death wondering how this curious reversal came to be.

*

Those who make a habit of flattery lack the capacity to love; flattery is always a sign of emotional impotence, seeking to achieve the effect in words it cannot attain in deed.

*

The most dramatic evidence that all of us live in airtight compartments, scarcely communicating from one room of the mind to the other, is the mathematician I know, an expert in probability theory, who invariably complains that he always holds "poor cards" at bridge.

*

The whole fallacy in an "ideological war" is that the ideologies aren't killed, but the people are; the ideologies simply reshape themselves under another name and banner and go marching on to further destruction; has the death of so many Caesars ever extinguished Caesarism?

*

The same person who sighs that life is short, and the days speed by, at the same time treats his money and his affairs as though he would live forever.

*

There is a kind of reverse perspective in opportunities; they always look larger when they are receding from us than when they are approaching us.

*

A cynic is not merely one who reads bitter lessons from the past; he is one who is prematurely disappointed in the future.

*

Principles are useless unless they are embodied in personalities; there is no such thing as an "abstract right," any more than there can be "abstract love"; and most mischief in the world has been perpetrated by cold and dedicated men of high principles whose living personalities did not irradiate their beliefs; by men who could make neither their wives nor children nor associates happy, but who somehow thought they could "make the world a better place" by imposing their ideas on it.

*

It is easier to forgive someone who injures us than someone who does us no harm but regards us with polite contempt; we can grudgingly respect power, but we can only resent the cool assumption of superiority.

*

One of the most malevolent and vulgar of traits is to encourage the confidences of those in whom we have little interest, and for whose problems we have no solutions; it is reprehensible to ask to look at a wound we have neither the ability nor the willingness to bandage.

*

Murder mysteries are so perennially popular because they enable us to satisfy two needs at the same time: to discharge our aggressive tendencies by vicariously murdering someone, and to assuage our conscience by seeing the murderer captured and punished. Mysteries are the classic literary example of having our cake and eating it, too.

*

Sons of famous or distinguished men generally tend to look much younger than they are far into middle age; a father who is a celebrity gives a son an expression of perpetual "juniorship."

*

It is no accident that so many women who think they yearn for a man to dominate them have married men they can twist around their fingers: for the fantasy of being dominated allows them to conceal from themselves their deep fear and resentment of being permanently subjected to such a relationship in real life.

*

When an applicant for a housekeeping job describes herself as a "plain cook" one may be sure she is not exhibiting modesty, but exuding optimism.

*

The gift for teaching must be accompanied by the passion for learning; the essential difference between a good and a bad teacher lies not so much in their disparate intellectual qualities as in their "openness" or "closedness" to further knowledge on their own parts.

*

Both pride and shame of ancestry are merely opposite sides of the same vice: the unwillingness to accept oneself as an individual, and to draw out of the past only those things which serve us in becoming more of what we are, and not those which serve us only as a means of self-congratulation or self-contempt.

*

Of all crackpots, the "realist crackpot" is perhaps the most dangerous; all he can see is what is in front of his nose, when our most pressing need happens to be a device for seeing around the sharp corners of tomorrow and tomorrow.

*

We seek advice when we feel weak, rather than when we feel strong; yet the insolence of strength is often much more in need of counseling than the flutterings of weakness.

*

Those censorious persons who are so convinced that current literature is corrupting morality seem never to have considered the even more plausible possibility that current morality is corrupting literature; for it is one of the inevitable marks of a narrow and rigid mind that it mistakes a symptom for a cause.

*

When love is not reciprocated, it is inwardly despised; and those who have a pattern of unrequited loves are secretly seeking for contempt to confirm their own low view of themselves.

*

One of the most ironic symptoms of our national schizophrenia is that while we have a great respect for "education" in the abstract, we have an equally great mistrust of the educated person in the particular; it is much like our religion, which abstractly worships the Christian virtues, but is scandalized by any individual who takes the teachings of Christ "too seriously."

*

There is no such thing as the "dead past" — it is the future that is dead, and whether or not it comes alive for us depends largely upon the lessons we draw from the past and utilize in the present. History, in fact, may be defined as the art of trying to understand and control tomorrow.

*

There seems something strained and twisted to me in those persons who venerate Nature to the exclusion, or denigration, of human beings; for human beings represent the quintessence of Nature, in all its glorious possibilities and horrible potentialities.

*

One of the hardest tasks for parents is to distinguish between the child and the act, behind the character and the stage the child is going through; to punish him for being bad without making him feel he "is" bad; to reprimand him for telling a lie without making him feel he "is" a liar; and our failure to make these distinctions implants the very traits we are trying to eradicate.

*

A man marries a woman because she reminds him of his mother, and then is irritated with her because she reminds him too much of his mother; or marries because she is quite different from his mother, and then resents her because she is so different from his mother. Such men, perhaps, should not marry at all — but they are the ones who marry first.

*

To look upon something inferior with distaste without at the same time taking credit for our distaste is the rarest and noblest form of discriminating . . . and one that moralizers are incapable of.

*

No woman is responsible for her face, but every woman is for her expression; and, especially after thirty, a woman's attractiveness is only one-fourth face, one-fourth artifice, but fully one-half expression; if the latter is greedy, or mean, or sullen, or discontented, the other half goes for nothing.

*

We think that our opinion of someone depends on what we see in him; it does not — in most cases, it depends on what he makes us see in ourselves.

*

Hardly one American in a hundred understands what the founding fathers meant by stating that all men are "created equal" — ninety-nine object to this phrase because they believe "equal" meant "similar" or "identical" or "all alike," which is not even remotely the meaning.

*

An injurious truth is justified in being expressed only when the one who expresses it is deeply sure that his basic motivation is a devotion to truth rather than a delight in injury.

*

I like the comment of the ten-year-old boy struggling through a book that was rather too difficult for him; asked by an uncle if he was a "slow reader," he answered, "Heck, no,

I'm a fast reader — it's just that the author of this book was a slow writer!"

*

According to recent astrophysicists the universe is steadily expanding at a terrific rate, with all the galaxies receding from one another at velocities approaching the speed of light; what is remarkable is that there are people who find no difficulty in believing this, but who reject religious conceptions because they are "inconceivable."

*

The basic contradiction in the human animal was summed up long ago by Seneca, when he observed: "We are always complaining that our days are few, and then acting as though there would be no end to them."

*

There is something in the makeup of the public man — even the good public man, like Lincoln — that militates against the happiness of his children; men who covet and exercise the power of public office rarely seem able to maintain the virtues of domestic felicity, especially in terms of their sons.

*

One of the greatest pleasures in life consists of being paid handsomely for doing what you would be willing to do anyway, without pay.

*

To know which illusions must be dispelled, and which are not worth puncturing, is the first and almost the whole art of being a good friend.

*

Women make better mothers than wives — which is a fortunate thing, because for every one man who is looking for a wife, ten are looking for a mother.

*

Foolish things done on impulse usually harm no one except the doer; but foolish things done for strong principles usually harm everyone else in the vicinity.

*

Women with the most romantic yearnings tend to marry the most prosaic husbands — for this is the only way they can safely retain their romantic yearnings without having them ruined by reality.

*

As technology enables the peoples of China, India, and Africa to leap into the twentieth century, one wonders what neurotic reactions will afflict the white race when it finally realizes it is the "minority group" in the world.

*

When we are young, we judge people by their attitudes toward us; as we get older, we judge them by their opinions; if we finally mature, we judge them only by the ways in which they act out their opinions, by their trueness to themselves, and not to us.

*

Duplicity requires a mask; but sometimes, also, so does innocence.

*

The greatest injustice in a collectivist state is not economic or political, but psychological — not merely the abolition of private property (which cannot be done), but the abolition of privacy itself, the exposure of the person to public scrutiny in every aspect of his life.

*

The pedigree of a dog is not nearly as important as its training; the most ignoble mutt can be trained to astonishing feats of intelligence, courage and loyalty; while the highest-bred of a line of champions can be ruined in a few months of cruelty, indulgence, stupidity, or neglect. And so, *a fortiori*, with human beings.

*

A personality divided against itself contains its own punishment.

*

A woman who gratuitously tells a strange man how wonderful her husband is, and what a happy marriage she has, is, surprisingly often, preparing to betray the former or abandon the latter.

*

There is no such thing as an "imaginary complaint," for the very act of imagination makes it real; a woman who believes she is ugly acts ugly and thus gives the impression that she is; a person who *feels* sick might as well *be* sick.

*

The toils of Sisyphus were not more incessant and ineffectual than the labors of husbands and wives who keep trying to change each other into someone else — not realizing that the "someone else" would have different defects they would try to change.

*

The one thing a woman wants from a man is *respect;* but, paradoxically, it is the one thing she becomes most easily dissatisfied with, in its undiluted form.

*

Discipline without talent can go a great deal farther than talent without discipline — for discipline itself is a kind of talent for making the very most out of the least.

*

The fundamental and unresolvable contradiction in the male nature is that no father of forty wants his daughter to do what he wanted other men's daughters to do when he was twenty.

*

Everything new represents not only a beginning, but also the end of something else; all true innovations are consequences as much as they are introductions, and their newness cannot be fully grasped unless we comprehend what they are replacing, not merely in the material sense, but in the history of human ideas.

*

What the arts most desperately need are not more talented artists but more talented audiences; the presence of a large body of uncultivated spectators is more fatal to the culture of an age than the presence of a large body of incompetent artists.

*

One of the most common mistakes is to confuse "strong will" with "self-will" — a baby is self-willed, it wants what it wants when it wants it; which is precisely why it does not have a strong will, which wants what it wants only at the right time, under the right conditions, and in a manner appropriate to the true needs of the person.

*

When we commit a piece of stupidity, we call it an "honest mistake" — as if most other people go around making dishonest mistakes.

*

A good teacher is one who warns his students about his own personal bias in a particular area, and urges them to lean against the pull of his preconceptions until the mind gives full assent to them.

*

The most false dichotomy we can make is between "mind" and "emotions" or "heart" and "head" — for thinking and feeling are inseparably linked to one another like the blades of a scissors, and we cannot cut anything accurately or cleanly unless both blades are operating in conjunction.

*

Children, until they are civilized, tend to laugh at cruelty, deformity, or misfortune; in short, at anything they consider alien or inferior to themselves; as we get older we discipline these reactions and no longer laugh at cruelty, deformity or misfortune in individuals — but, rather, we transfer such reactions to large and anonymous groups of people who, we permit ourselves the luxury of feeling, are alien and inferior. But are we any better than the children?

*

In a surprisingly large number of families, the wrong member is going for psychiatric help: the more disturbed one who is rigidly opposed to getting help has driven the more flexible and less disturbed one into treatment — which can hardly have a satisfactory solution.

*

Every true artist is a moralist who knows better than to preach; it is only when there is a deficiency of art that the moralizing seeps through to the surface and spoils the work.

*

It can be seen that a woman is a more complex creature than a man, for it is much easier to define manliness than womanliness — if a man lacks but one quality, courage, he is less than a man; but no single quality, or its absence, can so delineate woman.

*

You have not found your vocation if the drudgery it involves is not also somehow a kind of pleasure.

*

To be "original" does not consist in saying what has not been said before; any madman can do this; it consists, rather, in the ability to combine and rearrange old thoughts in such a manner that they can never again be separated and viewed in the old dimensions; and this is precisely the greatness of such "original" thinkers as Freud.

*

The last lesson that despotisms ever learn is that a government without an opposition is, eventually, the easiest to topple; for an opposition keeps a government sharp, muscular and flexible.

*

People who look down upon games as a "form of escapism" rarely stop to consider that, for them, work may be a form of escapism: indeed, for many, a kind of alcoholism which permits them, in socially approved fashion to elude their deeper responsibilities as human beings, and sometimes as parents.

*

Those who persist in making what they call "bad choices" in love are really not exercising choice at all, but are driven by forces they are scarcely aware of; where there is no freedom, there is no choice.

*

Many people are willing to be generous who are not willing to be just; their generosity is the price they agreeably pay for withholding justice when it suits their purpose.

*

For all the furor about "education" in this country, ask a dozen persons what, in their estimation, the proper end of education is, and you will receive a dozen different answers; until we can agree on the goal, how can we evolve any rational program or even know what we are talking about when we use the word "education"?

*

A marriage will flourish when it is composed of two persons who will nurse each other; it may even survive when one is a nurse and the other an invalid; but it is sure to collapse when it consists of two invalids, each needing a nurse.

*

Those who inordinately enjoy Mardi Gras and such masked festivals must feel extremely repressed when dressed in civilian clothes with their faces showing; for it is only when they are costumed and masked that they feel free to express themselves — a curious psychological reversal, when concealment becomes a form of disclosure.

*

We succeed best in those enterprises which not merely call upon our virtues and talents, but which also in some way are able to make use of our defects; as, for instance, the neurotic psychoanalyst who employs his defect in the service of his craft.

*

Political questions will not, and cannot ever be settled on the political level; they must be settled, if at all, on the emotional, moral and spiritual level; and history seems to repeat itself precisely because all purely political settlements are circuitous and self-defeating.

*

It's curious that the same people who are fond of quoting Jesus' remark that "The poor ye have always with you" as a justification for gross inequalities in wealth never quote His advice to the rich young man to give everything he had to the poor; picking and choosing among Biblical quotations is the favorite vice of the falsely devout.

*

Many a deep secret that cannot be pried out by curiosity can be drawn out by indifference.

*

The best method for investigating one's beliefs was prescribed by Simone Weil, when she said: "As soon as we have thought of something, try to see in what way the contrary is true."

*

A zealot is somebody who berates us for not having the courage of his convictions.

*

Everyone admits that "the truth hurts," but no one applies this adage to himself — and as soon as it begins to hurt us, we quickly repudiate it and call it a lie. It is this tendency toward self-deception (more than any active sin) that makes human progress slow and almost imperceptible.

*

Marriage remains so precarious a relationship because the very qualities that attract us to a person of the opposite sex are not usually the qualities that bind us — and the qualities that bind us are not readily discoverable under the feverish conditions of romance.

*

The mind works fast, but never so fast as the instincts; and we cannot learn to do any task proficiently until we are able to stop thinking about it, and can rely on the unconscious reflex, as all athletes and musical performers, among others, have painfully learned.

*

One of the minor advantages of having a high degree of literacy is that you can read a whole page while thinking of something entirely different.

*

The invariable remark of a father who fails to understand his growing children is "When I was your age . . ." As far as children are concerned, a parent was never their age — and rightly so, for it was a different age in a different time.

*

"If most of those idiots didn't take their cars downtown, for no good reason whatever, we wouldn't have such traffic jams and parking problems," muttered the idiot who was taking his car downtown, for no good reason whatever.

*

Men of great strength usually call it "strenth."

*

When a girl tells her escort that "I never kiss a boy goodnight on the first date," he cannot be blamed for wondering what sort of private timetable she keeps for the ultimate intimacy.

*

A "Professor," in American journalism, has come to mean anyone connected with a university staff, even an extension lecturer — which makes about as much sense as calling a hospital orderly "Doctor."

*

And, speaking of quaint journalist practices, it always annoys me to see a headline: "Plane crashes with 67 — 3 Yanks Aboard," as if the sixty-four foreigners were only incidental to the tragedy.

*

It is fallacious to believe that having a child can "save" a marriage; it has been my observation that children make a good marriage better, but a bad marriage worse.

*

I've never known a talented actress who wasn't content to remain exactly what she was, while most talented actors I've met have wanted to be directors, or writers, or something "more" than they were — which confirms my feeling that acting is, to a large extent, a feminine craft. (Not that actors are necessarily feminine in any way, but that their masculine creativity somehow seems finally unsatisfied by miming.)

*

Why is it that mayors, policemen and landladies are the same the world over? All national differences are blurred by these occupational similarities.

*

The best and briefest advice on reading was given by Flaubert, in a letter to Mlle. de Chantepie: "Do not read, as children do, to amuse yourself, or like the ambitious, for the purpose of instruction. No, read in order to live."

*

When a book doesn't require much thought from its reader, we may be sure it didn't require much from its author, either; when we go through a book "easily," it goes through us just as easily.

*

As soon as we begin "giving the Devil his due," we find more and more due to him.

*

Whenever I hear of a man well into his thirties who is still "pursuing" his studies, I begin to fear he will never overtake them. Scholarship should be a way of *penetrating* reality, but for many it is merely a way of *evading* it.

*

People who call for a return of the "old-fashioned virtues" forget the old-fashioned vices that went with them; nostalgia is just an emotional resistance against coping with the present.

*

Both the ignorant man and the educated man are satisfied with themselves; the ignorant man calls his ignorance "common sense," and the educated man calls his information "knowledge"; it is only the wise man who knows how little knowledge he has and how useless is his common sense for solving uncommon problems.

*

It's singular that the men who want to revert to their grandfathers' economics would not dream of reverting to their grandfathers' plumbing; they demand change in all the material aspects of life while resisting change in its economic aspects.

*

One can tell more about the character of a person from the pleasure he chooses than from the vocation he is engaged in; our vocations often choose us, by accident or inevitability, but our pleasures are voluntary selections made from the deepest parts of our nature.

*

Nations, like individuals, rarely know what is good for them in the long run; the loss of the battle of Waterloo was viewed as a calamity by all Frenchmen, but it was actually the making of modern France as a free republic.

*

A certain kind of calculated "tolerance" is worse than an insult; no one wants to be tolerated, and everyone wants to be respected.

*

Those who live by the maxim "to thine own self be true" rarely stop to consider that their own self might need considerable changing before it is worth the faith they give it.

*

One of the chief ingredients of maturity is the calm recognition that the best one can get out of life is a draw.

*

People who think they're generous to a fault usually think that's their only fault.

*

Never say you know a man until you have seen him as a heavy loser in a poker game; and never say you know a woman until you have observed her behavior in a divorce proceedings.

*

An empty stomach is the worst political adviser in the world; but the stomach is acting as secretary of state for half the population of the globe today.

*

Unlike half a loaf, half a love is *not* better than none; for the absence of the other half only embitters the taste of the half we possess.

*

There is a clock in every man, but no calendar; and a calendar in every woman, but no clock; thus, men remember times, but are weak on dates, like anniversaries; whereas women remember dates, but are weak on time, and seven o'clock is as good as six to them.

*

A person who has no genuine sense of pity for the weak is missing a basic source of strength; for one of the prime moral forces that comprise greatness and strength of character is a feeling of mercy. The ruthless man, *au fond*, is always a weak and frightened man.

*

All philosophies, if pushed to their logical and ultimate conclusion, are nonsense — for the universe is too vast, too varied and too subtle to be contained in any structure or system of thought.

*

I have never understood why prostitutes are arrested, but their customers are set free; and the only reason I can think of is that laws are made by men, and not by women.

*

When a person imagines that he or she is "in love" with two different people at the same time, all this means is that neither of the love-objects meets the full specifications.

*

Once a slang phrase really catches on and puts its roots deep down into the language, it's hard to conceive what was used before it as an equivalent; for instance, until "it's for the birds" came into use, what did we say to express the same attitude?

*

Patience is at the heart of every art, every craft, every science; and the real charge against the beatnik artists is not their morals or their manners but their lack of *inner* discipline, their refusal to work quietly, steadily and patiently, perfecting their craft in private.

*

Women are slaves to the past, and men are slaves to the future; a woman tends to look back at yesteryear's romance, and a man to look forward to next year's enterprise; she wonders what she has lost, and he calculates what he has to gain.

*

Of all the foolish and futile experiments, "living together" before marriage is the silliest; it is no better an indication of what the marriage will be like than sailing a paper boat in a bathtub is an indication of one's prowess in steering a real sailboat through a storm.

*

The highly conscientious person who will not put off until tomorrow what should be done today always puts off until tomorrow what can be *enjoyed* today; he will not violate his maxim where duty is concerned, but always where pleasure is concerned, and this inconsistency is what makes his life spiritually bleak and emotionally ungratified.

*

Architecture is such a frustrated craft because most architects want to build houses for other architects, but they are forced to build them for laymen.

*

What a marvelous literature we would have if only our books were as imaginative, as tasteful and as striking as our bookjackets.

*

Speaking of books, what is called a "psychological novelist" is commonly an author who doesn't know enough psychology to write a text, and doesn't know enough about the art of fiction to write a straight novel.

*

It may be true that "only the brave deserve the fair," but that's because only the brave can live with the fair; it takes a man who is quietly confident of his powers to handle a beautiful woman.

*

Whatever the social perils of a city, it is not nearly so lonely a place for a stranger as a small town where he is not accepted; there is something for everyone in a city, but a small town is rigidly constructed of "ins" and "outs."

*

A politician is a man who is invariably seen with his wife on two occasions — before an election, and after an indictment.

*

All public speakers fall into geometrical patterns: those who have no depth try to make up for it in length, and those without breadth make up for it by going around in circles.

*

Ninety per cent of the world's problems would be solved if the people with the proper goals had the practical judgment necessary to reach those goals, and if the people with practical judgment could be persuaded to adopt the proper goals.

*

The difference between an adolescent boy's "escapade" and his "delinquency" lies in the social status of his parents.

*

Speaking of boys, the surest way to ruin two children is to hold up one as a "good example" to the other — which only succeeds in turning the latter into a rebel and the former into a prig.

*

Men are those inconsistent creatures who want to violate every attractive woman they can — and then become indignant when the attractive woman they marry turns out not to have been inviolable.

*

The really intolerable thing about poverty is that it is so frightfully expensive.

*

I don't mind people who merely dislike modern art, in any form; but I do mind those who compare it unfavorably with traditional, or classical art, which they don't really understand, appreciate or cultivate — and would have disliked just as intensely if they had lived during the period it was created.

*

Virtuous people have no right to preach; if all the pulpits were filled with reformed sinners, the congregations would sit up and take more notice.

*

Those sects in which piety is allied with penuriousness have always struck me as quite alien to the genuinely magnanimous spirit that must be at the root of all true religious feeling.

*

Abstractions influence people only on a full stomach: to talk to a hungry man about "freedom" is as futile as talking to a blind man about color — for the stomach, as Cato said long ago, has no ears.

*

Piety without social responsibility leads to a selfish introspection, while social responsibility without piety leads to idolatry of the state or of some elite; only a firm combination of the two gives "salvation" any meaning, either for society or for the individual.

*

The natural grace in children is often repressed by "dancing lessons," just as the natural instinct for painting in children is often prevented by "art lessons."

*

It is true that success may spoil some, but the way a man behaves when he *loses* money is a much surer indication of his basic character.

*

When we say we are "doing our best," we always mean *under the circumstances;* for no one knows what his best really is until he faces the ultimate crisis — and then we realize potentials we scarcely knew existed.

*

It is axiomatic that the person who is not pleased with others is never pleased with himself, no matter how egocentric he seems to be; the chronic faultfinder is always projecting a profound sense of dissatisfaction with himself.

*

When we are young, we believe that "speaking the truth" is the most important thing; as we grow older, if we ripen, we learn that speaking the truth *lovingly* is the only way to make it count — for truth without love merely cuts without curing.

*

People should hang out their minds for an airing every so often, if they want their opinions to smell as fresh and sweet as their linens; the sour odor of stale convictions clings to most of us like a mist.

*

Bad marriages do not collapse nearly so often as uncomfortable ones — for the same reason that it is easier to stand a pain than an itch.

*

Unless we understand the grounds of our own opinions, then we do not understand our opinions; to comprehend *why* we believe often tells us more about ourselves than *what* we believe.

*

I am always saddened and amused by our unconscious arrogance in speaking of the "Dark Ages" — as if we were living in the age of light, reason and humanitarianism.

*

It is foolish to suggest that the skillful burglar or confidence man could make as much, if not more, if he expended his talent and energies in legitimate pursuits; of course, he could, but his vocation appeals to him not because of the gain involved (although he himself may even think it does) but, more deeply, because it is a way of cheating society and of retaliating for buried injuries suffered, if not remembered, in childhood. The criminal never chooses his métier for gain; that is merely his conscious rationalization.

*

A woman finds nothing quite so unsatisfactory as a friend without faults she can talk about.